Deleuze, Cinema and National Identity

In loving memory of my grandparents,
Joshua and Mary Clarke and
David and Isabel Martin-Jones

Deleuze, Cinema and National Identity

Narrative Time in National Contexts

David Martin-Jones

Edinburgh University Press

Edinburgh University Press Ltd
22 George Square, Edinburgh

First published in hardback by
Edinburgh University Press Ltd in 2006

Typeset in Monotype Ehrhardt by
Servis Filmsetting Ltd, Manchester, and
printed and bound in Great Britain by
Antony Rowe Ltd, Chippenham, Wilts

A CIP record for this book is available from the British Library

ISBN-13 978 0 7486 3585 6 (paperback)

Contents

Illustrations

Acknowledgements

An earlier version of Chapter 3 appeared in *CineAction*, volume 64 (2004), under the title 'Two Stories, One Right, One Wrong: Narrative, National Identity and Globalization in *Sliding Doors*'. It is reprinted with the permission of *CineAction*. The diagram of Bergson's cone is reprinted with the permission of Zone Books, New York.

As this project has taken shape over the best part of ten years there are a number of people to thank. For reading drafts and providing me with feedback at various stages I owe a debt of gratitude to the following people: Dimitris Eleftheriotis, Bill Marshall, David Rodowick, Laura U. Marks, Patricia Pisters, Gill Plain, Damian Sutton, Sarah Leahy, Bettina Bildhauer, Ian Garwood, Douglas Kellner, Peter Hutchings and John Mullarkey. Thanks also to Geoff King, who sent me chapters of *American Independent Cinema* prior to its publication, to Victoria Pastor-Gonzalez for her advice on Kieslowski and to Paul Coates for a copy of the paper on Kieslowski and Tykwer that he gave at the 2005 *Society for Cinema and Media Studies Conference*. Finally, for stimulating discussions that enabled me to work through my ideas I would like to thank Amy Herzog, András Bálint Kovács, Angelo Restivo, Dina Iordanova, Belen Vidal, Gary Needham, Julianne Pidduck and Jonathan Murray.

I have given a number of conference papers drawn from this material, and extend my thanks to the organizers of the following events: the *Cinema in Europe: Networks in Progress Conference* (Amsterdam 2005), the *Society for Cinema and Media Studies Conference* (London 2005), the *Security Bytes Conference* (Lancaster 2004), the *Northumbria University Gendered Subjects Research Group* (Newcastle 2003), the *Culture/Gender/Power Conference* (Glasgow 2002), the *9th Laterna Magica Conference* (Pécs, Hungary 2002), the *Automobility Conference* (Keele 2002), the *12th Screen Studies Conference* (Glasgow 2002) and the *21st Century French Studies Conference* (Davis, USA, 2001). Thanks also to the AHRC for providing funding for both my MSc at the University of Edinburgh, and my PhD at the University of Glasgow. I should also like to extend my thanks to the staff at these institutions, as well as those at The Glasgow School of Art, Northumbria University and especially those at the University of St Andrews who provided me with additional time in which to realise the project. Many thanks too to Sarah Edwards at Edinburgh University Press, for patiently guiding me through the process.

Finally I should like to thank my family, especially my mother, father, brother and my nephew Tim. I am sorry I am never around, thank you for being so patient with me. Thanks also to Lynn Buchanan and Sarah Nelson for putting me up when I was broke, and for always being there. Thanks finally to Soledad Montañez, thanks for coming back and for all the laughter and dancing.

Introduction: Deleuze, Film Studies and National Identity

This book uses Gilles Deleuze's philosophy of time to engage with a range of contemporary films from a number of different national cinemas. It illustrates how Deleuze's theories can broaden our understanding of the way national identity is constructed in cinema. At the same time, the conjunction of Deleuze and the study of national identity adds an, until now, untheorised dimension to Deleuze's categories of the time- and the movement-image. Understanding the construction of national identity in cinema, it will be seen, also broadens our understanding of Deleuze.

The films under discussion have all emerged within the very limited time span of the last ten years, from approximately the mid 1990s to the mid 2000s and have been chosen for two reasons. Firstly, they each share a common concern with the manipulation of narrative time. This is true of both the multiple narratives of *Sliding Doors* (Britain, 1997), *Too Many Ways to be Number One* (Hong Kong, 1997) and *Run Lola Run* (Germany 1998), and the disrupted, jumbled or backwards narratives of *Chaos* (Japan, 1999), *Memento* (USA, 2000), *Peppermint Candy* (South Korea, 2000) and *Eternal Sunshine of the Spotless Mind* (USA, 2004). Secondly, they all use their unusual narratives to examine recent transformations of national identity.

During times of historical transformation, films often appear that experiment formally with narrative time. The various European new waves of the 1960s and 1970s, for instance, can be interpreted not only as comments on the state of their respective national cinemas, but also on the changing postwar conditions each nation experienced. A jumbled, fragmented, multiplied or reversed film narrative then, can be interpreted as an expression of the difficulty of narrating national identity at a time of historical crisis or transformation. Such narratives formally demonstrate a nation's exploration of its own 'national narrative', its examination of the national past, present and/or future in search of causes, and possible alternatives, to its current state of existence.

This process of national self reflection was most clearly evident in the new waves of postwar Europe. As opposed to the 'linear' narratives of the classical Hollywood paradigm, many of these films contained 'non-linear' narratives, characterised by a fragmented, jumbled, multiple or reversed structure. Thus, many films to emerge from Europe's defeated, shattered or divided nations formally expressed modernity's confrontation with its own limitations as a defining metanarrative. The dominance of the nation as a framework within which identity could be structured was now in question, and would suffer a series of further crises in the incipient postcolonial era. The disrupted narratives that helped identify many of these art films as works of national cinema also illustrated how national identities that had previously been based on a notion of enlightened historical progression, had been disrupted by the war. It is perhaps rather ironic, then, that the 'non-linear' narrative form that formally acknowledged the difficulties European nations faced in the postwar era often became the internationally recognised face of a number of 'national' cinemas.

Deleuze's work on time in cinema mainly developed out of his focus on the European new waves, especially on a range of films that formally disrupted narrative time. For this reason his work is, with some qualifications, extremely well suited to explore the international surge of films with disrupted narratives that have emerged in the ten years since the mid 1990s.

Analysing the editing of European and American cinema, Deleuze drew a distinction between two types of image, that he called the time-image (broadly speaking the cinemas of the new waves which experimented with discontinuous narrative time), and the movement-image (broadly speaking an unbroken, linear narrative, based upon the continuity editing rules established by the Hollywood studio system). These categories of image can help us understand the way in which the films under discussion here envisage time, as so many of them appear to contain qualities usually associated with the time-image (especially a 'non-linear' or often labyrinthine model of time) but strategically deploy this non-linear model of time within a more broadly classical, linear, movement-image structure. As Deleuze posited the time-image as an alternative to the movement-image, these 'hybrid' (movement-/time-image) films enable both a rethinking of Deleuze's categories, and provide a range of new contexts within which to apply his terms.

I am not, however, advocating that this diverse range of films be unproblematically viewed as a genre solely due to their formal qualities. This is primarily because Deleuze's categories of movement- and time-image are too broad to be used to define a genre in this way, at least without some major qualifications. More importantly, as I argue at various points throughout the book, attempts made since the emergence of these films to group several of them together as though they were a genre have left important questions unanswered. It is, nonetheless, worth considering their more apparent similarities. Like any genre, these films are recognisably similar in aesthetic terms, in this case due to their formal experimentation with narrative time, and their meditation on character memory as an allegorical hook through which to explore national identity. Indeed, like any genre, manifestations of this type of film appear slightly differently in different national contexts. Finally, like many genres they are also marketed in a way that identifies certain types of target audience.

Yet the term 'genre' sits rather uneasily here as most of these films would normally be said to belong to a 'type' of cinema, rather than a genre. Loosely speaking they are recognisable to western viewers as either 'art' or 'independent' films. These are categories which, like those of the various genres themselves, are as much marketing strategies as they are descriptive terms. However, as many of these films attempt to use their 'hybrid' movement-/time-image status to cross the elitist-art versus popular-genre boundary, to label them a genre is perhaps not such a misnomer after all. For instance, both *Run Lola Run* and *Eternal Sunshine of the Spotless Mind* appeal to audiences who enjoy watching popular genre films (the action movie and the rom-com respectively) and also to those who prefer a more 'arty' or independent film.

The important point here is not the interminable question of 'what is a genre?' Rather it is this. If these films are so obviously similar in their aberrant time schemes and their focus on memory and character identity as filters through which to examine changes in national identity, how do they negotiate the same issues differently in their different contexts? How have devolution in Britain, national reunification in Germany, the handover of Hong Kong to China, the bursting of Japan's postwar bubble economy, the crash of South Korea's tiger economy, the First Gulf War and 9/11 all created variations on the same type of film? In attempting to answer this question one of the advantages of using Deleuze becomes clear. His philosophical categories of image enable a grouping together of disparate films in a manner that previously existing genre definitions do not. Indeed, I am not the first to use Deleuze to make this particular manoeuvre. As I have noted elsewhere,[1] in *The Skin of the Film* (2000), Laura Marks' use of Deleuze helps her group together a disparate range of international films as works of 'intercultural' cinema. In a similar manner existing models of genre are sidestepped by my use of Deleuze, enabling me to examine an international body of films that self-consciously manipulate narrative time in order to negotiate transformations of national identity.

Over and above the matter of genre then, this book examines how Deleuze's philosophy of time can help us understand the process through which the manipulation of narrative time is used to construct national identity. As I discuss at several points, classical narratives like Frank Capra's *It's a Wonderful Life* (1946) briefly toyed with a labyrinthine notion of time by presenting two possible parallel worlds, one with and one without George Bailey (James Stewart). However, this temporary departure from a singular, linear view of time was used to reinforce the legitimacy of the one true time, and indeed, to conflate this 'correct' view of time with the film's one true vision of postwar American national identity. Thus, whilst evoking the labyrinthine model of time found in many time-images, this movement-image quickly returned its narrative to a classical framework. At the other end of this spectrum however, European art films by directors such as Alain Resnais and Federico Fellini are equally famous for questioning this 'right' and 'wrong' binary view of time and, by extension, national identity. As I will elaborate in Chapter 2, films such as Fellini's *8½* (1963) used a disorienting editing pattern to represent the equal validity of various parallel universes. By representing these labyrinthine variables as indiscernible from any one 'correct' version of reality, *8½* expressed the seeming impossibility of finding one informing, linear national narrative at a time of historical transformation in postwar Italy. In essence, time-images like *8½* use their disrupted narratives to comment on the illusion that movement-images, such as *It's a Wonderful Life*, attempt to create, that is to say, the illusion that there *is* one 'correct' narrative of national identity. In the chapters that follow each hybrid film will be examined to see how far, or to what degree, it can be seen to exist as a movement- or a time-image. This enables a greater understanding of the political stance of each film, in relation to its particular narrative of national identity.

The theoretical ramifications of this question will be thoroughly examined in Chapter 1. Here I propose an interactive model of the time- and movement-image, which necessitates a slight rejigging of Deleuze's categories from *Cinema 1: The Movement-Image* (1983) and *Cinema 2: The Time-Image* (1985), in line with his earlier work with Félix Guattari, *A Thousand Plateaus* (1980). I make a case for understanding how the two images interact as a mutual struggle of deterritorialisation and reterritorialisation, a process that Deleuze never explains in the cinema books. Reterritorialisation entails a constraining of a narrative into one linear timeline; evidence of this suggests the presence of a strong movement-image. Deterritorialisation, on the other hand, enables a displacement of narrative into multiple labyrinthine versions. Evidence of deterritorialisation suggests the unruly presence of a strong time-image.

In the first instance described above, *It's a Wonderful Life* displays the strong reterritorialising pull exerted by the classical narrative. Here the movement-image co-opts an aspect of the time-image (the labyrinthine model of time), but ultimately reterritorialises it by returning to the one 'correct' narrative. Effectively it uses the labyrinth to strengthen its claim to legitimacy as the dominant narrative form. In Fellini's film, by contrast, the time-image has almost completely deterritorialised the movement-image, throwing its linearity into disarray, along with its claim to normative legitimacy. In each case national identity is similarly re- (*It's a Wonderful Life*) or deterritorialised (*8½*).

With each of the films discussed, the question I will answer is, to what degree does the film de- or reterritorialise narrative time and, with it, national identity? To what extent is each film an attempt to reassert a linear narrative of national identity (a reterritorialisation of narrative time), or alternatively, to question the options that are open to national identity (a deterritorialisation of narrative time)? These hybrid films are seen as existing on interactive planes – struggling between the restraining, actualising powers of the movement-image, and the disruptive, virtual forces of the time-image – in an attempt to open up new possibilities, or close off alternative views of national identity. In general, then, it is the current state of national identity (the degree to which the national narrative has been disrupted or recuperated) that is negotiated by a film's de- or reterritorialised narrative. It will be seen that all these hybrid films are, to a greater or lesser degree, *time-images 'caught in the act' of becoming movement-images*. It is a question of degree as to exactly what state they are 'caught' in.

Using Deleuze's work enables a greater understanding of the ways in which narrative time is used to construct national identity in cinema. It illuminates how films with disrupted, multiple, jumbled, or reversed narratives (films that appear to be hybrid movement-/time-images), formally demonstrate the renegotiation of national identity at times of historical transformation. In this my approach correlates with that of certain postcolonial theories (as I discuss in Chapter 1), but ultimately it is different from these in that it provides a unique approach that can be applied to mainstream genres as well as art and independent cinemas from a number of different nations.

Deleuze and Film Studies

This is the first book to tackle the intersection between Deleuze's work and the construction of national identity in cinema. Yet this may not initially appear to be an obvious meeting point for – with the exception of one chapter of *Cinema 1* that analyses four national cinemas in terms of their montage practices, and of a brief section in *Cinema 2* on 'modern political cinema' – it was not a topic that Deleuze addressed in any real depth.[2] Admittedly his work on modern political cinema (which has since become known through D. N. Rodowick's pioneering work on Senegalese filmmaker Ousmane Sembene as 'minor cinema') has had an impact upon the field.[3] Named after Deleuze and Félix Guattari's work on minor literature,[4] minor cinema is a product of attempts made by marginalised or minority groups to create a new sense of identity. Minor cinema is 'revolutionary' in its appeal to colonised, minority, postcolonial, neocolonial, or otherwise marginalised peoples to establish a new sense of identity. However, this does not necessarily entail the creation of a new *national* identity. In fact, the work to emerge so far on this subject has stressed the ability of minor cinema to question established notions of national identity. See for instance, Bill Marshall's *Quebec National Cinema* (2001), Alison Butler's *Women's Cinema* (2002) and my own article from 2004 that analyses Peter Mullan's *Orphans* (1997) as a work of minor cinema from post-devolutionary Scotland.[5] All these pieces have carefully trodden around the issue of national identity, in contexts where the 'national' is at best a contested category that exists as a greater or lesser degree of de- or reterritorialisation. This book exists in parallel with this growing body of work on minor cinema. Although it was never Deleuze's intention to apply his ideas to the context of the nation, as his ideas continue to be adopted by Film Studies (a discipline still extremely engaged with national contexts), such a use of his work is increasingly likely to occur.

I will elaborate. In spite of the ever-growing body of work on Deleuze and cinema, in Anglo-American Film Studies Deleuze has a somewhat ambiguous position. His philosophical concepts have now become everyday terms in many areas of academia, yet some scholars remain concerned about his value for Film Studies. Such reservations are undoubtedly due to a number of the problems that exist with Deleuze's work, not least of which are his Parisian elitism, his disdain for popular culture, his dismissal of television, his at times convoluted style, his lack of concrete filmic examples and his disregard of film scholarship outside of the pages (and limitations) of *Cahiers du cinéma*. Most obviously however, Deleuze does not sit well with many in Anglo-American Film Studies due to his deliberate avoidance of history.

Deleuze published his twin cinema texts in the 1980s: *Cinema 1: The Movement-Image* in 1983, and *Cinema 2: The Time-Image* in 1985. English translations emerged in 1986 and 1989 respectively. The difficulties that Anglo-American Film Studies experienced accommodating his philosophy at that time are by now well documented,[6] and I do not wish to rehearse them in any detail here. Suffice it to say that it was not until 1993 that the first book emerged which seriously engaged with Deleuze and cinema, Steven Shaviro's *The Cinematic Body*. Indeed, even after over a decade of published material on Deleuze, it is still not always apparent – to Film Studies students and scholars alike – exactly how his work can be utilised in relation to existing debates in the field. In his challenging contribution to Gregory Flaxman's edited collection, *The Brain is the Screen* (2000), András Bálint Kovács notes that it was partly the timing of Deleuze's work that created this difficulty of assimilation:

> Deleuze's cinema books appeared at a time when film studies had just reached the state of an 'established science'. The institutions growing up around this discipline were just beginning to firm up, certain accepted methods of analysis were gradually acquiring wide currency, and the production of cinema studies was becoming a 'major industry' on both sides of the Atlantic. One of the major symptoms of this process was a turn away from 'pure theory', which was paralleled by a renaissance of historical research.[7]

In fact, as Kovács points out, in philosophical terms Deleuze did have an historical project. Unfortunately it was somewhat different to that of Film Studies as it was then establishing itself. His aim was to categorise the different formal ways in which cinema expressed our changing conception of time, focusing in particular on the caesura that occurred around the time of the Second World War, and the broad way it effected American and European cinema. This project appeared directly at odds with the move towards much more localised, national contexts that was then developing in Film Studies. To those unaware of his philosophical project, Deleuze's work undoubtedly smacked of the reductive binary previously proposed by such works as David Bordwell's 'Art Cinema as Mode of Film Practice' (1979).[8] Here, tacitly assuming Hollywood's aesthetic to be the norm, Bordwell theorised Europe's various art cinemas as its aesthetic other. As a result, he not only ignored the distinctiveness of indigenous European popular genres, but he also homogenised many European art cinemas on the strength of, as it were, their textual 'nonHollywoodness'. As early as 1981, in 'Art Cinema as Institution', Steve Neale pointed out that this type of approach was too universal in intent, and did not take account of the different, localised, contextual factors (institutional, industrial, commercial, cultural etc.) that influenced the construction of the different national cinemas of Europe.[9]

Thus Film Studies scholars reading Deleuze's *Cinema 1* and *Cinema 2* purely as works of film theory would have been understandably bemused. On first glance they appear somewhat anachronistic, produced by an outsider who was apparently not aware of the most recent developments in the field. In an attempt to salvage Deleuze from this reception this book addresses one of the major contributing factors to this difficulty, the localised historical dimension of the nation that is so apparently absent from his work. In fact, my contextual approach provides a fresh perspective on Deleuze's movement-/time-image model for a number of reasons. Firstly, these numerous hybrid films are themselves evidence of a blending of these positions, expressing therein the interaction that now exists between various cinematic styles once associated with, or at least marketed as belonging to, different parts of the globe (generally speaking, classical Hollywood cinema with the movement-image, and postwar European art cinema with the time-image). Purely by existing they question the legitimacy of a model that posits one narrative style as the accepted international norm, and homogenises a variety of different styles as its other.

Secondly, the various European art and American independent films discussed are viewed as products aimed at specific markets, rather than as either commercial pap or products of an *auteur*'s genius. Thus, even though in Chapters 4 and 5 I contrast hybrid American independent films such as *Memento* and *Eternal Sunshine of the Spotless Mind* with the more mainstream commercial successes *Saving Private Ryan* (1998), and *Terminator 3* (2003), this is not to draw a clear distinction between time- and movement-image, rather, this is done to stress the extent to which the former deterritorialise the national narrative that is evident in the heavily reterritorialised movement-images of the latter. These hybrid images demonstrate how once clearly demarcated styles of filmmaking are now blending together in an attempt to cross over into different markets (including those whose audiences' political orientations may have deterritorialised from the accepted view of national identity), thereby increasing the profitability of a film. This is not a case of *either* art *or* culture industry then, but rather of niche products and their relationship to national identity.

Thirdly, and for the same reason, each chapter situates its hybrid film or films as thematically consistent with a broader examination of national identity seen in various other contemporary films to emerge from the same nation. This approach avoids the pitfalls of positioning Hollywood-produced movement-images as the supposed 'norm' against which these hybrid films should be judged, and of conflating a nation's cinema with a minority of their more 'unusual' art cinema narratives.

Fourthly, although the dominance of Hollywood in the postwar era does correlate with its triumphal position after the Second World War, and although the movement-image's dominance in US (hereafter American) cinema can be explained as a consequence of this unbroken national narrative, a closer examination of North American cinema in Chapters 4 and

5 demonstrates that the Europe versus America postwar model adopted by Deleuze also needs refining. This is especially so if the American hybrid images discussed in this book are to be fully understood in terms of national identity.

Finally, Chapter 6 examines three South Asian films. The aberrant narrative structures of European art films on which Deleuze primarily based his concept of the time-image also exist in films from Hong Kong, Japan and South Korea. This broadens the theoretical horizons that Deleuze's work makes available to Film Studies away from his at times rather limited, Eurocentric vision. It also further illustrates the need to examine these unusual hybrid films in their respective national contexts. Time-images were first identifiable in postwar Europe, but as expressions of national turmoil they are just as likely to emerge in any nation at a time of crisis or transformation. The geographical and chronological closeness of the postwar European new waves made this phenomenon easily identifiable. However, it was not an isolated phenomenon but a concentrated outburst of a recurring trend, as the existence of these Asian films demonstrates. Moreover, these Asian films provide a unique perspective on the themes evident in many of the European and American films discussed in this book. Like much of Asia, Hong Kong, South Korea and Japan all encountered modernity as a colonial import from the West. It is interesting then, that at a time when the nation state is redefining itself in relation to globalisation, they have also appropriated the time-image's modernist critique of modernity to reimagine the nation's role in a new, global context.

For all these reasons, a focus on national identity enables me to bring together an apparently ahistorical philosophy of cinematic time, with a consideration of historical context. Admittedly nowadays such methodological liminality is not unusual. A great many Film Studies texts utilise aspects of both film theory and history, even whilst being packaged as primarily engaging with one or the other. As various works on different national cinemas have shown (especially those focusing on Asian, African and South American nations), aspects of 'theory' (for example gender, race, sexuality) that were once treated ahistorically are now viewed rather differently once historically contextual factors are taken into account. Hence this book is motivated by the desire to illustrate the continuing relevance of Deleuze's theory for Film Studies, in an era when acknowledging historical context is increasingly important.

Deleuze himself advocated a form of philosophical sodomy as the most productive manner of working with another person's ideas ('I saw myself as taking an author from behind and giving him a child that would be his offspring, yet monstrous').[10] For this reason I am sure he would have approved of the at times invasive reappropriation of his work found in *Deleuze, Cinema and National Identity*. On a personal note, working with Deleuze's often convoluted and inadequately demonstrated theories over the last decade has been a labour of love during which I have often exclaimed, 'oh bugger Deleuze'. Yet despite the limitations of his work, I find it every bit as suggestive as, say, Marxism, psychoanalysis, structuralism, Derridean deconstruction, cognitive psychology and any number of other theories that have been brought into Film Studies in the past.

Deleuze and National Identity

The films analysed in this book come from a variety of different national cinemas because my aim is to use Deleuze's work to show how – despite their formal similarities – each film negotiates national identity slightly differently in a different context. In this respect this book is different from previous examinations of national identity in Film Studies, which generally focus exclusively on one nation. In choosing which national cinemas to study I remained close to those in which I already had an interest. Understandably then, a great many are noticeable by their absence. Films and nations that only get a mention in the Conclusion include France, from whence *Irreversible* (2002) and *5×2* (2004) only emerged several years after the project had already taken shape. Discussion of *Before the Rain* (1994) is also missing, a fascinating film, but both beyond my field of expertise and already much discussed. There are countless other such examples. For instance, although in Chapter 6 I do discuss one South Korean film, *Peppermint Candy* (2000), there was simply not room to discuss as well films such as *The Virgin Stripped Bare by Her Bachelors* (2000), which also fits the remit of the book. Finally, I have deliberately not discussed the films of directors like Alain Resnais, Jacques Rivette, Jean-Luc Godard, Michelangelo Antonioni, Andrei Tarkovsky and so on. This is due to both the amount of coverage their work has already received, and to a desire to position this work in contrast to a more traditionally *auteur*-based approach. Indeed, as Deleuze formulated his theory of the time-image on the works of such directors, it seems a little redundant to rake over the same territory once again.

Instead, the weight of evidence that I bring by discussing Britain, Germany, America (before and after 9/11), Hong Kong, Japan and South Korea – as well as, in passing, Italy and Poland – sufficiently illustrates my case. On a number of occasions I use already existing material to summarise the current stance on a national cinema in the 1990s before examining the films under discussion in relation to Deleuze's work. Thus

I uncover what Deleuze can illuminate of their meditation on narrative time and the construction of national identity. As will be seen, in several instances the use of Deleuze enables me to draw a significantly different conclusion to that of the field as it currently stands.

As for the ever expanding body of work on national identity, as Chapter 1 illustrates, the most useful crossover between Deleuze's work on time and our understanding of the construction of national identity occurs through Homi K. Bhabha's work, and in particular his ideas in response to Benedict Anderson's now famous *Imagined Communities* (1983). Connecting Deleuze and Bhabha enables this work to enhance our understanding of exactly how formally disruptive films narrate the nation. In this respect my approach is similar to that of Marshall, although my emphasis on the formal structure of a range of films from different national cinemas is very different to his work on Quebec.[11] I also position my own work in line with the conclusions of writers such as Dimitris Eleftheriotis, Gertjan Dijkink and Robert Burgoyne, who have all drawn similar conclusions to mine, only from different starting points.

Finally, although discussing national identity, I do not engage with the ongoing debate over how to define a national cinema. As Philip Schlesinger's recent analysis of the stances of critics like Andrew Higson, Susan Hayward, John Hill and Pierre Sorlin suggests, the answer to this depends on the approach taken and the cinema in question.[12] With so many cinemas examined in the book it was paramount that I examine each film in relation to its specific context, and the manner in which it constructs national identity. For instance, whilst American independent films like *Memento* and *Eternal Sunshine of the Spotless Mind* undoubtedly use their narratives to deterritorialise dominant myths of American national identity, they do so in a manner typical of the American independent film, by smuggling in a political message under cover of generic conventions. Although these films can be seen to be extremely deterritorialising of the national narrative, this may only appear to be the case to a certain niche demographic of both their national and transnational audiences. The way in which this is done in other contexts is entirely different, due to the different markets and audience expectations anticipated by filmmakers in various European and Asian nations. As no one model of this process can be applied universally, defining what a national cinema is is beyond the bounds of this work.

Deleuze, Cinema and National Identity

In relation to the books that already exist on Deleuze and cinema, or that use Deleuze's ideas as part of a broader project to examine film, where does this one fit? Its initial influence was Rodowick's *Gilles Deleuze's Time Machine* (1997). Using Rodowick's conclusions as a jumping-off point enabled me to construct the interactive model of movement- and time-image on which my conclusions concerning the construction of national identity followed. In thinking through these issues I am also indebted to the respective stances of Angelo Restivo and András Bálint Kovács, on Deleuze and film history, in *The Brain is the Screen* (2000). Laura Marks' criticism of Deleuze from a postcolonial perspective in *The Skin of the Film* (2000) was also of great significance to my research.

However, this book is also quite unlike these predecessors in that it attempts to show how Deleuze can be used to examine both art films and examples from more popular genres. In particular, as I show in Chapters 4 and 5 through my discussion of the war film *Saving Private Ryan* and the science fiction film *Terminator 3*, there is as much to be gained from understanding the movement-image as there is from analysing the more unusual aspects of the time-image. In this respect the most influential texts were undoubtedly Steven Shaviro's *The Cinematic Body* (1993), and Patricia Pisters' *The Matrix of Visual Culture* (2001), although the book also shares some common ground with Julianne Pidduck's *Contemporary Costume Film* (2004), Barbara Kennedy's *Deleuze and Cinema* (2000) and Anna Powell's *Deleuze and Horror Film* (2005). Significantly however, this work departs from all these predecessors in its focus on national identity, in which its closest companion is Marshall's *Quebec National Cinema* (2001). Chapter 6 breaks new ground altogether by using Deleuze to analyse both popular and art films from different countries in East Asia.

Chapters 1 and 2 introduce and clarify the theoretical concepts that feature in the following chapters. In Chapters 3 to 6 the hybrid films are examined. Chapter 1 introduces the Deleuzean concepts that the book engages with, explaining what time- and movement-images are, the different conceptions of time that accompany them, and how I am mobilising them to examine contemporary films that contain characteristics of both. This is the only purely theoretical chapter, although a number of films and film movements are mentioned as examples that illustrate my stance. Also in this chapter I use Bhabha's work on time and national identity to illustrate how Deleuze's work is problematised by postcolonial theory, and yet how it can still be deployed to help us understand how narrative time constructs national identity.

Chapter 2 delves into the representation of memory in the movement- and the time-image, to enable a greater understanding of how the national past is rendered in cinema. It begins with an examination of Henri Bergson's philosophy of time – on which Deleuze drew significantly in developing his own theories – which is clarified through an analysis of Alfred Hitchcock's *Vertigo* (1958) and Fellini's *8½*. The final third of the chapter reexamines *Vertigo* and *8½* to uncover how a character's experience of the past is used to portray allegorically the search for national identity (in America and Italy respectively), and how the movement- and the time-image use different narrative structures to negotiate national identity construction.

Chapter 3 focuses on *Sliding Doors* and *Run Lola Run*. These two European films of the late 1990s both use multiple narratives to examine recent transformations in British and German national identity. In both cases a labyrinthine model of time is deployed to offer stark 'right' and 'wrong' choices between slightly different conceptions of national identity, based around the need for the national capitals (London and Berlin) to be reconfigured as global cities. Hence, whilst these films initially appear to valorise a performative identity based on a labyrinthine model of time, they are actually only contemporary manifestations of *It's a Wonderful Life*. As in the chapters that follow, each film is examined in light of its national cinema, with parallels and contrasts drawn with other films from the same decade. In this way it is possible to discern the similarities between these formally unusual films and their more mainstream national contemporaries, whilst also acknowledging their distinctive use of narrative time. This approach also demonstrates how films with similar narrative patterns that emerge from different nations are divergent in the context-specific manner in which they negotiate localised changes to national identity.

Chapters 4 and 5 examine certain American films from the 1990s and the 2000s. Chapter 4 contrasts the successful, mainstream movement-image *Saving Private Ryan* with the popular cult movie, *Memento*. *Memento*'s disrupted narrative, coupled with its protagonist's memory loss, is seen to offer a critique of American cinema's typical use of the movement-image to construct a triumphalist national narrative. This typical use is seen in *Saving Private Ryan*, a film that reflected the reconstruction of national identity after the First Gulf War. Chapter 5 examines how 9/11 created a similar distinction within American cinema, of successful mainstream movement-images that reconstructed a defensive national identity based on a return to Cold War politics, and somewhat critical independent films that – like *Memento* – smuggled in a political critique through a self-conscious play with narrative time. Here the examples used are *Terminator 3* and *Eternal Sunshine of the Spotless Mind*. Both films are examined as products that appeal to different markets (as opposed to opposites in an art/popular culture binary), thereby enabling a greater understanding of the degree to which they de- or reterritorialise national identity.

Chapter 6 examines three Asian films. Firstly, *Too Many Ways to be Number One*, a triple narrative gangster comedy that is similar in structure to *Run Lola Run*, but which uses the labyrinthine model of time to examine Hong Kong's identity in the face of the handover to China in 1997. Secondly, Hideo Nakata's *Chaos*, a *noir* thriller with a jumbled narrative somewhat similar to *Memento*. *Chaos* draws on the conceit of a doubled *femme fatale* (as seen in *Vertigo*) to examine changes to Japanese national identity brought about by the end of the economic boom in the early 1990s. Finally, from South Korea, *Peppermint Candy* is analysed, a reverse narrative film that self-consciously seeks out the moments in the national past when history could have branched off in a different direction, but did not. Its unusual narrative structure is used to deconstruct the way in which national identity is typically created by movement-images, by constraining the past into one, linear view of time.

The conclusion briefly examines *Blind Chance* (1981), a seminal film for this study that is referenced by many of those analysed in Chapters 3 to 6. I show how, although it is formally similar to both *Run Lola Run* and *Too Many Ways to be Number One*, it is actually closer to *Peppermint Candy* in the manner in which it examines the options open to its protagonist. Here it is the similarities between the political conditions of Poland and South Korea (rather than the similarities between the narrative structures of the two films), that are more pertinent for understanding the way their narratives construct national identity. To conclude I also suggest various other films, albeit existing beyond the constraints of space offered by this particular book, which offer further space for an examination of Deleuze, cinema and national identity.

Notes

1. David Martin-Jones, 'Laura U. Marks, *The Skin of the Film*', *Screen*, 43:4 (2002), pp. 442–6.
2. Gilles Deleuze, *Cinema 1: The Movement-Image* (London: The Athlone Press, [1983] 1986), pp. 29–55, Gilles Deleuze, *Cinema 2: The Time-Image* (London: The Athlone Press, [1985] 1989), pp. 215–24.
3. David Rodowick, *Gilles Deleuze's Time Machine* (Durham and London: Duke University Press, 1997), p. 139.
4. Gilles Deleuze and Félix Guattari, *Kafka: Towards a Minor Literature* (Minneapolis: Minnesota University Press, [1975] 1986).
5. Bill Marshall, *Quebec National Cinema* (Montreal: McGill-Queen's University Press, 2001), Alison Butler, *Women's Cinema* (London: Wallflower, 2002), David Martin-Jones, '*Orphans*, a work of minor cinema from post-devolutionary Scotland', *Journal of British Cinema and Television* 1: 2 (2004), pp. 226–41.

6. For instance, see the preface to David Rodowick, *Gilles Deleuze's Time Machine*, or the introduction to Gregory Flaxman (ed.), *The Brain is the Screen: Deleuze and the Philosophy of Cinema* (Minneapolis: University of Minnesota Press, 2000).
7. András Bálint Kovács, 'The film history of thought', in Gregory Flaxman (ed.), *The Brain is the Screen*, pp. 153–70, p. 154.
8. David Bordwell, 'Art Cinema as Mode of Film Practice', *Film Criticism*, 4:1 (1979), pp. 56–64.
9. Steve Neale, 'Art cinema as institution', *Screen*, 22:1 (1981), pp. 11–39.
10. Gilles Deleuze, *Negotiations* (New York: Columbia University Press, 1990), p. 6.
11. Bill Marshall, *Quebec National Cinema*.
12. Philip Schlesinger, 'The sociological scope of "National Cinema" ', in Scott MacKenzie and Mette Hjort (eds), *Cinema and Nation* (London: Routledge, 2000), pp. 19–31, pp. 24–9.

Part I

Deleuze and Narrative Time

CHAPTER 1

History

This chapter introduces the different definitions of time that are found in Deleuze's cinema texts, *Cinema 1: The Movement-Image* and *Cinema 2: The Time-Image*. It then interrogates the debate surrounding how the movement-image and the time-image interact. This is of crucial importance because how these images are understood to coexist greatly influences the conclusions drawn when using Deleuze to analyse films. I argue that their interaction is such that many of the recent movement-images that express characteristics previously thought typical of the time-image (particularly a multiple, jumbled, reversed or otherwise non-linear narrative time scheme) should not be seen as evidence of a radical change in our conception of time. They do not illustrate the end of the movement-image's dominance as Deleuze's work suggests. Rather *these 'hybrid' movement-/time-image films are time-images, to a greater or lesser degree, 'caught in the act' of becoming movement-images*. In spite of the increasing manipulation of narrative time in recent cinema, the reterritorialising strength of the movement-image ensures its continued dominance.

This conclusion is reached through an examination of the way history and identity are explored through narrative time, and the implications of this for the construction of national identity. In particular I make reference to Homi K. Bhabha's 'DissemiNation'[1] (his now famous contribution to *Nation and Narration* (1990)) for the insights it offers concerning narrative, time and the narration of national identity. I conclude that the many hybrid films made since the mid 1990s and discussed in the following chapters use their unusual time schemes to negotiate transformations of national identity. Thus by contextualising Deleuze's work within the parameters of the nation I am able to critique the often universalising conclusions that he draws from the interaction between the two images.

Ungrounding Cinema

For Deleuze, cinema in the twentieth century expressed two different conceptions of time. *Cinema 1* and *Cinema 2* thereby illustrated the changing

Western philosophical understanding of the relationship between movement and time. The movement-image expressed a 'classical' conception of time, whereas the time-image, emerging after the Second World War, a 'modern' conception.[2] Yet Deleuze theorised the emergence of the time-image primarily by drawing evidence from European art cinema, even though in the mainstream (at least in the popular cinemas of America and Europe) the movement-image retained its dominance in the postwar era. Deleuze's conclusion then, was quite an ambitious extrapolation from his limited observations of one style of filmmaking. Nonetheless, with the emergence of a number of more popular, mainstream films that seem to share characteristics of both, which of the two images is thought to be dominant is now of great importance. Is it the movement-image, suggesting that we still conceive of time in a very classical way, or is it the time-image, suggesting that we have departed from this way of thinking?

Deleuze's philosophical terms can cause some confusion due to the fact that they overlap with certain categories that already exist in Film Studies. Deleuze's 'classical', for instance, does not solely apply to films of the classical Hollywood style. Rather, it expresses a range of movement-image cinemas, including those of the French, American, Russian and German prewar montage styles. In fact, Deleuze's term refers to all cinemas that create the 'image of thought'[3] that has characterised the Western conception of time from antiquity to the present. However, the type of movement-image which came to dominance in the inter-war periods, the action-image, is typified by continuity editing, and it is here that the classical model of time is most easily seen. At the risk of conflating action-image with movement-image, this is the manifestation of the movement-image that I will focus on from now on.

Although in classical narratives the time experienced by characters in the film may appear to be consistent with the time of the story, in actual fact (as everyone knows) time in movies is actually shown in a very condensed form. Events that transpire across days, months or even years are rendered in a matter of hours. Put another way, the movement-image provides an indirect expression of time. To retain narrative coherence it illustrates time through a character's movement through space. In the classical narrative of the action-image time is both spatialised and rendered linear by the protagonist's sensory-motor continuity. The causal movement of the protagonist – from the perception of their surroundings, to an action based upon this perception – is used as a means of indirectly expressing time's passing. The protagonist is able, by acting upon what he or she sees, to directly influence his or her situation. Thus for Deleuze, action-images are most commonly characterised by a movement from an initial situation, through an action (or series of actions), to a changed situation. This process has already been explained in detail elsewhere (not least by Deleuze himself)[4] so a brief example should suffice. Let us consider the old joke about Hollywood star, Tom Cruise.

It is commonly held that the narratives of most Cruise vehicles follow a set pattern. Cruise is initially established as being a racing car driver/fighter pilot/military lawyer/vampire/futuristic cop/sports agent and so on. This is the situation. Typically, Cruise then suffers a crisis of faith in his abilities. He responds decisively (action) and thereby ensures his return to prominence (changed situation). This is exactly the trajectory of the action-image, from situation, through action, to new situation. The time of the narrative condenses around the body of the protagonist, the rules of continuity editing ensuring that the narrative focuses on their physical movement through space. As the protagonist is central to the narrative, extraneous details are expelled from the frame to ensure the focus and clarity of their story. No matter how disjointed the spaces are through which they travel, or how elliptical the narrative's movement between them, the physical actions of the protagonist provides the logical link. In *Top Gun* (1986) for instance, we have no difficulty following a narrative that rapidly progresses from aircraft carrier, to briefing rooms, to crowded bars, to volleyball courts, to aircraft hangers, and to the skies over both Kansas and the Indian Ocean. We are led through these otherwise disjointed spaces by the continuous presence of Cruise, and his linear agency as motorcyclist and fighter pilot. Thus in the action-image there is always a causal, linear progression to the narrative. The protagonist's ability to act evidences an unbroken sensory-motor continuum, and the passing of time is rendered subordinate to a character's movement through space. This focus on the protagonist's body is one of the major reasons why the movement-image is described as an 'organic regime'.[5]

In the movement-image time never appears directly, or 'in its own right'. It would be unusual after all, for a Cruise vehicle to chart the passing of time by lingering on an empty space from which he has just departed, in the manner we might expect of a director like Michelangelo Antonioni or Yasujiro Ozu. This would only conceivably be the case if the space contained the causal result of Cruise's action, such as a villain dying, a car crashing or a plane exploding. Even in such a case we would be seeing time via the movement of objects in space, rather than directly watching it unfold. Similarly, with the exceptions of *Eyes Wide Shut* (1999) and *Vanilla Sky* (2001), it is unusual for Cruise to suddenly experience a discontinuous movement of time. Whereas, for instance, we might expect it in a Fellini movie, we do not expect to see a disjointed series of flashbacks to Cruise's character's childhood or adolescence, or to slip into a dream or fantasy that seems indistinguishable from reality. In the movement-image then, we do not directly witness the spectacle of time passing in and for itself. Rather we see – quite literally – an edited version of time. Thus, at least in the dominant form of the movement-image, the protagonist's movements ensure that the classical form of time is singular and linear. As I shall further show in Chapter 3, because of its spatialised nature (and despite Deleuze's designation 'classical') it is also a four-dimensional time. After all, to render time visible through a movement through space is to illustrate 'space-time'.

By contrast, the time-image provides a direct image of time. We see the passing of time in itself, without the mediating influence of the protagonist's body. Moreover, this 'modern' image conceives of time not as a straight line but as a virtual and expanding whole. In the time-image, then, Deleuze saw a shift in the image of thought. Beyond the individualist ethos exemplified by the action-image (in which the individual's ability to alter his or her situation was beyond doubt), in the time-image the individual no longer has the power to influence his or her situation. The sensory-motor link is broken, or at least suspended, and – unable to always react in order to influence his or her physical context – the protagonist of the time-image becomes dislocated from the linear continuity of spatialised time. They begin to slip through the virtual whole of time, whose aberrant movement is glimpsed as it invades the interval between perception and action. The cinema's previous privileging of the protagonist's motor reaction to sensory data is replaced in the time-image by an emphasis on the movement of time itself. Time now appears in a pure state, in a '*pure optical situation*',[6] in which the protagonist can only visually record time's passing. The difference between the two images is perhaps most memorably summed up in Deleuze's phrase: 'This is a cinema of the seer and no longer of the agent'.[7]

Again, a brief example or two should help to clarify this. In the films of directors such as Chris Marker, Alain Resnais and Federico Fellini, protagonists are often caught in moments of reverie. Physically stilled because of an inability to act, they directly experience the passing of time. Suspended in the interval between perception and action, the seer of the time-image travels within time, perhaps on a trip through memories, as in Fellini's *Intervista* (1987), or in fantasies of a future meeting, as in Resnais' *Providence* (1977). One more recent example of this technique, *The Jacket* (2005) sees its protagonist Jack Starks (Adrien Brody) drugged, straitjacketed and locked in a morgue drawer. This suspension of his sensory-motor continuity enables him to travel in time, even though he remains physically stationary.

In such a situation, as D. N. Rodowick shows using Chris Marker's *La jetée* (1962), time in the time-image is discontinuous, rather than linear. Thus the interval between perception and action might throw up images from the past, the present or the future in any order. Now it is movement (virtual movement) that occurs in time, rather than vice versa. As Rodowick has it: 'Time no longer derives from movement; 'aberrant' or eccentric movement derives from time.'[8] Thus, rather than witnessing time through the medium of a character's movement in space, we now witness time's movement around the immobile character. The narrative traverses the many discontinuous spaces seen in a film like *Top Gun*, but without the physical movement of a protagonist like Cruise to provide a linear coherence to this mapping. This shift in emphasis ensures that, as Deleuze puts it, in the time-image 'the only subjectivity is time, non-chronological time grasped in its foundation, and it is we who are internal to time, not the other way round'.[9] In the time-image we see 'a little time in the pure state',[10] for, as opposed to an organic regime, the time-image expresses a 'crystalline regime',[11] for reasons I will examine below.

Labyrinth and Line

Each image has a corresponding model of time. In *Cinema 2* Deleuze grafts a labyrinthine model of time onto Bergson's concept of 'duration'[12] in order to further explain the functioning of time in the time-image. This is a labyrinth without a centre, whose pathways expand outwards infinitely, or to use a Deleuzean term, 'rhizomatically'.[13] Drawing on a famous idea from a short story by Jorge Luis Borges, Deleuze posits the existence of what amounts to multiple parallel universes. These parallel universes exist (or rather, insist, or subsist) in a virtual state, and become actual in the present along a series of infinitely bifurcating pathways. The infinite possibilities of labyrinthine time always exist virtually, as matter in a state of flux. The one pathway that we perceive is time in its actual state, solidified matter. According to Deleuze, in *The Garden of Forking Paths*,

> nothing prevents us from affirming that incompossibles belong to the same world, that incompossible worlds belong to the same universe. 'Fang, for example, has a secret; a stranger calls at his door . . . Fang can kill the intruder, the intruder can kill Fang, they can both escape, they can both die, and so forth . . . [Y]ou arrive at this house, but in one of the possible pasts you are my enemy, in another, my friend . . . ' This is Borges' reply to Leibniz: the straight line as force of time, as labyrinth of time, is also the line which forks and keeps on forking, passing through *incompossible presents*, returning to *not-necessarily true pasts*.[14]

Each bifurcation of the pathway through the labyrinth leads to two 'incompossible presents', two possible, and possibly contradictory, outcomes to any one situation. However, in the labyrinth this is not a paradox, as the potential for both outcomes always exist virtually, and both are always both played out (albeit in different parallel universes), in their respective actual manifestations. Moreover, the past becomes 'not-necessarily true' for at least one outcome, thereby destroying the notion of a single, linear time. Rather than a direct causal chain of development there is the emergence, with each fork in the path of labyrinthine time, of multiple virtual pasts. These fluctuate in and out of existence depending upon how they are realigned in the present.

Reduced to their most simplified expressions we have two models of time, the straight line (the movement-image) and the labyrinth (the time-image). Yet it would be a mistake to think of these times as an either/or. These two times do not exist independently of each other. Rather they are different manifestations of the same time.

Time exists in a virtual state, but what we generally perceive of as time is its actualised form. Thus we will normally only be aware of one actualised path through the many that exist in the virtual labyrinth of time. Deleuze came to this conclusion because his philosophical project attempted, in many different contexts, to break free from the constraints of binary reasoning. For instance, rather than understanding the world as philosophers of the Hegelian tradition do, as the existence of Being and its defining other, Nothingness, Deleuze was a philosopher of becoming in the Nietzschean/Bergsonian tradition.[15] He conceived of matter as existing simultaneously in two states, the molar and the molecular. The molar form was a solidified version of matter that we experience empirically, such as a tree, a chair, a person and so on. Matter conceived at the molecular level was exactly the same matter, but understood as changing (or rather, becoming) even if it does so in a manner that we do not necessarily perceive empirically. After all, when observing a chair it is normal to consider that it is stationary and unchanging. However, we also know that it will inevitably rot away over time. Therefore we must conclude that even as we watch, the chair must be changing at a molecular level. It was because of this type of reasoning that Deleuze also conceived of time not as an actual line and its virtual labyrinthine other, but as a virtual whole that is constantly in the process of becoming-actual, as a labyrinth in the process of becoming a line.

The movement-image expresses the classical conception of time because it only shows one 'True' time, and marginalises, expels or eradicates all others from the frame. Based upon the defining absence of all other times, the one time that is seen attains the form of the true. This is most evident in the action-image because one of the basic principles of continuity editing is the removal of everything (effectively all other times) that are extraneous to the one 'true', condensed time of the narrative. By reducing all other times to the position of other, the movement-image disavows its virtual origins, establishing the labyrinth as the defining other of the straight line of time. Thereby the movement-image disguises the fact that its linear narrative is actually only one manifestation of the labyrinth, and ensures that the virtual and the actual appear to be binary opposites.

In the time-image, by contrast, we begin to grasp that time is, at a virtual level, constantly in a process of becoming-actual. In the labyrinth of time the form of the true is replaced by the Nietzschean inspired 'powers of the false'.[16] These are not 'false' in the sense of the opposite of true. Rather, these multiple times express the potential for multiple ungroundings of time's actualised form. Their power is to 'falsify' the singular form of the true. Thus in the time-image the virtual and the actual are not considered to be separate, but rather to coexist in an interactive relationship. In the time-image, time becomes actual along multiple, divergent paths with each fork in the labyrinth of time. Each such movement cannot help but falsify at least one of the pasts that preceded it. Thus whilst in the movement-image time returns (or repeats) in the same form, in the time-image, time (paradoxically) has the potential to return in difference.

As I shall further show, the interaction between these different conceptions of time has huge ramifications for the construction of the national past, and national identity, in cinema. Before I turn to that particular question, however, it is first necessary to understand how these two models of time interact. This is crucial to our understanding of the way films with aspects of both movement- and time-image construct national identity. To demonstrate this I will refer to Deleuze and Guattari's *A Thousand Plateaus*, a text that emerged in 1980, three years prior to *Cinema 1*.

Two Planes

In *Cinema 1*, Deleuze theorised the existence of all matter (on a molecular level) as light, existing on what he called a 'plane of immanence'.[17] Put simply, a plane is a layer of matter in a more or less virtual or actual state. Rodowick drew on Deleuze's position to argue that the cinemas of the movement- and the time-image actually create 'two distinct planes of immanence'.[18] For Rodowick these planes are defined by the different way in which each image expresses time and truth. I will now take this interactive model as my point of departure, and place a slightly different emphasis on Rodowick's conclusions. This is possible because Deleuze's *oeuvre* contains certain seeming inconsistencies as his ideas develop in different contexts.[19] If we take *A Thousand Plateaus* as a starting point it is therefore possible to draw slightly different conclusions than those of Rodowick.

For Rodowick, the movement-image's plane of immanence, or rather what he terms 'the plane of consistency' which it creates through its assembling of images, is: 'the open totality in movement that gives rise to the model of the True as totalization' in which 'images are linked or extended according to principles of association and contiguity'.[20] The plane of consistency which the time-image creates, by contrast, is one in which: 'Succession gives way to series' and images are strung together only as 'disconnected spaces'.[21] Indeed, these definitions are very much as I have described the two images so far, with a film like *Top Gun* illustrating the 'principles of association' of the movement-image, and a Fellini film the 'disconnected spaces' of the time-image. However, these planes do not exist in isolation. Rather, the movement-image emerges as a reterritorialisation of the time-image. This is evident if we consider the following statement from *A Thousand Plateaus*:

> The plane of organization is constantly working away at the plane of consistency, always trying to plug the lines of flight, stop or interrupt the movements of deterritorialization, weigh them down, restratify them, reconstitute forms and subjects in a dimension of depth. Conversely the plane of consistency is constantly extricating itself from the plane of organization . . . scrambling forms by dint of speed or slowness, breaking down functions by means of assemblages . . .[22]

Using the definition of the two planes found in *A Thousand Plateaus* the movement-image and the time-image can now be seen to exist in an oscillating movement between the plane of *consistency* of the time-image, and the plane of *organisation* of the movement-image. The plane of consistency is an ungrounding, or deterritorialising force. The plane of organisation, a reterritorialising, or grounding force. Their interaction functions roughly as follows.

In its reterritorialising dominance there is the plane of organisation (Deleuze and Guattari also dub this a 'plane of transcendence'),[23] which: 'always concerns the development of forms and the formation of subjects'.[24] This is the plane on which the movement-image exists. This is the plane of the actual on which time is always seen in its indirect form, as an expression of movement, as it is in *Top Gun*. On the plane of consistency, by contrast, the time-image emerges as a deterritorialisation of the movement-image. A direct image of time is glimpsed in the time-image, and the crisis of truth (as a singular entity) becomes evident. It is here that the powers of the false offered by the labyrinthine model of time become visible, as they do in a Fellini film.

Whether an image is a movement- or a time-image depends on the degree to which it de- or reterritorialises time. The closer it is to establishing a linear narrative, the more likely it is to be a movement-image. By contrast, the more visible the labyrinth, the closer to the time-image. In the interaction between these two planes then, time- and movement-images are formed as different degrees of de- and reterritorialisation. As an example of the deterritorialising process described in *A Thousand Plateaus*, Deleuze and Guattari discuss Godard's cinema's ability to unground the totalising form of representation that is the plane of organisation. 'Godard . . . effectively carries the fixed plane of cinema to this state where forms dissolve, and all that subsists are tiny variations of speed between movements in composition.'[25]

Using this view of Deleuze's work the two images can be seen to interact as contrary but simultaneous movements of de- and reterritorialisation towards differing images of thought. On the plane of organisation, truth is created through the contiguous succession of images of the movement-image. Time appears indirectly on this plane, seen through the movement of an organic form, which provides coherence to the narrative. This molar form is ungrounded, deterritorialised or otherwise put into crisis by the time-image's discontinuous, labyrinthine movements on the plane of consistency. Here time can be glimpsed directly without the need for a continuous linear movement through space. Rather than a molar form, the protagonist is shown as constantly coming into existence, a discontinuous entity who (as will become clearer in Chapter 2), simultaneously exists in multiple times. Here time exists in itself, and is glimpsed in its multiple, or discontinuous virtual becomings. The movement-image, however, will usually have the last say, as it constantly struggles to reimpose form upon, to 'restratify', the discontinuous flux that the time-image suggests. In general, the movement-image's plane of organisation takes, to use Brian Massumi's terms, the '*both/and*' of the time-image, and reterritorialises it into a binary division, an '*either/or*'.[26] In general the powers of the false are no match for the form of the true, and the plane of organisation maintains its dominance through the movement-image.

Two Pasts

The way in which the past is aligned on the two different planes is also crucial to an understanding of how the national past is constructed differently in the two images. On the plane of organisation of the movement-image the past maintains a linear trajectory. It is chronological, evolves in a causal fashion, and begins with a first cause. This is the teleological time of official history. On the plane of consistency of the time-image, by contrast, the labyrinthine time of *Aeon* (as opposed to that of *Chronos*) effects a past that begins with the present moment and works backwards in order to uncover the many pasts that may, or may not necessarily be true.[27] The two views of the past created by these different processes are most easily summarised as continuous (movement-image) and discontinuous (time-image).

For instance, the first type of time is characterised by Freudian psychoanalysis, with its perpetual recourse to first causes in the past to explain psychological difficulties experienced in the present. The second way of conceiving the past is analogous with certain types of philosophical thought, especially the works of Nietzschean-inspired philosophers such as Deleuze and Foucault.[28] Patrick H. Hutton describes the two different methodological approaches that exist to uncover the past thus:

> The intellectual historian seeks to account for a theoretical viewpoint by fathoming its intellectual sources. His intent is to return to its earliest conceptualization and then to reconstruct the continuous narrative of the modifications that lead to its present formulation. The genealogist, in contrast, traces patterns of intellectual descent from the present backwards without seeking to ascertain their formal beginnings.[29]

The historical recovery of the past which begins with a first cause and works up to the present is a device frequently used by the movement-image, as I shall further show in Chapter 4. This is often achieved through the use of a flashback structure that begins with the end of the story and flashes back to the 'beginning', thereby establishing a teleological progression and a false origin from which the narrative stems. In this temporal scheme there is no scope for a bifurcation of the path which the narrative will take through time. To allow such deviation would be to threaten the already established ending.

The genealogical recovery of the past of the time-image, by contrast, begins in the present and attempts to trace a path backwards through the labyrinth 'without seeking to ascertain formal beginnings'. It looks for the past which, from all those which are not necessarily true, makes the most sense in retrospect. Looking back across time in this way falsifies histories that may previously have seemed to have a directly causal relationship with the present. In the time-image several histories are often offered without any one being specifically given as 'correct'. The virtual nature of these possible pasts is further emphasised, as I will show in Chapter 2, by confusing the 'real' past with the cinematic past.

The construction of the past in the two images is a contrast between the past envisaged as a return of the same (the movement-image), and a return of difference (the time-image). Positing a false origin to explain the present suggests a coherence to time that equates the past with the present. Any different or discontinuous view of time is therefore marginalised, or left out of history. Thus the past appears to evolve logically in only one way, creating one true past. Looking back across the labyrinth of time, by contrast, the present no longer appears in a causal relationship with the past. History now has the potential for different routes of return, as the past may or may not be the direct cause of the present.

To reterritorialise the labyrinth the movement-image must perpetually reimpose a single straight line. This is achieved through the privileging of one past, denying difference and excluding all other possible labyrinthine pasts. This illusion of continuous linear time is threatened, however, whenever the presence of the labyrinth is glimpsed. It is often in denial of this ungrounding force that the notion of one true national identity is posited.

In films that contain aspects of both movement- and time-image, this struggle is dramatised in the film's disrupted narrative, which literally reflects a moment of historical transformation in which national identity is renegotiated. However, before I turn to the construction of national identity in time it is necessary first to examine how individual identity is constructed in time. This is important for two reasons. Firstly, several of the films under discussion in later chapters use character identity in order to examine broader issues of national identity. Secondly, the process of individual identity formation correlates with that of national identity creation.

Two 'I's

Deleuze credits Kant with the discovery of a schizophrenic subject, and the initial movement towards the realisation of the virtual whole of time. In his deconstruction of Descartes' *Cogito*, Kant illustrated that the 'I' that Descartes describes is split into an I that contemplates (I think) and an I that is (I am).

> For Kant, it is a question of the form of time in general, which distinguishes between the act of the I, and the ego to which the act is attributed . . . Thus time moves into the subject, in order to distinguish the Ego from the I in it. . . . It is in this sense that time as immutable form, which could no longer be defined by simple succession, appeared as the form of interiority (inner sense) whilst space, which could no longer

> be defined by coexistence, appeared for its part as the form of interiority. 'Form of interiority' means not only that time is internal to us, but that our interiority constantly divides us from ourselves, splits us in two . . .[30]

Time, 'no longer defined by simple succession' or subordinate to a movement through space, is now the force which splits the subject in two. It is this view of time that is uncovered by the time-image. Here the subject is both an I that acts, and an Ego that both endures and contemplates the I that acts. The implications of this division of the subject by time were explored more fully by Bergson, who conceived of the bifurcation in time (of each fork in the labyrinth of time) as the point at which time splits into a present that passes, and a past that is preserved. The subject, then, is at once an actual self that acts in the present, and a virtual self that insists, or subsists, as the past. Deleuze quotes Bergson to this effect:

> Our actual existence, then, whilst it is unrolled in time, duplicates itself along with a virtual existence, a mirror-image. Every moment of our life presents the two aspects, it is actual and virtual, perception on the one side and recollection on the other . . . Whoever becomes conscious of the continual duplicating of his present into perception and recollection . . . will compare himself to an actor playing his part automatically, listening to himself and beholding himself playing.[31]

The point at which time splits Deleuze terms the 'crystal of time'.[32] It is the crystal that is glimpsed in the time-image. Here anyone gaining intuition of their doubled self as it splits in time will be aware of their becoming-other much as one would who compares themselves to an actor playing a part. In this way the binaries which are usually upheld by the subordination of time to movement (such as inside/outside, and self/other) are disrupted by the virtual whole of time. In the crystal we glimpse time splitting. Therefore we become aware that the subject is at once both inside and outside, self and other, virtual and actual, recollection and perception and, indeed, past and present. The masquerade in which the subject is now involved, the falsifying of the self and the forever making contingent of the past, is a return of difference which destroys the linear causality of the model/copy (past/present) binary of *Chronos*. As in the Kantian view of time, in the time-image subjectivity is multi-faceted, or crystalline.

The implications of this temporal view of the subject are wide reaching. For instance, Deleuze's work on time provides the metaphysical justification for Judith Butler's early work on identity. For Butler, both gendered and biologically defined sexual identities are social constructs. Male and female gender roles are not the effect of an original sexual divide (man/woman), but rather, this illusionary origin is retroactively created through the continuous repetition of gender roles. Gender is a performance that, when its roles are repeated in the exact same manner, constantly reestablishes the accepted norms of heterosexuality. In 'Imitation and Gender Insubordination' (1991) she argues that

> heterosexuality must be understood as a compulsive and compulsory repetition that can only produce the *effect* of its own originality; in other words, compulsory heterosexual identities, those ontologically consolidated phantasms of 'man' and 'woman', are theatrically produced effects that posture as grounds, origins, the normative measure of the real.[33]

Our sexual identity is but the continual reimposition of a seemingly originary but actually illusory biological division, through the repeated playing out of established heterosexual gender roles. The creation and maintenance of compulsory heterosexuality is a causal process which establishes an illusory first cause in the organism. It maintains its hegemony by ensuring its perpetual return in the same form, as all attempts to perform these roles differently are immediately marginalised as other. The single, linear timeline immediately apparent in the construction of the heterosexual division of 'man' and 'woman' thereby ensures its contribution to chronological views of history and patrilineal reproduction as the norm.

Yet this construction of gender, and indeed, sexual roles through a 'compulsory repetition' also contains the potential for its own possible ungrounding. Just as the labyrinth exists as the ungrounding of the straight line, so too does the repetition of difference haunt the repetition of the same that perpetuates compulsory heterosexuality. Butler continues, stating that

> if heterosexuality is compelled to *repeat itself* in order to establish the illusion of its own uniformity and identity, then this is an identity permanently at risk, for what if it fails to repeat, or if the very exercise of repetition is redeployed for a very different performative purpose? If there is, as it were, always a compulsion to repeat, repetition never fully accomplishes identity. That there is a need for repetition at all is a sign that identity is not self-identical. It requires to be instituted again and again, which is to say that it runs the risk of being *de*-instituted at every interval.[34]

Should the repetition of the same which informs the straight line ever be made to stutter, to branch off into a repetition of difference, then the straight line would begin to become a labyrinth. Consequently, the self would no longer be 'self-identical', but becoming-other, multi-faceted, or crystalline. The potential for the de-institution of identity exists in attempts to perform identity differently. For, if sexual and gender identities are but roles that are legitimised through the repetition of the same, then to perform one of these roles differently is to unground the illusion of the continuous, evolving self. The most obvious examples of such a practice would be drag, although the labyrinth of time should, in theory at least, enable anybody to perform their identity differently.

However, this view of identity often seems to be a utopian dream at an individual level. This owes much to the strength of the powerfully reterritorialising form of the true, against whose reactive forces the powers of the false continuously struggle. Yet in terms of the performance of national identity and its representation in cinema, this process can be seen whenever a historical transformation requires a new masquerade of national identity. It is the officially sanctioned image of national identity that the time-image perpetually resurfaces to 'queer', deterritorialise or unground.

National Identity

The Time of the Nation

As I will now show with reference to Bhabha, national identity is constructed and renegotiated using time in a manner that correlates with Deleuze's two images and their time schemes. Films that construct or critique national identity using multiple, jumbled or reversed narrative times can therefore be examined in relation to the various different aspects of the interactive model outlined above. Determining the extent to which these films are movement- and/or time-images is an integral part of determining exactly what view they take on the national past.

In his seminal study, Benedict Anderson famously argued that the nation was 'an imagined political community'.[35] With the emergence of the nation in the late eighteenth century, the simultaneity of its peoples' existence was predicated upon 'an idea of "homogeneous, empty time" that was objectively measured for all its inhabitants "by clock and calendar"'.[36] In other words, time came to be understood in a way that stressed the simultaneous existence of the nation's people. Clock time ensured that even if you never met anyone in the neighbouring city, you knew that as you started work at 9 a.m., so did they. Further, calendar time meant that your linear measure of time's passing was also the same as that of the rest of the nation. The time of the nation was linear and progressive, ensuring that the nation came to be defined as 'a solid community moving steadily down (or up) history'.[37]

In *Nation and Narration* (and further in *The Location of Culture* (1994)) Bhabha, critiquing Anderson's work from a postcolonial viewpoint, offered a slightly different conclusion. He argued that the nation was actually narrated in a double time. It was defined by a progressive, teleological view of the present that problematically established its origins in an ancient or almost timeless past. It was performed in the present in such a way as to both erase and then recuperate this past. Bhabha states:

> The language of culture and community is poised on the fissures of the present becoming the rhetorical figures of a national past. Historians transfixed on the event and origins of the nation never ask, and political theorists possessed of the 'modern' totalities of the nation . . . never pose, the awkward question of the disjunctive representation of the social, in this double time of the nation. It is indeed only in the disjunctive time of the nation's modernity . . . that questions of nation as narration come to be posed. How do we plot the narrative of the nation that must mediate between the teleology of progress tipping over into the 'timeless' discourse of irrationality?[38]

Despite its relatively recent emergence, the nation called upon an informing past found in 'rhetorical figures' that often predated the era of the nation-state. National identity was thus maintained through a circuitous process in which the present was seen to be a continuation of a past, that was itself a construction of the present! In the present it is decided which 'rhetorical figures' (which flags, salutes, wars, founding fathers, invasions, revolutions, religious allegiances, racial characteristics and so on) constitute the nation's origins. However, those that are excluded or forgotten in the process still subsist, and await recall in the future should a change of origin become necessary. Such a change may be determined necessary by, for instance, a new form of government.

This time of the nation was considered by Bhabha to be pedagogical in that it aimed to establish one dominant view of national history, and identity. In this sense it functions much as Deleuze's classical conception of time does. Its linearity is based upon the ability to make the present appear to be a repetition of the past, a repetition of the same that guarantees the status of official history as a singular truth. As I will show in Chapters 4 and 5, this use of a posited (or 'false') origin to suggest continuity with the present is still evident in the use of flashback in recent American cinema.

Yet this particular construction of national identity through the equating of the past with present is not the whole story. As I have stated, for Bhabha the double time of the nation was a process that was perpetually in the process of being narrated and renarrated. In this process there is a performative rethinking of the past in the present that, to use a Deleuzean term, constantly reterritorialises national identity. However, constantly threatening to unground the immemorial status of the people of the past are the people in the present. Their performance of national identity should always ensure the return of the pedagogical discourse. Despite its ever-transforming nature, this performance should always retroactively ensure a reterritorialisation of the nation as a repetition of the same. Despite what 'should' happen however, within this process there also lies the possibility of its very ungrounding. Bhabha continues:

> We then have a contested cultural territory where the people must be thought in a double-time; the people are the historical 'objects' of a nationalist pedagogy, giving the discourse an authority that is based on a pre-given or constituted historical origin or event; the people are also the 'subjects' of a process of signification that must erase any prior or originary presence of the nation-people to demonstrate the prodigious, living principle of the people as that continual process by which the national life is redeemed and signified as a repeating and reproductive process. The scraps, patches, and rags of daily life must be repeatedly turned into the signs of a national culture, while the very act of the narrative performance interpellates a growing circle of national subjects. In the production of the nation as narration there is a split between the continuist, accumulative temporality of the pedagogical, and the repetitious, recursive strategy of the performative. It is through this process of splitting that the conceptual ambivalence of modern society becomes the site of *writing the nation*.[39]

By establishing national identity as stemming from certain historical origins a nation's often diverse peoples are provided with a sense of continuity that erases the difference between the past and the present. The population is thereby assured that a match exists between past and present, that things as they were then are things as they are now. Yet this process is ongoing, due to the constant need to renegotiate identity in the present. After all, the people in the present can only prove that they are the cutting edge of a progressive linear development if they can also establish their dissimilarity from their predecessors. If they are the 'new', then the people of the past must be the 'old'. Paradoxically, things as they are now must also be better than they were then. This constant eruption of a disparity between an 'us' and a 'not us'[40] is then closed again by the placing of yet another origin, and so on.

This process demonstrates exactly the same fragility that Butler noted surrounding the discourse of compulsory heterosexuality. Its repetition of the same illustrates the perpetual possibility of the resurgence of difference that constantly threatens to erupt and unground its illusory linearity. Bhabha argues from a postcolonial perspective that with each acknowledged change in the population the national past must be rethought. Yet should the nation be performed (or 'written') differently in the present, then a discontinuity will emerge between its present status and its myths of origin. For Bhabha, colonialism was the founding other upon which modernity (and therefore the nation) posited its dominance. The possibility of ungrounding the nation's dominance, then, is most evident when the reemergent histories of postcolonial or diasporic populations, 'threaten' the maintenance of the pedagogic view of national identity. By extension, as Bill Marshall summarises: 'The nation can . . . be considered to be a site of conflicting or at least plural temporalities, marked by class, ethnicity, gender'[41] and race. Thus in the 'heterogeneous histories of contending peoples'[42] within the nation, we glimpse once again the ungrounding potential of the labyrinth of time.

As was the case with the labyrinth and the straight line of time, so too is the construction of national identity a struggle between contrary pulls towards de- and reterritorialisation. In the gap, or 'time-lag'[43] opened up by a deterritorialising of the national narrative in the present, it is sometimes possible to glimpse the performance of national identity as a repetition of difference. This is the ungrounding potential that 'underwrites' national identity, and it is this which pedagogical time must perpetually work to reterritorialise. This process of de- and reterritorialisation of national identity is perhaps easiest to consider in terms of a series of recognitions, or perhaps appropriations, of previously marginal minorities into the mainstream. Take postwar Britain for instance. The sixty years since the end of the Second World War have seen the accepted face of national identity deterritorialise, and then reterritorialise to incorporate (to a greater or lesser degree) feminism, queer sexualities, postcolonial histories, post-industrial identities, and more recently, the devolved identities of Scotland, Wales and England.

What is most surprising about Bhabha's argument is that as a concrete example of the potential deterritorialisation of the narrative of the nation he discusses a film, *Handsworth Songs* (1985). Admittedly this film could be argued to reflect or illustrate the transformations in British society that led up to the Handsworth riots. Yet Bhabha's choice is interesting because it also suggests that – although we might expect to consider physical examples of this process, perhaps in theories of everyday rebellion such as Michel de Certeau's *The Practice of Everyday Life* (1984) – the 'performance' through which national identity can be deterritorialised could be filmic. *Handsworth Songs* is used by Bhabha because it both illustrates and formally demonstrates the ungrounding of national identity that can occur in the double time of the nation. As Kobena Mercer argues, *Handsworth Songs* critically foregrounds the ideological naturalisation of race normally effected by the British documentary realist aesthetic.[44] Similarly, in this book the formal construction of narrative time in the films under discussion is examined to discover the extent to which their demonstration of recent renegotiations of the national narrative critiques (deterritorialises), or emphasises (reterritorialises), this process.

To ensure that what I am suggesting is clear, I will briefly consider Bhabha's description of the way minority cultures are able to destabilise the national narrative in Deleuzean terms. Despite not directly engaging with the issue of national cinema in his cinema texts, Deleuze was concerned with what has come to be known as 'minor cinema'.[45] Minor cinema is named after Deleuze and Guattari's work on minor literature;[46] it describes films created by colonised, minority, postcolonial, neocolonial, diasporic or otherwise marginalised peoples who are attempting to establish a new sense of identity. Primarily using examples drawn from postcolonial countries in Africa and South America, Deleuze discusses how this type of cinema imagines a people who are missing, or who do not yet exist. To do so it takes a major cinematic voice and makes a minor use of it, making it stutter or stammer. It is in this sense that minor cinema is 'revolutionary'. Although this process does not necessarily have to impact upon national identity, as I noted in the Introduction in the 2000s several works have argued that it can, including those of Bill Marshall on Quebec, Alison Butler on women's cinema in a variety of different nations, and my own work on Scottish cinema.

For Bhabha, the presence of a minority discourse 'reveals the insurmountable ambivalence that structures the *equivocal* movement of historical time.'[47] The difference that inhabits the process of national narration when a minority discourse speaks forces a reconsideration of the national narrative. This process correlates with that of a 'minor' discourse. Here, rather than opposing the pedagogical 'Truth' of the nation, a deterritorialising minority uses the language of the dominant, major voice, but makes it speak in a minor way. In the case of *Handsworth Songs* the ungrounding of official history is seen in the continual return to, and reiteration of, the moment of migrant arrivals on British shores in the 1950s. Thus the film demonstrates 'the filmic time of a continual displacement of narrative'.[48] Originally filmed by British news crews, this archive footage of diasporic origins is reappropriated by the Black Audio Collective, who make a minor use of the nation's major voice, demonstrating that in the present the ex-colonial people of Britain are 'always just emerging'[49] from the boat. Official linear history is ungrounded through the disruption of narrative time in a repetitious performance that exposes the multiple origins of British national identity.

However, this is not to claim that the films under discussion in this book are works of minor cinema. They are not. After all, minor cinemas usually emerge either in nations 'peripheral' to modernity, or from sections of the populace whose existence is peripheral to the dominant narrative of the nation. What these films do illustrate in their content, and demonstrate in their non-linear narrative time schemes, is the process of national identity de- or reconstruction. Thus it is possible to view them in terms of the minor actions they perform upon the major discourse of national identity. It is here that the politics of each film appears. For this reason, and despite Deleuze's reticence to discuss the nation, I follow Marcia Landy in finding his work on cinema illustrative of the process through which 'particular cinematic styles signal important cultural changes closely tied to pedagogical conceptions of the nation or its critique'.[50]

The non-linear time schemes of these hybrid films demonstrate, to a greater or lesser degree, the ungrounding influence of the time-image on the movement-image. Subsequently they demonstrate the renegotiation of national identity at times of crisis or transformation in a number of different contexts. They reflect upon the process of de- and reterritorialisation of national identity, and the extent to which the major voice retains its hegemony, or is fractured by its minor enunciation. The question that will be addressed in each of the following chapters is, to what extent do the specific films in question deterritorialise the major voice of national identity?

In some cases the reterritorialising forces of the national narrative are so strong that all we see is the process already reterritorialised. In Chapter 3, for instance, the multiple narratives of *Sliding Doors* and *Run Lola Run* appear to render literal a fork in the national narrative, only to reduce the options they offer to the very familiar pattern of one true/several false times. These films are thus firmly coded as movement-images in their inception. Other films however, especially those appearing very shortly after major national traumas and those from nations acutely aware of their reterritorialising institutions, offer a more radical critique of the pedagogical time of the nation. In particular this is the case with the South Korean film *Peppermint Candy*. The filmic performance of narrative time in such films demonstrates the potentially ungrounding power of the labyrinth. However, even these films are rarely time-images. The reterritorialising power of the double time of the nation is still evident, and can most usefully be described as being formally demonstrated, or rendered literal, by the film's narrative structure. The only difference here is that, unlike the films discussed in Chapter 3, this demonstration of national identity reterritorialisation is done without the same celebration of the new. Rather, such films critique the process of reterritorialisation itself.

In either case what we see in these non-linear films is a crisis of national identity formally rendered literal by multiple, jumbled or otherwise discontinuous narrative time. As such these films are time-images 'caught in the act' of becoming movement-images. This is different from what is seen in the time-image, which depicts a deterritorialising event that has yet to actualise (and that actively resists actualising) into a form. Instead these hybrid films illustrate the reterritorialisation of the time-image's labyrinthine conception of time into a form.

By using Deleuze's interactive model and by assessing each film on its own terms, it is possible to reconsider the binary trap of equating art films with time-images, and popular genres with movement-images. This is an obstacle that theorists have stumbled over in the past, not least of which was Deleuze. The very existence of these hybrid films, after all, renders boundaries such as that between art and commerce extremely hard to define. Although I am not suggesting that all movement-images are by definition expressions of a hegemonic view of national identity, the model of time on which they are built is likely to make their narrative reterritorialising in intent. Thus they will be more or less pedagogical, depending on the film. However, I do not conclude that only art and *avant-garde* cinema can offer an 'alternative' to the mainstream. Rather, the mainstream exists at varying degrees of de- and reterritorialisation.

Put another way, a film does not have to be a time-image, or a hybrid image to critique the dominant ideology usually found in the movement-image. Many movement-images critique the dominant view of national identity in their narratives. However, it is rare for one to also *demonstrate* this critique formally. Indeed, when it does so, its deterritorialising movement ensures that it becomes a hybrid image. This is the added dimension that hybrid films are able to negotiate, a formal demonstration of the process of national identity de- or reterritorialisation examined in their narratives. Although the demonstration of national deterritorialisation found in these films often turns out to be a lesson on how national identity is currently reterritorialising, it always contains the potential to enact a minor deterritorialising of the time of the nation. Thus, as well as the intercultural films that Laura Marks discovered on the margins of the nation in *The Skin of the Film* (films which often function as time-images), there is also always the potential for a deterritorialisation of the national narrative in more mainstream, hybrid films. Although they inevitably tend towards reterritorialisation as movement-images, they still formally demonstrate the double time of the nation, that which perpetually threatens to unground its normalising narrative.

There is a canonical position within Film Studies with which this study correlates: the debate on the negotiation of ideology through form and content introduced by Comolli and Narboni in 1969.[51] Sean Cubitt has recently argued that nowadays the most successful films are unlikely to conform to Comolli and Narboni's '"category 'e'", the film that tries to present the dominant ideology but does so in a contradictory way that reveals the working of ideology itself'.[52] For Cubitt this is because most successful films attempt to divorce themselves from the 'social and material world'.[53] In fact, as time-images 'caught in the act' of becoming movement-images, many of these hybrid films demonstrate the internal contradictions that characterise Comolli and Narboni's famous category e.

> The films we are talking about throw up obstacles in the way of the ideology, causing it to swerve and get off course. The cinematic framework lets us see it, but also shows it up and denounces it. Looking at the framework one can see two moments in it: one holding it back within certain limits, one transgressing them. An internal criticism is taking place which cracks the film apart at the seams.[54]

Yet as so many of the films under discussion ultimately reterritorialise as movement-images, the 'dislocation'[55] between their apparent stance and the way it is constructed is very often disavowed. In many instances the forces that hold the film 'back within certain limits' are much the stronger, ensuring that any transgression is actually a controlled realigning of the present with the past that sutures over a period of historical transformation. In Chapter 3, *Sliding Doors* and *Run Lola Run* are both considered to function in this manner. Indeed, although it is not my aim to label each film systematically in this way, I will show in passing that some of these hybrid films are actually closer to Comolli and Narboni's categories b and c – films which either challenge the dominant ideology in their narrative and form (b), or in their form 'against the grain'[56] of an otherwise seemingly innocuous narrative (c). In particular, *Peppermint Candy* corresponds to category b, and *Memento* and *Eternal Sunshine of the Spotless Mind*, category c. Cubitt is right that these are not, financially speaking, particularly 'successful films'. However, they do reflect the potential for deterritorialisation of the dominant ideology that these hybrid films contain.

Contextualising Hybrid Films

To conclude this chapter I will examine my stance in relation to Patricia Pisters' *The Matrix of Visual Culture* (2003). This serves two purposes. Firstly, Pisters is the only person so far to provide a sustained explanation for the surge of mainstream films that contain characteristics of both the movement- and the time-image such as those discussed here. It is necessary then, to assess my conclusions in light of hers. Secondly, Pisters' work provides an opportunity to discuss just how my focus on the nation provides a different set of conclusions from those offered by the much broader context within which Deleuze couched his own argument.

Pisters argues that certain recent popular films, including *Fight Club* (1999) and *Pulp Fiction* (1994), are 'time-images "disguised" as action-images or action-images that take on characteristics of the time-image'.[57] She continues: 'Both Fincher and Tarantino present images that play with the status of the movement-image that has become "contaminated" with characteristics of the time-image.'[58] Using the interactive model of the two images I outlined above it is possible to see the contamination that Pisters observes as the ungrounding of the plane of organisation that the time-image constantly attempts, that deterritorialising movement which the movement-image constantly struggles to reterritorialise. What Pisters sees as 'time-images "disguised" as movement-images' are actually time-images 'caught in the act' of becoming movement-images. This somewhat different conclusion is drawn by my focus on how these films negotiate transformations in national identity. It is this use of a localised context that marks the contrast between my work and Pisters'.

Pisters rightly notes that Deleuze's philosophy provides a different way of understanding cinema to more established models in Film Studies, such as psychoanalysis. She argues that this approach is particularly pertinent nowadays because we have entered an age in which we are increasingly encountering a new type of cinematic culture, an age where

> the cinematic apparatus . . . has become only one aspect of contemporary culture and . . . the apparatus has changed. From a transcendental apparatus, designed to give the subject the illusion of control but actually controlling the subject, the apparatus has become an immanent one, to the point where the whole universe becomes cinematic. . . . [W]e have entered an age where a new camera consciousness makes clear distinction between the subjective and the objective impossible; the past and the present, the virtual and the actual have become indistinguishable.[59]

For Pisters we have entered an age where a new camera consciousness ensures the indistinguishability of virtual and actual that Deleuze described as typical of the time-image. However, whilst this is perhaps true in many ways, Pisters is only able to draw her conclusion for certain slightly unusual films, like *Fight Club* and *Pulp Fiction.* Whilst these films do suggest a certain degree of hybridity, she herself notes how other popular films like *The Matrix* (1999), with its clearly demarcated realms of the virtual and the actual, do not. Indeed, she points out in her introduction that 'the traditional transcendental model of the cinematic apparatus is still vigorously alive'.[60] As I noted above, the cinema in the period discussed in this book illustrates a contested territory between a transcendental time of representation, and its immanent labyrinthine ungrounding. As I have also shown, however, this power of reterritorialisation actually functions in the construction of national identity.

Like Deleuze before her, Pisters sees the contested territory in global terms. This is the major difficulty with Deleuze's broad contextualising of the caesura between movement- and time-image. For Deleuze, using cinema to chart the shift from a classical to a modern conception of time necessitated recourse to a major, global event as determining factor. Deleuze thus chose the Second World War. Indeed, Deleuze's decision makes a great deal of sense, especially when we consider the correlation that Angelo Restivo has noted between Deleuze's cinema texts and the work of other French poststructuralists (in particular Foucault and Lyotard), who also tackled mammoth philosophical and historical questions in their work.[61] In very general terms, the shift from movement- to time-image can be read as an epistemic shift marking the end of the modern era.

Yet despite the link between Deleuze's approach and that of his contemporaries, there is still much to be critical of. One of the most obvious is his reiteration of a certain bias that used to structure Film Studies before it turned to a more historical approach to localised, national contexts. In general, Deleuze equates the dominant movement-image forms with Hollywood cinema, and the emergence of the time-image with European art cinema. As I noted in the introduction, by doing so he evokes the same homogenising tendency that was displayed by David Bordwell in 'Art Cinema as Mode of Film Practice' (1979), who assumed Hollywood's aesthetic to be the norm, and theorised Europe's various art cinemas as its aesthetic other. Deleuze's work on time reflected Bordwell's homogenising binary approach to American and European cinema. Focusing on the nation however, as Steve Neale's work showed shortly afterwards, provides some slightly different conclusions.

To illustrate the ramifications of this I will briefly consider the existence of movement- and time-images in a couple of national cinemas. As Rodowick has shown in *Reading the Figural*, the emergence of the time-image in France (primarily in the films of certain new wave directors) directly reflected the cultural and intellectual changes taking place in France during the 1960s.[62] In particular, it bears testimony to the emphasis on Nietzsche of philosophers like Foucault and Deleuze during that period in French history. In this sense Deleuze's decision to extend the category of the time-image to cover the cinemas of several countries could be seen as an overemphasising, or universalising of French thought in 'global' terms. Indeed, Deleuze charts the development of the time-image, from Italian neorealism, to the French new wave, to New German Cinema, to the American *auteurs*, in a manner that betrays a linear emphasis in his thought previously noted by András Bálint Kovács.[63] Ironically Deleuze appears to be suggesting an evolution of the time-image that contradicts the (as Angelo Restivo has shown) genealogical approach to history across the two volumes. Undoubtedly these different national cinema movements would have influenced each other, but, as Neale's work showed, they would also have been conditioned by their own national contexts. The fact that the time-images that emerged in France negotiate a slightly different national context than those which emerged in Italy, Germany, Japan and even America, then, goes a long way towards explaining the many subtle differences that exist between the time-images of these different cinemas.

Take France for instance. In *Popular Cinemas of Europe* (2001) Dimitris Eleftheriotis notes that the *nouvelle vague* – famously conceived as an alternative to the 'tradition of quality'[64] – was soon renegotiated into the national narrative in the manner Bhabha described. Eleftheriotis argues that one of the most important defining characteristics of the *nouvelle vague* 'is the importance of what is seen to be an almost revolutionary newness that challenges the national hegemony and fragments in this sense the unity of the national discourse. The latter is divided along lines of the old and new (the New Wave vs. *le cinéma du papa*), conservative and progressive, commercial and art, and so on.'[65]

Although these films were a challenge to previous conceptions of what 'French cinema' was, they also came to represent French cinema internationally. As Eleftheriotis demonstrates, to reincorporate this movement into the dominant national narrative, de Gaulle's government emphasised the artistic merit of the *nouvelle vague*. This ensured that the movement's 'new' qualities – whilst they 'must erase any prior or originary presence' of *le cinéma du papa* – could at once supplant and reinvigorate the 'old'. Here, as I will further show in Chapter 2, the figure of the *auteur* enabled the reterritorialising of the new within the old. The paradox that arises from this, of the *international* face of the *national* that the *auteur* promotes, merely illustrates the different attitude to the nation's role in the global marketplace that emerged after the Second World War.

Another example can help us to understand how this 'struggle between old and new . . . is a recurring story in histories of post-1960s European cinemas'.[66] Take Italy in the postwar era. It is entirely possible to chart, as Deleuze did, the emergence of the time-image in Italian cinema, from neorealism to the *auteur* cinemas of Antonioni, Fellini, Bertolucci et al. Yet during the postwar years it was popular genres like the western, the comedy, the *peplum* and the *giallo* that dominated the screens.[67] Deleuze discretely ignores these films, their absence almost suggesting that only time-images emerged in postwar Italy. These popular genres were movement-images and, typically, action-images. Even if they did not all express the linearity of the classical Hollywood narrative, they still maintained the focus on the protagonist's organic form, and his sensory-motor continuity. Thus, although it was possible to theorise a global shift in thinking occurring after the Second World War as Deleuze did, had he acknowledged the existence of these films then it would have been just as possible for him to theorise this shift in thinking as occurring at a national level.

A radical change in the image of thought was evident in Italian postwar time-images, but it makes more sense to see it as a change in the image of national identity. After all, the fork in the labyrinth of national identity that these films (often time-images) created, coexisted alongside its continuity in the popular genres. In fact, both of these contrasting cinematic forms renegotiated the postwar transformation of Italy's national identity, they simply did so in different ways. As I will show in Chapter 2, the time-images of directors like Fellini exposed disruptions in the national narrative. This was evident both in their narrative content and in their formal construction of non-linear narrative time. Yet they were also reterritorialised within the national narrative through the *auteur*'s role as artistic individual. On the other hand, it is possible to see how the resurgence of the *peplum* during this period also enabled transformations of national identity to be negotiated in movement-images. Here, however, rather than a deterritorialising critique of national identity, the *peplum* reterritorialised national identity, again in the manner described by Bhabha.

As Richard Dyer has shown, in the *peplum* the postwar reconception of a rapidly industrialising working-class masculinity was at stake.[68] Negotiating the devaluation of rural white-male prowess under industrialisation, these films returned to prewar images of the strong white man. This time, however, his strength was valued in and for itself, rather than for its economic worth in a rural context. Their use of the same type of image, but with a different emphasis, suggested a continuity that sutured over the devaluation of rural white-male prowess under industrialisation. The *peplum* chose an aspect of its previous incarnation (the display of masculinity) and used it to create the illusion of continuity between its past and present incarnations. The return of this prewar genre thus gave the impression that the years under fascism were an easily eradicated blip in an otherwise continuous national narrative. In this movement-image we see the reterritorialisation of national identity through the realigning of the old and the new. This is perhaps most obviously seen in a genre that used mythical male figures from antiquity to inform male experiences of the industrial present.

As these two brief national examples illustrate, Deleuze's conception of the divergence evident in the time-image makes more sense when viewed in a national context. Rather than a European time-image and a Hollywood movement-image, we now have Italian movement- and time-images, French movement- and time-images and so on. Thus, as I will show throughout the book, many time-images (or indeed, hybrid films that incorporate characteristics of the time-image) are often not amazingly dissimilar to their movement-image contemporaries. In fact, they very often explore the same themes, but with the added dimension of a formal examination of national de- or reterritorialisations. Although time-images do tend to deterritorialise the national narrative with the hybrid image it is a question of just how far they are able to do so. My emphasis on the nation thus ensures that what Deleuze considered 'classical' and 'modern' views of time can now be reconsidered as different ways of illustrating old and new versions of national identity. As I argue below, this approach also suggests slightly more muted, politically focused conclusions than those drawn by Deleuze. Rather than evidence of a global shift in the image of thought, or an epistemic shift marking the end of the modern era, the hybrid films negotiate transformations of the national narrative in a variety of different contexts. Only by examining them in relation to these contexts can the full implications of their use of temporal narratives be uncovered.

I am not the first to note the need for this national focus. In the era of globalisation it is a common misconception that identities are now post-national. Of the many voices, noticeably including Bhabha's,[69] which oppose such a conclusion I will consider just two. In *National Identity and Geopolitical Visions* (1996), Gertjan Dijkink states:

> The Second World War has been the most pervasive influence on geopolitical visions in the past half-century. Since war and revolution are the most disturbing events in the life of individuals and nations, this conclusion is not surprising. However, knowing an influence does not imply that one knows its consequences. Geographical location, history and the amalgamation of both in a national self-concept ultimately determine the effect that worldwide crises or other threats will have on the mind of a people . . . The world is a system of messages but they are understood differently in different places.[70]

Whilst films with non-linear narrative time schemes might initially appear to express the crisis of truth of the postwar time-image they actually use narrative time to renegotiate the 'national self-concept' in the face of major postwar 'events' and movements such as globalisation. Here Robert Burgoyne is in agreement. In *Film Nation* (1997) he states:

> Recently, several influential theorists have argued that the category of nation has been superseded by the globalization of economics and by the spread of information technology, that national boundaries have been effectively dissolved. Social, cultural, and economic life in the twentieth century, the argument goes, is increasingly organized in transnational ways; real power is draining away from the nation-state, and it is only at the political level that the nation-state retains its identity. Yet the importance of the imagined community of nation in the cultural and emotional life of even the most cosmopolitan societies should not be dismissed.[71]

Although major economic and technological advances have undoubtedly had an effect on the nation in the manner stated, Burgoyne's concluding point concerning the construction (imagining) of its identity remains extremely valid. In the second half of the book I will show how this is so in a number of contexts. For instance, in Chapter 3 I examine the way multiple narratives are used to construct images of national identity in Germany and Britain. Although globalisation is indeed the major factor that links these films, it is ultimately to restructure national identity in the face of the new global economy that they utilise a non-linear model of time. Again, in Chapters 4 and 5 I examine the way American history has been renegotiated through narrative time after two major global events, the First Gulf War and 9/11. Finally, Chapter 6 discusses films from three East Asian countries: Hong Kong, South Korea and Japan. Each examines national identity in relation to the widespread economic crises faced by several Pacific Rim countries in the late 1990s, but also to the specific challenges that each nation faced.

As a final warning about the difficulties of Deleuze's approach it is worth noting the Eurocentrism that structures his argument. Deleuze chose the Second World War as the point at which to situate the break between the two texts for more concrete reasons than solely the disruption of time evident in the time-image. It was amongst the rubble of Europe's major cities that he specifically saw the crisis in truth emerge. He argued that the creation of 'any-space-whatevers' in time-images replaced the determined direction through city spaces that had previously distinguished the realist cinema of the movement-image.[72] Consequently he argued that connections between spaces became discontinuous, and the ability of the subject to react to what they encountered in these spaces became similarly questionable. Yet it would be a mistake to think that once Europe's cities were rebuilt the crisis of truth ended. The return to dominance of the movement-image, and the dying out of the time-image in European and American cinemas did not signal an end to the struggle between the two. With the gradual dissipation of the postwar political crisis in Western Europe, the crisis of truth may have been eradicated from our immediate perception of its spatial expression. Yet this does not mean that it is not still an ongoing crisis.

As the interactive model of the two planes shows, truth is always in crisis whenever it encounters its virtual ungrounding. It is not just in crisis when the cities of Europe are in ruins. The fact that, globally, there is always a city somewhere that has been reduced to rubble can only confirm this fact. Indeed, as Laura Marks points out in *The Skin of the Film* (2000),[73] the subject's inability to extend its sensory perception into a motor action – that which accompanies the creation of any-space-whatevers in the postwar European, urban landscape – is a crisis that perhaps most strongly effects the postcolonial and diasporic populations who came to dwell in these cities after the war. Truth is always in crisis then, in any number of ways, and it is the narrative of official history that obscures this from our view. Marks' work illustrates that even though the time-image is an unusual image, it is still to be found in certain marginal, or marginalised cinemas. It may only rise up in mainstream cinema during times of national crisis, and then only in hybrid images. Yet for those populations within a nation that constantly question its pedagogical narrative of belonging this crisis is permanent. Thus it is in their 'intercultural' cinemas that Marks rediscovers the time-image, illustrating once again how the bias in Deleuze's approach is ungrounded by postcolonial thought.

From this new perspective it is possible to see how the shift that occurs in postwar cinema's conception of time is simply the realisation of the ungrounding of the pedagogical time of the national narrative. The fact that the time-image emerged in so many different cinemas after the Second World War simply reflects the broad impact that the war had. Admittedly this crisis can also be seen as a broader crisis of modernity, and the stuttering of Enlightenment ideals of progress caused by the war, but these ideals were themselves embodied in the idea of the nation. Thus, although there has been a global shift, as Deleuze and Pisters both note, it is in the context of the nation that we can most clearly see this shift being renegotiated, and ultimately reterritorialised.

Notes

1. Homi K. Bhabha, 'Dissemination: time, narrative and the margins of the modern nation', in Homi K. Bhabha (ed.), *Nation and Narration* (London: Routledge, 1990), p. 291–322.
2. Gilles Deleuze, *Cinema 2: The Time-Image* (London: The Athlone Press, [1985] 1989), p. xi.

3. Gilles Deleuze, *Difference and Repetition* (London: The Athlone Press, [1968] 1997), p. 129.
4. Gilles Deleuze, *Cinema 1: The Movement-Image* (London: The Athlone Press, [1983] 1986), pp. 141–215.
5. David Rodowick, *Gilles Deleuze's Time Machine* (Durham and London: Duke University Press, 1997), p. 12.
6. Deleuze, *Cinema 2*, p. 2.
7. Ibid. p. 2.
8. Rodowick, *Gilles Deleuze's Time Machine*, p. 5.
9. Deleuze, *Cinema 2*, p. 82.
10. Ibid. p. xi.
11. Rodowick, *Gilles Deleuze's Time Machine*, p. 13.
12. Henri Bergson, *Creative Evolution* (New York: Dover Publications Inc., [1911] 1998), p. 4.
13. In fact, Borges' labyrinth is perhaps more of an influence on Deleuze's thought than is often acknowledged. It seems to have affected Deleuze and Guattari's concept of the rhizome, of Chapter 1 of *A Thousand Plateaus*, with whose dispersive shape it has much in common. In fact, the term 'labyrinth' is perhaps a little misleading, as Borges/Deleuze's labyrinth has no centre. See, Gilles Deleuze & Félix Guattari, *A Thousand Plateaus* (London: The Athlone Press, [1980] 1987), p. 3.
14. Deleuze, *Cinema 2*, p. 131.
15. For a fuller analysis of this see David Rodowick, *Reading the Figural, Or, Philosophy after the New Media* (Durham and London: Duke University Press, 2001), pp. 170–202.
16. Deleuze, *Cinema 2*, p. 126.
17. Deleuze, *Cinema 1*, p. 60.
18. Rodowick, *Gilles Deleuze's Time Machine*, p. 175.
19. Deleuze's reasoning concerning what the plane of immanence actually is proceeds in a rather circuitous way. The plane of immanence in *Cinema 1* is figured as a, 'set of movement-images . . . a series of blocs of space-time' whilst the plane of consistency (itself necessarily a plane of immanence) which is defined in *A Thousand Plateaus* is thought to be that which enables a 'freeing of time, Aeon'. This is a development of the concept '*Aion*' from *The Logic of Sense*. Aeon and space-time, however, are not compatible as definitions of time. Aeon roughly corresponds to labyrinthine time, as it is found in the time-image, whilst space-time is exactly that which is created by the subordination of time to a movement through space in the movement-image. Deleuze's thinking of the plane of immanence, then, is not always consistent. For the purposes of this discussion, Deleuze's conclusions concerning the plane of immanence in *Cinema 1* should be understood as descriptive of the plane of immanence of the movement-image, but not that of the time-image. In this way can the plane of immanence (actually, organisation) of the movement-image exist as described in *Cinema 1*, as blocs of space-time,

and the plane of immanence (actually, consistency) of *Cinema 2* be that of Aeon. See: Deleuze, Gilles, *The Logic of Sense* (London: The Athlone Press, 1990), p. 61, Deleuze, *Cinema 1*, pp. 58–61, and Deleuze, *A Thousand Plateaus*, pp. 265–72.

20. Rodowick, *Gilles Deleuze's Time Machine*, p. 177.
21. Ibid. p. 178.
22. Gilles Deleuze and Félix Guattari, *A Thousand Plateaus*, p. 270.
23. Ibid. p. 265.
24. Ibid. p. 265.
25. Ibid. p. 267.
26. Brian Massumi, *A User's Guide to Capitalism and Schizophrenia* (Cambridge, MA: The MIT Press, 1992), p. 112.
27. Gilles Deleuze and Félix Guattari, *A Thousand Plateaus*, p. 262.
28. In *Reading the Figural*, Rodowick shows how the shift in thinking found in the break between the movement- and the time-image is analogous to the shift in thinking (in post-'68 French philosophy at least) from the Hegelian inspired existentialism of Sartre, to the Nietzschean inspired post-structuralism of Deleuze and Foucault. Chapter 6 explains in some depth the difference between the two approaches to history which these methodologies define. Rodowick, *Reading the Figural*, pp. 170–202.
29. Patrick H. Hutton, 'Foucault, Freud, and the technologies of the self', in Luther H. Martin, Huck Gutman and Patrick H. Hutton (eds), *Technologies of the Self* (Amherst: University of Massachusetts Press, 1988), pp. 121–44, p. 129.
30. Gilles Deleuze, *Kant's Critical Philosophy* (London: The Athlone Press, [1963] 1984), p. ix.
31. Deleuze, *Cinema 2*, p. 79.
32. Ibid. pp. 68–97.
33. Judith Butler, 'Imitation and gender insubordination', in Diana Fuss (ed.), *Inside/Out* (New York: Routledge, 1991), pp. 13–31, p. 21.
34. Ibid. p. 24.
35. Benedict Anderson, *Imagined Communities* (London: Verso, 1983), p. 6.
36. Ibid. p. 24.
37. Ibid. p. 26.
38. Bhabha, 'Dissemination', p. 294.
39. Ibid. p. 297.
40. Bill Marshall, *Quebec National Cinema* (Montreal: McGill-Queen's University Press, 2001), p. 9.
41. Ibid. p. 9.
42. Bhabha, 'Dissemination', p. 299.
43. Homi K. Bhabha, *The Location of Culture* (London: Routledge, 1994), p. 263.
44. Kobena Mercer, *Welcome to the Jungle* (London: Routledge, 1994), p. 58.
45. Rodowick, *Gilles Deleuze's Time Machine*, p. 153.
46. Gilles Deleuze and Félix Guattari, *Kafka: Towards a Minor Literature* (Minneapolis: Minnesota University Press, [1975] 1986).

47. Bhabha, 'Dissemination', p. 308.
48. Ibid. p. 306.
49. Ibid. p. 306.
50. Marcia Landy (ed.), *The Historical Film* (London: The Athlone Press, 2001), p. 6.
51. Jean-Luc Comolli and Jean Narboni, 'Cinema/ideology/criticism', in Bill Nichols (ed.), *Movies and Methods* (Berkeley: University of California Press, [1969] 1976), pp. 22–30.
52. Sean Cubitt, *The Cinema Effect* (Cambridge, MA: The MIT Press, 2004), p. 243.
53. Ibid. p. 243.
54. Comolli and Narboni, 'Cinema/ideology/criticism', p. 27.
55. Ibid. p. 27.
56. Ibid. p. 26.
57. Patricia Pisters, *The Matrix of Visual Culture* (California: Stanford University Press, 2003), p. 79.
58. Ibid. p. 104.
59. Ibid. pp. 43–4.
60. Ibid. p. 13.
61. Angelo Restivo, 'Into the breach: between the movement-image and the time-image', in, Gregory Flaxman (ed.), *The Brain is the Screen* (Minneapolis: University of Minnesota Press, 2000), pp. 171–92.
62. Rodowick, *Reading the Figural*, pp. 170–202.
63. András Bálint Kovács, 'The film history of thought', in Gregory Flaxman (ed.), *The Brain is the Screen* (Minneapolis: University of Minnesota Press, 2000), pp. 153–70.
64. François Truffaut, 'A certain tendency of the French cinema', in Bill Nichols (ed.), *Movies and Methods* (Berkeley: University of California Press, [1954] 1976), pp. 224–36, p. 225.
65. Dimitris Eleftheriotis, *Popular Cinemas of Europe* (New York: Continuum, 2001), p. 40.
66. Ibid. p. 40.
67. Christopher Wagstaff, 'A forkful of westerns', in Richard Dyer and Ginette Vincendeau (eds), *Popular European Cinema* (London: Routledge, 1992), pp. 245–61, p. 251–2.
68. Richard Dyer, *White* (London: Routledge, 1997), pp. 165–80.
69. Bhabha, *Location of Culture*, p. xv.
70. Gertjan Dijkink, *National Identity and Geopolitical Visions* (London: Routledge, 1996), p. 139.
71. Robert Burgoyne, *Film Nation* (Minneapolis: University of Minnesota Press, 1997), p. 10.
72. Deleuze, *Cinema 1*, p. 212.
73. Laura U. Marks, *The Skin of the Film* (Durham: Duke University Press, 2000), p. 27.

CHAPTER 2

Memory

This chapter explores how memory functions in the movement- and the time-image. This entails a focused exploration of the individual's existence in time, which builds upon the 'two "I"s' section of Chapter 1. As memory functions differently in the two images so too is the subject (here the character within the film) envisaged differently in each case. Understanding this distinction is of great importance as many films explore the temporality of character identity to negotiate transformations of national identity allegorically. Most obviously this is achieved through the use of a character's memory to represent the reconstruction of the national past. In the films discussed in later chapters, however, this process is also reflected in the narrative's structure. Mirroring the character's experience of memory these narratives visualise the process of national identity reterritorialisation, the reconfiguring of the national past that is examined allegorically in the diegesis. Exploration of memory in the two images enables a much fuller understanding of how hybrid films which may initially appear to function as time-images, are actually structured around a character memory typical of the movement-image. Thus, although their narrative time schemes may appear aberrant, they often offer only very limited, or temporary deterritorialisations of the normative narrative of national identity.

In this chapter I firstly provide an explanation of habit and attentive recollection, the two types of memory found in Bergson's *Matter and Memory* (1896). Using *Vertigo* (1958) these two types of memory are shown to characterise memory in the movement-image. Next I turn to Deleuze's work on the three syntheses of time from *Difference and Repetition* (1968). The first two syntheses draw upon Bergson's two memory types. However, they are ungrounded in a third synthesis, based upon Nietzsche's eternal return. This third type characterises memory in the time-image, and is illustrated through an examination of *8½* (1963). For the sake of clarity I have kept these sections separate, detailing the theory first, before using the respective films as illustrations. Finally, I conclude by relating the construction of character memory in these two films to their respective constructions of national identity. As these are already much discussed films I keep this final section brief and limit it to the individual films, intending it as an introduction to the more original, in-depth analysis of the contemporary films that follow.

Movement and Memory/Time and Memory (*Vertigo, 8½*)

Bergson and Memory

In *Cinema 1* Deleuze reworks Bergson's two memory types from *Matter and Memory*, habit and attentive recollection. These memories become visible in the present, in the interval between perception and action. Yet, although they have the potential to either confirm or unground the subject's sensory-motor continuity, they both ultimately confirm it.

Habit is an empirical form of recollection based upon a logical, linear, sensory-motor link between the subject and its surroundings. It is the instinctual recognition of the everyday reality that surrounds the subject. Habit is a recognition that extends into action, rather like the reflexive closing of the leaves of a Venus Fly Trap plant upon feeling the touch of its prey. It is formed by a building up of repetitions of same actions, the storing up of the past as bodily habit. The example given by Bergson is that of the student learning a text by heart, in which what is remembered is not each separate reading of the text, but the mechanical operation of repetition by which the words gradually come to be linked together.[1] When such learned habits are performed (or remembered) the interval between perception and action is minimal. In fact, there is almost no time lag, no interval, in which an attentive recollection can intervene between what is perceived and the mechanical setting into motion of the action that is performed upon it. Thus the continuity of the sensory-motor subject is maintained.

On the other hand, and in contrast to habit, attentive recollection is the return, or rather the becoming-actual, of the past (which exists as a stored, virtual memory-image) when it encounters a corresponding image in the present. Attentive recollection is the emergence of memories of the past within the interval between perception and action. Unlike habit, the automatic setting in action of a mechanism of stored bodily actions in response to certain stimuli, recollection involves an active effort of mind. Attentive recollection, moreover, ensures that the subject becomes temporarily suspended in the sensory-motor interval, and is unable to immediately act upon that which it perceives. Even so, this is not yet enough to completely liberate the subject from its sensory-motor continuity. Both habit and recollection then, serve to prolong the subject's continuous movement through space.

Before I describe the operation of attentive recollection in full I will first examine Bergson's conception of the past. Due to the perpetual splitting of time into a present that passes and a past that is preserved, the stored, virtual past is envisaged by Bergson as cone shaped.[2]

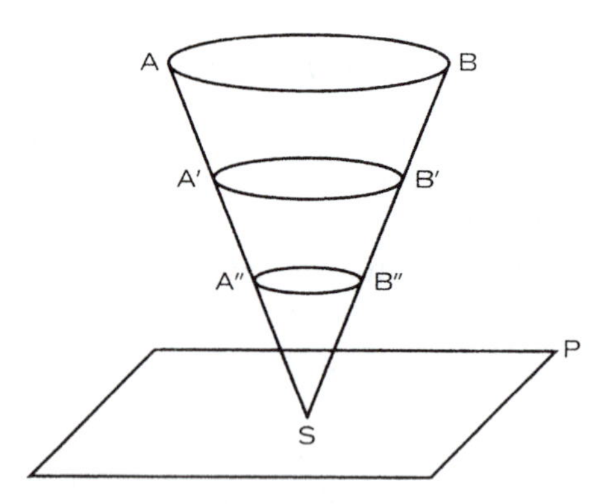

Figure 2.1 Bergson's cone of time (Source: *Matter and Memory*, p. 162)

Bergson's cone represents duration, time as a virtual whole. The point of the cone, S, corresponds to the present moment, the most contracted level of the past. The subject at this point exists as the condensed memory of repeated previous bodily attitudes. As time splits, the action of the storing up of pasts creates the cone shape, SAB. Each layer of this is a more or less relaxed level of the past. As the present, at S, is the most contracted level of the past, the layer AB is the most relaxed. Here all of the past exists as distinct and separate images, the antithesis of the condensed memory of habit. The myriad layers in-between, represented here as A′B′ and A″B″, are infinite in number. The virtual weight of the past serves to push the present moment forward into its point of interaction with the area marked P, the universal plane of images that is our perceived vision of reality. Thus the cone ensures a linear direction to time. At S the subject exists at the interval between perception and action, which is also the point of time's splitting into passing present and preserved past. The subject's unbroken sensory-motor continuity maintains their existence within the present moment. A suspension of this continuity however, creates an interval (a moment of indeterminacy) in which they become engaged with the past, usually through memory recall.

The question remains of exactly how this virtual past is recalled by attentive recollection? How does memory come to insert itself into the interval between perception and action? One might expect that, if the subject at S is defined by its sensory-motor continuity, its habits, or at least the body's physical position, would play an important part in this process. However, our habitual tendency to extend perception into bodily action – which usually serves to block the return of memories by closing off the interval into which time seeks to flow – cannot help but also encourage it. Bergson explains this paradox, saying,

> just because the disappearance of former images is due to their inhibition by our present attitude, those whose shape might fit into this attitude encounter less resistance than the others: if, then, any one of them is indeed able to overcome the obstacle, it is the image most similar to the present perception that will actually do so.[3]

The body's physical position plays a decisive role in attentive recollection, as it allows the recollection-image from the past that is 'most similar' to the image perceived in the present, to surge forward into the interval. Attentive recollection is based upon the same mechanical recognition as those learned, bodily repetitions of habit, but it distinguishes itself from habit by facilitating a much more complex encounter with the past. It is not simply the body's physical posture that calls forth the recollection-image. Memories also force themselves out to meet the image perceived, and with a greater degree of success when the subject's physical posture creates a shape that they can match. An attentive recollection, then, does require an adaptation of the body, a physical positioning that facilitates the entry of the recollection-image. This in turn requires a certain inhibition of movement of the subject. At the very least, a brief pause, or time lag, in the sensory-motor continuum is needed for reflection upon the past. Accompanying this motor positioning, however, there must also be a corresponding movement of the past, pushing forward into the present. Therefore, the subject is not always consciously in control of memory recall. This conclusion is borne out by Proust's modification of Bergson's theory, in which he describes involuntary memory recall caused by the sensory recollection of tastes, sounds and smells.[4] In these instances time surges forward unsolicited. Entering into the interval it brings forward recollection without an attentive effort of mind. Time, it would seem, has as big a part to play in recollection as the physical movement of the subject.

In attentive recollection, images from the past are grafted onto perception-images in the present. The return of the past is an effective *recognition* of the past, when it creates a match with the present. To return to Bergson once again:

> Every *attentive* perception truly involves a *reflection*, in the etymological sense of the word, that is to say the projection, outside ourselves, of an actively created image, identical with, or similar to, the object on which it comes to mold itself.[5]

This is the process of the becoming-actual of a virtual image, which comes to abide with the actual image that is perceived by the individual. As the virtual image comes forward from memory it enters into a circuit of indiscernibility with the actual image. In this 'circuit' of 'mutual tension',[6] the recollection-image overlays itself upon the image of the object perceived (the perception-image) until it is impossible to tell them – the respective past and present images – apart.

For Bergson, the process through which a recollection-image is recovered from its virtual storage in the past and brought forward to meet the present, breaks down into three inter-linked stages. These are, the leap into the past in general, the search through the layers of the past, and the bringing forth through translation–rotation of the appropriate layer as a recollection-image.[7] Firstly there is the leap into the past in general, the purely virtual realm. This ensures that the subject is detached from the present and that there is a momentary pause in the sensory-motor continuum. This initial movement, moreover, is accompanied by the search for the particular region of the past that contains an image corresponding to that perceived. If we return to Bergson's cone momentarily this process can be explained more clearly. Each section of virtuality, each layer of time (A′B′, A″B″ etc.) contains the entire past. Moreover, each such layer exists as a different degree of contraction and/or expansion of the past, uniquely divided with particular starring memories (different for each layer) and a supporting cast of lesser memories. It is for this reason that different associations take us to, and bring forth, different layers of the past, different ways in which we remember events. This explains why Proustian involuntary memories can abruptly return us to layers that we have previously attempted to recover in vain when using the Bergsonian process of attentive recollection. We may have previously been attentively searching on a layer where the memory sought plays a minor role, and is therefore not immediately apparent. An involuntary memory trigger (a taste, a sound) on the other hand, may leap us directly back to the layer within which the memory we seek plays a starring role.

Finally, once within a particular layer of the past it remains for the memory found there to be brought forward into the present. This occurs in a two-fold movement of translation–rotation that Bergson refers to as 'a work of adjustment, something like the focussing of a camera'.[8] During this process the cone simultaneously contracts the region of the past that contains the appropriate recollection-image and rotates the cone to bring that particular region of the past to bear upon the sensory-motor present. The body, for its part, assumes the posture most likely to receive said memory-image, to allow it to become actual. There is, then, a part to be played by the physical positioning of the body in the attentive recollection of memory-images, although it is not without a corresponding forward movement of the past pushing itself forward into the present. For this reason the recollection-image belongs to the movement-image. The organic regime of the movement-image, whilst momentarily paused by the emergence of the past, is ultimately restored to action after a brief interval. Thus, as I will further demonstrate shortly, attentive recollection is usually rendered as a conventional flashback. During the process of recollection the subject is involved in a double movement, always oscillating between AB and S, the virtual and the actual. The subject

> consists in the double current which goes from the one to the other – always ready either to crystallize into uttered words or evaporate into memories . . . This amounts to saying that the sensori-motor mechanism figured by the point S and the totality of the memories disposed in AB there is room . . . for a thousand repetitions of our physical life . . .[9]

With each leap into the past there is an expansion, a dissipation of the self into multiple past selves, 'a thousand repetitions' amongst all the many layers of the past. With each contraction of the past by contrast, there is a becoming-actual of one particular self. These coexistent past selves, myriad layers of the past, and their relevance for the subject in the present will be further examined in relation to Fellini's time-images. In the cinema of the movement-image however, the return to the singular self of the present is always retained. The reason why the recollection-image is not quite the same as the time-image will now be seen through an analysis of a single scene from Hitchcock's *Vertigo*. Here the return of the past as a process of expansion and contraction (translation–rotation) is readily apparent.

Hitchcock, Memory, Movement-image

The scene under discussion takes place in Judy Barton's (Kim Novak) room at the Empire Hotel. Scottie (James Stewart), having almost completed his makeover of Judy into Madeleine, awaits her exit from the bathroom. Judy/Madeleine enters the room, with hair blonde and tied back as per Madeleine. Scottie moves towards her, they embrace and begin to kiss. At this point the camera moves behind Scottie and begins to pan to the right, circling the couple. Scottie, sensing a change in his surroundings, opens his eyes. The scenery behind the couple now changes. The backdrop moves as the camera continues to appear to circle, from the interior of the room, to black, and then to the livery stables of the San Juan

Bautista Mission. This was the original setting for the kiss with which Madeleine parted company with Scottie before her flight up the bell tower. Recognising his surroundings, Scottie closes his eyes again. The kiss resumes, and the backdrop rotates back to the room interior. This is a perfect example of the action of translation–rotation whereby the past comes to be overlaid upon the present, entering into a circuit of mutual tension between the actual perception-image, and the (virtual-becoming-actual) recollection-image.

The process starts with the kiss. The position of the bodies creates a certain stillness of Scottie's sensory-motor continuum, and enables the memory-image to push itself into the interval. Yet it is not solely the characters' bodily posture that brings forward the recollection-image. Until Judy had effectively become the image of Madeleine, Scottie remained unable to access the particular layer of the past that would return the memory to him. Indeed, until the completion of his transformation of Judy into Madeleine he had been unable to adopt this physical position and kiss her passionately on the lips. Only with Judy's makeover into the image of Madeleine completed does Scottie find the correct associative image to enable the movement of past into present to be completed. Whilst this process is indeed aided by the physical posture they adopt during the kiss, the recollection-image also required a perception-image to match before it could surge forward into the present. With its match found in the present, in the made-over image of Judy, the memory of Madeleine pushes itself forward to create a Judy/Madeleine circuit of indiscernibility, a recollection-image.

When the room begins to circle we see the centripetal movement of time as it rotates the cone of the past. This simultaneously contracts the layer of the past in which the kiss in the livery stable is the most akin to the kiss Scottie experiences in the hotel, and pushes that particular layer forward into the present. This is the movement of translation–rotation akin to the focusing of a camera which Bergson discusses. The indiscernibility between the actual and the virtual-becoming-actual that this creates – the setting up of the circuit of mutual tension in which the past and present 'careen one behind the other'[10] – is seen in the way in which the backdrop changes from room to stable, to room again. Moreover, Scottie's facial recognition when he sees the stable around him confirms that the correct image has been found, and that the perception of kissing Judy in the present matches that of kissing Madeleine in the past.

This overlaying of identities continues to deepen as, immediately after the kiss, Judy forgets herself for a moment (as it were) and makes the mistake of putting on Madeleine's necklace. This was the necklace previously worn by Judy, playing Madeleine, playing Carlotta, when she initially ensnared Scottie. As Scottie is fixing the clasp behind her neck he catches sight of the necklace in the mirror. This transforms the image seen into the recollection-image of the necklace worn by Carlotta in the portrait seen earlier in the film. As the camera pulls back from this image of the painting, we discover Madeleine in the art gallery looking at the painting, with her back to Scottie. Here once again the situation in the present becomes overlaid by the recollection-image of the past. Madeleine seen from behind by Scottie in the past, is the image brought forward by Scottie's memory to match, to deepen, to enter into a circuit with, the image in the present. The image which matches that of Judy, standing in front of Scottie, looking at the image of Madeleine that she is becoming, is that of Madeleine, looking at the image of Carlotta that she was then becoming.

For Deleuze the successful completion of a circuit between a corresponding past and present image enables the 'sensory-motor flux to take up its temporarily interrupted course again'.[11] In the scene from *Vertigo*, Scottie pauses momentarily to take in the image of the stable, to witness the overlaying of matching recollection- and perception-images (the Judy/Madeleine match). Once he is satisfied with the match he resumes kissing. Essentially then, the recollection-image functions as a flashback, and as such, it maintains linearity. As Deleuze has it:

> the flashback is a conventional, extrinsic device: it is generally indicated by a dissolve link, and the images that it introduces are often superimposed or meshed. It is like a sign with the words: 'watch out! recollection'. It can, therefore, indicate, by convention, a causality which is psychological, but still analogous to a sensory-motor determinism, and, despite its circuits, only confirms the progression of a linear narration.[12]

Although the flashback renders the interval between perception and action visible, it actually enhances the linear unfolding of time. It posits an origin for the present in the past, and ensures a singular history to the narrative. In so doing it retroactively places the present as the *telos* to which the past seems to have inevitably led. It does not permanently threaten the subject's sensory-motor continuity, or its consequent subordination of time to a movement through space. What is seen in the recollection-image is the return of elements of the past that maintain the subject's continuity. Scottie is the classic example of this process of perpetual self-affirmation, a man forever struggling to be, as he says, 'free of the past' who must repeat the past in order to become so! In fact, *Vertigo* is itself marked by a narrative repetition that tends towards the same with a doomed, entropic and ultimately cliched finality. A flashback then, ensures that the classical narrative is a closed loop. Even in the scene chosen from *Vertigo*, which is an exceptional flashback and which verges on becoming a time-image, the linear trajectory of the movement-image is ultimately retained.

Clearly Hitchcock's conception of time has much in common with Bergson's. It may not be entirely coincidental that Scottie's moments of vertigo when looking down the stairwell of the bell tower are figured in the shape of a cone. This queasy elongating effect was achieved using a simultaneous zoom in and track out of the camera.[13] This double movement catches Scottie in the interval between perception and action, his glimpse of the bell tower's receding stairwell causing his sudden loss of agency. It suggests Scottie's realisation of his existence in time, with the cone shaped past – as it were – falling away 'beneath' him. Moreover, the spiralling vortex which emerges from the eye in Saul Bass's opening title sequence again suggests a cone shape seen from above. In this way Scottie's vertigo is shown to be as much a fear of the past as it is a fear of heights. His dizziness is brought on by a confrontation with the past, glimpsed whenever he stares into the cone. The fear that haunts Scottie from the opening death of his colleague is that this past will reappear and break his sensory-motor continuity. For this reason he recreates the past once again, by making Judy over into Madeleine, closing off the distance between the two, returning himself to agency with the kiss and reaffirming his sensory-motor continuity. Ironically, however, this process of ensuring linearity also seems to necessitate the death of Madeleine. At the end of the film the image in the present is still the same as that in the past, with Scottie staring down at a figure lying dead on the ground below him. Tampering with the linearity of time's cone, with the match of images of the recollection-image, is apparently not something that can be achieved in the cinema of the movement-image.

Indeed, following Bergson's theory, when the past returns in both recollection-images (that of the stables and that of the necklace) it creates but a momentary pause to the continuity of Scottie's sensory-motor present. *Vertigo* then, perfectly illustrates the way in which the past returns in the movement-image, whilst always retaining the primacy of a singular, linear present and a self-same subject. Admittedly, at the conclusion of *Cinema 1* Deleuze describes Hitchcock's cinema as illustrative of the crisis that the action-image faced when it neared the realisation of its own completion. Pisters also notes how Scottie aimlessly wanders through much of the film in the manner Deleuze described as typical of the seer of the time-image.[14] Yet *Vertigo* ultimately does not conceive of the subject's relationship to the past as the time-image does. It remains a movement-image, in which the return of the past is resolved in the actualisation of a recollection-image.

Even though *Vertigo* comes close, it does not manifest the direct expression of time found in the time-image. Admittedly the recollection-image is an 'optical and sound situation',[15] a moment in which the sensory-motor continuum is suspended very like those moments which characterise the time-image. However, it is only a temporary pause in continuity that, once reterritorialised, always ensures a return to agency. It does not yet, as the crystal does, capture the moment of time's splitting, the point of deterritorialisation. For this to happen the sensory-motor link must be completely severed. Only with perception unable to continue into action can the subject travel within a purely virtual past. After all, in its return from the past (in order to meet the perception-image in the present), the recollection-image always becomes actual. Thus, 'the recollection-image is not virtual, it actualises a virtuality . . . on its own account. This is why the recollection-image does not deliver the past to us, but only represents the former present that the past "was".'[16] The recollection-image is not quite a direct image of time, for the emergence of the recollection-image always involves its becoming-actual as it overlays itself upon the present. By returning in such a way as to explain the present situation, its function is necessarily truth confirming, and causal. In its becoming-actual it verifies the singularity of the past that 'was', and eliminates the falsifying potential of the virtual past that endures, the past that 'is'. In this way the recollection-image effects the reterritorialisation of the past that characterises the movement-image. In the time-image by contrast, something else occurs.

Deleuze and Memory

In the time-image we glimpse the crystal of time that I introduced in Chapter 1. The crystal exists in 'disturbances of memory and . . . failures of recognition'[17] that break up the logical progression of the self in time, and expose the virtual realm that Bergson distinguished as 'pure-recollection'.[18] The crystal is the mutual coexistence of an actual and a virtual image, of the actual and the purely virtual. It shows the present and a past that 'is', rather than the present and a past that 'was'. It is the image of time at the moment of its labyrinthine splitting into a present that passes and a past that is preserved. The crystal is a double-sided image, in which neither virtual or actual has yet crystallised, but in which both are caught up in the process of so doing. It is this lack of finality to the time-image that ensures the total suspension of the subject in the sensory-motor interval. As long as the past remains purely virtual the sensory-motor link remains permanently suspended.

Both habit and attentive recollection are ways of recognising the past as it returns to meet its match in the present. At either an instinctive, or an attentive level, they make manifest a continuity of past and present. For instance, Scottie must complete his makeover of Judy into a matching image of Madeleine before his flashback can occur. In the crystal of time, by contrast, the past is always misrecognised. It is not necessarily that which corresponds to the present which it mismatches. The time-image's labyrinthine falsifying of causality ensures that what returns, the memory of the past, can be used to create the memory of the future. This is the falsifying of the past, and the creation of different directions through the labyrinth that is enabled by the realisation of time's perpetual forking. As I described in the previous chapter, the labyrinth provides the potential for the past to be made over as not necessarily true, and it is this that creates a new memory capable of activating a new future.

Deleuze's work went beyond Bergson's through his engagement with Nietzsche. In *Cinema 2*, it is Nietzsche's eternal return that provides the ungrounding impetus to Bergson's conceptualisation of time as a virtual whole (duration). This same Bergsonian/Nietzschean assemblage had previously enabled Deleuze to formulate the three passive syntheses of time in *Difference and Repetition*. Beyond habit and recollection Deleuze argued, there exists the memory of the future. This is the pure or 'empty form of time'[19] which ungrounds Bergson's (ultimately linear) cone of time. It is this that makes visible the simultaneous becoming-actual of the virtual, and corresponding becoming-virtual of the actual, in the crystal of time.

The third form of memory also emerges in Deleuze's work on Kant in which he uses time to critique the Cartesian *Cogito*. Although I discussed this in the previous chapter, it is worth recapping at this point. Following Kant and Bergson, Deleuze argued that time divides the subject in two, just as time itself is perpetually splitting into a passing present and a preserved past. There is, then, always an aspect of the subject in both past and present, an actual I in the present, and a virtual I in the past. These aspects appear as either active or passive: active in the actual I of the present, and passive in the virtual I (or 'Ego' as Deleuze differentiates)[20] of the past. As I will show in Chapters 4 and 5, in American cinema the Cartesian I is at times celebrated (especially in heavily reterritorialised movement-images) and at others critiqued (mostly in movement-/time-image films) in order to negotiate transformations of national identity. Deleuze's take on Kant's divided I, however, is most easily seen in the crystal of time. To understand why this is we must first understand how the I synthesises time.

In *Difference and Repetition*, Deleuze identifies three ways in which time can be synthesised, three ways in which it can be experienced by the subject. The first and second of these roughly correspond to Bergson's habit and recollection. Habit is the first passive synthesis of time, the contraction of a series of presents into habitual actions. The second passive synthesis is that of the past that is preserved in Bergson's cone. As the present only comes to pass because of the storing away of the virtual past effected by the cone (the storing up of preserved pasts), recollection 'grounds' time[21]. Thus, whilst habit is a passive synthesis of many different passing presents, recollection is a passive synthesis of many different layers of the past.[22]

The subject seen through habit is formed by a synthesis of passing presents, through repetitions of actions that tend towards the same. The subject in recollection exists in a more dynamic relation to the past, as a synthesis of several pasts – the action of relaxation and contraction between points SAB of the cone. However, the second synthesis of time, when seen in the subject's actions at the level of representation, appears as an active synthesis of time.[23] For, with the successful actualisation of the recollection-image, the subject's spatial continuity in the present can once more be resumed. The active representation of the second synthesis thus maintains the illusion of both the subject's inevitable extension into action (despite its more fundamental existence as a passive synthesis of time) and its existence as the singular I of Descartes' *Cogito*. The reterritorialising of the past in the recollection-image ensures that in the movement-image the positioning of the body seems of greater importance than the movement of time itself, and the subject appears organic, linear and continuous.

Yet the first and second passive syntheses, constitutive of the present and past respectively, are themselves suggestive of an 'ungrounding'[24] of time, a third passive synthesis that belongs to the future. This is the third type of memory, Deleuze's formulation of the eternal return as the pure form of time. Here we see time released from spatial succession. It is the synthesis of time peculiar to the split, or doubled subject of the time-image. The third synthesis of time is an ungrounding or *möbius* loop:

> There is eternal return only in the third time: it is here that . . . the straight line of time, as though drawn by its own length, re-forms a strange loop which in no way resembles the earlier cycle, but leads into the formless and operates only for the third time and for that which belongs to it.[25]

Unlike the circular, self-identical loop of the 'earlier cycle' (that which, like the flashback, returns in the same form) in the eternal return the virtual empty form of time folds itself into a self-reflexive loop. It creates the oscillation peculiar to the crystal of time. Rather than a loop that tends towards the same – as in the actualisation of a recollection-image – this is a 'strange loop' that tends towards difference. The 'formless' into which it opens is the labyrinthine whole of time that is created when the linear drive of the memory cone is ungrounded, and the subject's sensory-motor continuum suspended. What returns in the crystal is always the other face of a *möbius* spiral, the other face of a discontinuous subject.[26] Thus the crystal of *Cinema 2* expresses exactly the 'hidden ground of time'[27] or the '*terra incognita*'[28] of the eternal return. This enables the crystalline subject to create the memory of the future, for, as I will momentarily demonstrate using *8½*, in Deleuze's crystal the subject exists in its becoming-actual, but it is never actualised as it is in the movement-image.

The subject of the time-image is a unique subject who 'belongs' only to that one repetition of itself-as-other. This is a subject who, unable to extend itself into an action through space, becomes-other in time. The suspension of its sensory-motor continuum defines the subject as a static (as opposed to active) synthesis of time. This is the synthesis of time enacted by an immobile spectator – like Jack Starks in *The Jacket*, locked away in the morgue drawer – whose sensory-motor continuity has been suspended. The subject now exists in a time in which change occurs, but which does not itself change. As I explained in Chapter 1, in the time-image all movement exists in time, rather than vice versa. Thus, in the time-image the subject's becoming-other involves an interminable slipping between different layers of the past. This is often a process through which characters come to explore their memories of the past, the myriad layers in which they exist as many different past selves. Now, when an image from the past enters into a circuit with that which is perceived in the present it does not become actual as the recollection-image did. Consequently, the past is not reterritorialised into a singular continuum in the present. Rather, the process of crystallisation allows the subject to slip into the past in general (the past that is, rather than the past that was) and to explore its myriad, not necessarily true layers. Here what is virtual and actual is now impossible to discern for, 'we no longer know what is imaginary or real, physical or mental in the situation, not because they are confused, but because we do not have to know and there is no longer even a place from which to ask'.[29] In the time-images of Fellini this synthesis is evident in the subject's slippages between the different virtual layers of the not necessarily true past.

Fellini, Memory, Time-image

Fellini's *8½* shows the subject as it exists in the third synthesis of time, especially the indiscernibility of virtual and actual that is manifested in its crystalline existence. The film was made in response to Fellini's experiences when he found his ability to act (to make the film) suspended by an artistic block. Similarly unable to extend perception into action, the film's protagonist Guido (Marcello Mastroianni), begins to slip through time. Through Guido's travels we see how in the time-image the past does not function as a first cause that informs the present. Rather, it provides a number of not necessarily true pasts that enter into virtual circuits with the present, to create a memory of the future.

The two meetings between Guido and the Cardinal provide excellent examples of this process. Guido visits his mistress, Carla, in The Railway Hotel. She has a fever from drinking spa water. Exhausted, Guido lies back on the bed and stares at the back of his hands. With his sensory-motor ability suspended his voiceover reflects wearily, 'What shall I tell the Cardinal tomorrow?' This is followed by an abrupt cut to the meeting of Guido with the Cardinal. Already we cannot be sure that this is actually the next day which we are seeing, a dream or a fantasy on Guido's part. With the subject's linear continuum suspended, the distinction between 'imaginary' and 'real' becomes increasingly difficult to make with any degree of surety.

Guido is walking through the woods where he is to meet the Cardinal to discuss the treatment of religion in the film. He is told by the Cardinal's assistant that his previous idea for a setting for the meeting won't work because 'the film's hero and a prince of the church can't meet in a mud bath . . . a prelate would have a private cubicle'. Again, this dialogue leaves us none the wiser as to whether we are seeing a genuine meeting or Guido's fantasy of this meeting within the film-within-the-film, which has to happen in the woods because it cannot happen in a mud bath.

As he sits with the Cardinal, Guido adopts the position of a naughty schoolboy, sitting on the edge of the seat with shoulders slumped, hat in hands and knees pointing inwards. As all around listen reverently to the Diomedes bird, Guido furtively glances around and sees a large woman walking towards him down the hill. As she hoists up her dress Guido looks directly at her exposed legs. In a gesture which epitomises the subject as 'seer' of the time-image, he pointedly moves his sunglasses down his nose to see her more clearly. This signals the movement through time that then occurs.

The movement is effected by another abrupt cut, this time shifting us back through time into the past, where we emerge into a schoolyard from behind a priest's head. The young boy Guido is being called away by his friends to visit La Saraghina, a large, beach-dwelling prostitute who dances a saucy rumba for money. As was previously the case with the recollection-image, the layer of the past chosen by Guido is that in which he finds a match for the image he perceives in the present. In this instance, it is a match between the Cardinal and the woman's legs in the present, and the Catholic school and La Saraghina's rumba in the past. However, unlike the recollection-image, this match does not extend into an actualisation of the past that thereby confirms the present.

Guido finds in this layer of the past the virtual double of the (actual?) situation in which he previously found himself. Yet how can this scene – which initially began as though it might be a dream, but equally might be the next day – be actual? In fact, the meeting with the Cardinal is actual even if it is not 'actually' happening. Whether it is actual or virtual is impossible to discern, so it effectively becomes actual once it enters into a circuit with another – virtual – image, a process that renders it indistinguishable (virtual? actual?) once more. Just as we cannot tell if the meeting with the Cardinal is actually happening or a fantasy, so the memory that Guido leaps into through the association with the woman's legs may or may not be a memory that is directly linked to the actual present. Unlike the actualisation of the past that accompanies the recovery of the recollection-image, here the past remains virtual. It cannot aid Guido in regaining his agency. Fellini's *8½* illustrates precisely how, in the time-image the subject proceeds through a series of memory 'failures', travelling through the past that is rather than reterritorialising it into a past that was.

The 'end' of this memory sequence abruptly cuts to adult Guido talking with the film critic Daumier. From here we move again, this time to the mud bath in which Guido is to meet the Cardinal. Again we must question whether this scene follows chronologically from Guido's visit to his mistress? If this is a return to the present then this would seem to place the narrative of *8½* very much within a movement-image schema. Should this be the case, Guido's fantasy/recollection is but the actualisation of a recollection-image, rather than the crystallising of a pure fantasy/recollection. However, we cannot assert this for sure. Is the meeting with the Cardinal that happens in the mud bath the actual meeting which Guido was so nervous about, or could it be another fantasy? The reference to the mud bath made by the Cardinal's assistant when Guido went to meet him in the woods earlier adds to our confusion, for in the mud bath the Cardinal actually has a 'private cubicle'. Is this the film within the film? Is it fantasy? Is it reality? We are no longer able to tell, for, subject to the movement of time, we no longer have 'a place from which to ask'.

Even if we are 'wrong' here, and the meeting is meant to be the actual happening that follows once Guido returns to reality from his fantasy, when he next visits the recollection of the meeting with the Cardinal, which will be the one that best fits the situation in which he finds himself?

Will the past that best matches the present be the first or the second meeting? How will the subject visiting a virtual layer of the past know if it is a fantasy or a reality? Which was the real meeting is a question that can and will only be answered in the future, a time that will make one of the meetings not necessarily true. In the future, when Guido calls upon this now virtual past he will not be able to tell its actual status from those versions of the same past that preceded and followed it. Thus, by slipping through the different layers of time it is possible to create a memory of the future, a not necessarily true 'origin' for some future present.

In fact, the Cardinal's private cubicle also seems to be in a process of oscillation with an image from Guido's childhood past. Specifically, it resonates with the boy Guido's enforced visit to a confessional after being caught with La Saraghina. This further illuminates the manner in which the subject exists differently in the memory of the future than it does in Bergson's recollection. It emphasises the interminable associative slippages between layers of the past that have occurred in Guido's virtual journey up to this point. The private cubicle implies that the scene in the mud bath is best conceived of as the image that fits most easily with his slippage from the past in which he (as a boy) is partitioned off from the priest within the confessional, into the present in which he is similarly partitioned off from the Cardinal in his 'private cubicle'. Rather than the actualisation of the past in a recollection-image ensuring the narrative's return to the present, Guido simply slips back into the present.

Let me elaborate. When the boy Guido is taken to confess his sin of rumba fascination, we see him disappear into the central of three monstrously gothic cubicles. When he steps out again, however, he exits one of only two monstrously gothic confessionals. There is no longer a cubicle to the right as we look, and the room has changed to include a wall that was not there previously. Within the confessional Guido has slipped between two different virtual layers of the past. In doing so he has become-other. The Guido that steps out of the confessional is the Guido who exists on the new layer that has been accessed. Guido in the present has therefore changed in this movement between the different layers of the past, the change in memory enabling a change in his future (now present), self. Thus the pure and empty form of time provides the conditions for self-creation, the utilisation of a not necessarily true past in order to create a discontinuous self and a new future.

Owing to this indiscernibility of the different layers, not only is there no longer a distinction to be seen between actual and virtual, but also, when Guido slips into the past 'initially', we cannot say with any certainty that the layer in which he finds himself is the virtual, or that the present which he left is the actual. After all, what would that then make the first layer of time from which he slips into the second layer? Where he moves from in the past (the layer which, for all we can tell, is the actual) is the double, the situation which best fits the posture adopted by that with which it oscillates. In becoming indiscernible in this way, the subject slips from an actual situation (even if it may appear to us to be a dream or a fantasy) into a virtual situation (new layer of the past) which in turn becomes the actual from which he will move into the next virtual, and so on. This is why the crystal is akin to the revolution of the *möbius*, effecting a shifting from an actual self, to a virtual self, to an actual self once more, and so on. The subject always coexists with its emergent double, due to the forking of time, and always becomes other through a movement within time.

In the time-image there is no necessity for the subject always to return to the present once the memory sought for has been uncovered in the past. When reviewed under the ungrounding conditions established by the third synthesis of time, Bergson's initial leap into the past in general is not so much a leap as a slippage into the past. Indeed, rather than being an originary act, this slippage is immanent to the subject's existence in time. In the time-image the subject in the time lag between perception and action now exists as a degree of expansion or contraction that is much more random than that theorised by Bergson. After all, Bergson was describing a subject who was still subordinate to a sensory-motor continuum, the subject of the movement-image. By infinitely deferring the actualisation of the past that occurs in the recollection-image, the time-image struggles instead to ward off the reterritorialisation of the past into a linear continuum, by maintaining the virtual nature of the past at all times. Becoming-other is not the same process as that which culminates in the actualisation of a recollection-image. Instead, reasons Deleuze,

> we constitute a continuum with fragments of different ages; we make use of transformations which take place between two sheets to constitute a sheet *of* transformation . . . which invents a kind of transverse continuity of communication between several sheets, and weaves a network of non-localizable relations between them. In this way we extract non-chronological time . . . at once a past and always to come.[30]

In the time-image the subject's return to the present may be due not to the actualisation of an appropriate recollection-image at all, but rather to an oscillating doubling, or match, between what is occurring there and the memory in which we existed previously. In this way, the present remains only one layer of the past (albeit the most condensed) that joins up with all the others through which the sheet of transformation moves. The sensory-motor continuity of the subject is thus undermined by the aberrant circuits of time, as it moves around the subject. For this reason, the second meeting with the Cardinal (in his 'private cubicle') is merely the double of the image in which Guido previously existed in the past, in which he was in the confessional as a boy.

At the end of the film, after his (fantastical? we cannot tell) suicide attempt, Guido finally reconciles himself to his sensory-motor suspension. At this point, asking forgiveness of all the characters in his life, he admits, 'Now everything's become as it was, confused . . . but this confusion is me.' Sitting in his car once again he is, as he was at the film's beginning, the immobile subject who travels within time. From the past, from his interaction with the confusion of selves that he is, Fellini is now finally able to begin his film. Hence in the carousel finish the boy Guido appears with the adult Guido, illustrating that the confusion of not necessarily true, virtual pasts can create the memory of the future.

In the final part of this chapter I will examine how the two different types of character memory seen in the two images are used to examine the construction of the national past.

Memory and Nation (*Vertigo*, *8½*)

Vertigo: *From miscegenation to economic-nation*

As I argued above, in *Vertigo* Scottie's confrontation with the virtual whole of the past disrupts his sensory-motor continuity. After resigning from the police force he only regains agency when he creates a recollection-image by making Judy over into Madeleine. In this section I will show how the match that this image creates, between past and present, illustrates the reconstruction of the national narrative that was ongoing at the time of the film's production.

Although *Vertigo* has received much critical attention in the past, it is only relatively recently that critics have begun to focus on its relationship with its Cold War context. For my purposes the most pertinent of these recent analyses is Robert J. Corber's chapter from *Alfred Hitchcock: Centenary Essays* (1999). Using Corber's analysis of the film enables me to illustrate how its use of the recollection-image mirrors its diegetic illustration of the construction of national identity, whilst my Deleuzean emphasis enables me to draw a slightly different conclusion to Corber.

For Corber *Vertigo* has a rather ambivalent relationship with its Cold War context. On the one hand it goes a long way towards exposing certain subjects usually thought taboo in American cinema of the 1950s. These include both the exploitation of America's various minority populations during the colonial past, and indeed, of certain sections of the population (especially the working class) during the 1950s. On the other hand, whilst the film equates these two processes it also separates them. This suggests that the racial segregation of the colonial past is a thing of the past, and that any exploitation that occurs in the present is purely a matter of class difference.

> Judy's relationship with Scottie duplicates the exploitative structure of her relationship with Elster. Like Elster, Scottie makes her over so that she conforms to his sexual fantasy, and then discards her after discovering the truth about her identity. Finally, in the film's final scene Judy throws herself away by jumping from the bell tower of the mission at San Juan Bautista, an act that links her not only to Carlotta, but also to the real Madeleine who is thrown from the bell tower by Elster. These parallels would seem to suggest that Judy's working-class identity plays a role in her exploitation that is analogous to the one Carlotta's Mexican heritage played in hers. In so doing, they acknowledge that working-class women are vulnerable to sexual exploitation by upper-class men. In the light of the ways in which cold-war ideologies obscured the formation of identity in relation to class, this acknowledgement is certainly remarkable. At the same time, however, the parallels occlude the entanglement of racial and class hierarchies in American society. Race and class emerge as discrete categories rather than mutually constitutive ones. There is no recognition that because of her racial privilege Judy's exploitation differs significantly from Carlotta's.[31]

This occlusion of the 'entanglement' of race and class was part of a much larger repackaging of America in the postwar era as 'leader of the "free world" '.[32] In order to effectively oppose Communism, Corber elaborates, it was necessary that developing countries should perceive America to no longer be racially segregated, regardless of the reality of this situation. In effect, the continuation of America's colonial heritage in the present had to be recoded as a matter of class or economic difference, if America's brand of market capitalism was to find a welcome reception abroad. In terms of national identity creation, America's 'new' economic colonialisation of the postwar era had to be reimagined in such a way as to create a continuity with the 'old' national past, but also to erase both past and present racial exploitations.

When viewed through a Deleuzean filter Corber's conclusion can be slightly altered. Rather, I argue that *Vertigo* uses the recollection-image to expose this very process. The film does in fact recognise the 'racial privilege' that makes Judy's case significantly different from Carlotta's, specifically by foregrounding the process through which this racial privilege is erased in the creation of a coherent national narrative of economic difference. The film illustrates precisely the separation of racial and class concerns in the postwar era by equating the two made-over versions of Madeleine in the recollection-image. By so doing it forces a consideration of their difference. In the second recollection-image in the hotel bedroom this difference is made clear when Carlotta's necklace reappears.

Writing on the horror film from a Deleuzean perspective, Anna Powell argues that a reappearance of the past (such as in the presence of a ghost) creates a confusion, or indiscernibility, between different layers of time. In a manner that describes precisely the effect of the return of the necklace on the recollection-image, Powell states:

> Ghosts conflate past and present as they linger to repeat their own present, refusing to let it be past. They compel present-day characters to abandon contemporaneity and to experience the history of others by enforced overlay . . . Tension is experienced as an unbearable dilation of time, whereas shock intensively collapses a temporal force felt like a physical blow.[33]

It is because of the necklace, this 'ghost' of the past, that Scottie drags Judy/Madeleine back to the Mission at San Juan Bautista where she dies. The necklace signifies Carlotta and the return of her Mexican heritage, and as such it forces Scottie to 'experience the history of others' which he has been working to eradicate. The necklace illustrates the threat of exposure that emerges when the makeover of the national narrative into one suggestive of economic, rather than racial difference is reinfiltrated by the return of a potentially ungrounding, colonial past. Hence it is precisely because the entanglement of race and class threaten to reemerge that Judy/Madeleine must die. Scottie has struggled to recreate an image of the present that denies racial and class entanglement, but the necklace renders the present and the past indiscernible once again. For this reason, Scottie is forced into action once again, to ensure the correct realignment of national identity. By recreating the death of Judy/Madeleine – itself a recollection-image – he eradicates the virtual past that is glimpsed in the necklace, and thereby restores his own sensory-motor continuity.

Prior to the reappearance of the necklace, *Vertigo* illustrates precisely the process described by Corber. Yet even here the functioning of the recollection-image is vital, as a few examples will illustrate. As I showed previously, the recollection-image through which Scottie regains agency illustrates how an image in the present is constructed that matches, and performs the same function, as one from the past. As a national allegory the disruption of Scottie's agency by the past, and its resumption once the past is actualised in the present by the made-over Judy/Madeleine, illustrates the reterritorialisation of the 'threat' that is created when previously excluded histories return to unground the national narrative. After all, the American national narrative was rethought during the Cold War precisely so that developing countries would not question America's role as 'leader of the free world'. The reappearance of previously occluded postcolonial histories threatened the national narrative, and for this reason the continuation of America's colonial heritage (its racial segregation of the present) needed to be erased from the national narrative. Hence, Corber points out, the makeover of Judy by both Elster and Scottie is coded as economically, rather than racially exploitative. By equating this process with the previous exploitation of Carlotta Valdez in the past, the film dramatises how the present is constructed to look like a certain image of the past, precisely illustrating how the racial segregation of the colonial past has been replaced by an economic definition of difference. Its visual equation of the two Madeleine's in Scottie's recollection-images illustrates how the new image of class difference functions to erase America's continued racial segregation. By equating the past with the present it retroactively suggests that the colonial actions of the past were as much about class as they were about race. The film thus illustrates how the past is also 'made over' to resemble the dominant view of the present as it supposedly is.

At a number of points the film illustrates how the makeover of Judy is an economic miracle that replaces and simplifies previous racial differences. As Corber points out, Judy's mimicry of the Mexican heiress Madeleine is possible because Madeleine adopts 'a mass-produced style of femininity that Anglicises her'.[34] The ubiquity of Madeleine's look is emphasised in the film, both in the 'assembly line'[35] environment of the beauty parlour where she is made-over, and in the besotted Scottie's mistaking of several women for the dead Madeleine.[36] In fact, I would add, not only is the beauty parlour figured as a production line, but the sales assistants also refer to the different dresses Judy tries on as 'models', much as one might a car. Thus the Fordist rationale behind the 1950s' consumer boom is highlighted, to illustrate how it constitutes a certain style or performativity that constructs and then perpetuates an ideal, Anglo-feminine image. Following Butler's rationale, the image functions as a homogenising repetition that tends towards the same; its ubiquity ensures that all American women appear the same, but its reappearance in the made-over Judy/Madeleine also foregrounds the continuity of the norm that it constructs by repeating in the same form. What previously appeared as a very reterritorialising erasure of the Mexican in Elster's wife Madeleine, is here shown to be refigured (through the makeover of Judy) as the erasure of class difference in the generic WASP look of Madeleine. To make this point most clearly the film situates the completion of the makeover in the

Hotel Empire. The new American export empire is figured as a place that represents status economically, rather than racially.

The recollection-image appears once again in Elster's office, and here too it is used to emphasise the creation of this particular national narrative. In the scene in which Scottie takes the case from Elster the film again foregrounds the process through which the present comes to selectively match the past. On the left-hand side of the image, the walls of Elster's office are covered in pictures of sailing ships. A model of a cruise liner also imposes itself upon one wall. On the right-hand side there is the backdrop of cranes either used in the construction of ships or for loading and unloading ships on the docks. They are also framed, this time by the window. Here San Francisco's past as a port, seen framed on the walls, meets its present status as a port, framed by the window. In this two-sided recollection-image the virtual and the actual create a match in which the virtual past is, quite literally, actualised in the present. Noticeably the national narrative here is realigned through the image of enterprise, as opposed to colonialism. This suggests that the maritime past was, like the tourist and export industries of the postwar present, a commercially oriented enterprise (which, admittedly, it was) but a commercially oriented enterprise *as opposed* to a colonial one. Once again the two-sided recollection-image is used to stylistically foreground how the colonial past is rendered a thing of the past, by the closing of the double time of the nation in the present. This process sutures over the contradictions that arise during a transformation of national identity. The ships that Elster builds after all, are designed to export the ubiquitous image of American national identity, constructed by its Fordist economy, to the expanding global market. It is literally in the context of the spread of market economics that Scottie agrees to police the normative image of the nation (in this case, Madeleine's mass produced look) against the disruptive return of the colonial past, Carlotta's possessive ghost.

For Corber the return of the colonial past is rendered as a return of the repressed through which the film 'undercuts' the reality of this historical exploitation by 'turning it into the stuff of melodrama'.[37] Leaving aside this bias against melodrama as a 'meaningful' form of expression, I would argue that the very obvious manner in which the recollection-image is deployed throughout *Vertigo* suggests that it is actually being used to foreground the process of national identity construction. Thus, with the reappearance of the necklace the film goes one step further than Corber acknowledges. Admittedly the return of the colonial past can be interpreted as a return of the repressed. However, if it is read as creating a confusion of past and present in line with Powell's work on the horror film, then the second recollection-image that appears in the hotel room can be seen as deliberately exposing the process of national identity creation for the construction that it is. As Scottie's reaction shows, the 'unbearable dilation of time' that the necklace evokes, creates the 'shock' like a 'physical blow' that he experiences.

In the first recollection-image, culminating in the kiss, Scottie makes over the present into the past that 'was', thereby assuaging his fear of the ungrounding past that 'is'. Thus he regains his sensory-motor continuity, and the national narrative is effectively reterritorialised in economic terms. Yet the Judy/Madeleine copy is only a selective match with an aspect of her image from the past. The one thing missing, Carlotta's necklace, is an accessory to the mass-produced look that would not have been (as the rest of it was) 'widely available to women in the 1950s, regardless of their class'.[38] When this signifier of the occluded racial other of America's past returns, threatening to undo Scottie's replacement of the image of a colonial past with an economic one, he is forced to act once more. He must replace this indiscernible crystal of time with a recollection-image, and to do so he must again confront the swirling whole of the past that 'is', that virtual whole which causes his vertigo. The necklace, then, points out the difference between Carlotta/Madeleine the racial other, and Judy/Madeleine, the economic other. Therefore, Scottie is not, as Corber contends, more horrified by class than racial difference,[39] but by the sudden reappearance of a racial heritage that threatens to undercut his carefully constructed economic image of national identity. Once again it is the past that 'is' that terrifies Scottie, due to the potential it has to confuse past and present, and perpetually suspend both his sensory-motor continuity and the national narrative. For this reason, when the necklace reappears Scottie takes Judy/Madeleine back to San Juan Bautista to put the Mexican heritage that it suggests back in its place as the past that 'was'. Judy/Madeleine's death, then, depicts the continued symbolic murder of the colonial past that must be maintained if the postwar image of economic difference is to maintain its dominance.

Vertigo is a movement-image that foregrounds how Bhabha's time lag in the national narrative is reterritorialised by a performance of national identity in the present. This realigning of history is effected by creating a match with a certain image from the past. The perpetual need for this action to be repeated is seen in the reappearance of the necklace. This unwelcome ghost of the occluded past necessitates that the process begins yet again, with the return to linearity of the national narrative (Judy/Madeleine's death) once more creating the conditions for its own potential ungrounding. To illustrate this process formally the film foregrounds the recollection-image, and the threat that the crystal offers to its reterritorialising dominance, making it an obtrusive special effect that demands attention. However, it does not attempt to deterritorialise this process, simply to show its almost cliched inevitability. Only in the time-image are things able to appear differently, once the national narrative is deterritorialised.

8½: *From Miracles to Economic Miracle*

In *Vertigo*, even though the film self-consciously foregrounds the process through which it happens, the movement-image schema ultimately reterritorialises the time lag in the double time of the nation. The national narrative is restored just as the protagonist's sensory-motor continuity is regained with the erasure of the colonial past. By contrast, although *8½* also expresses the consequences of a national transformation on national identity, this time we see the time lag in the national narrative as a spectacle in its own right. Rather than reterritorialising the national narrative, the film captures the moment of deterritorialisation, which it both illustrates in its protagonist's temporal malaise, and demonstrates in its aberrant movements of narrative time. Here both character and national identity are captured, adrift in the sensory-motor interval, as they seek in vain for an informing past.

In Fellini's film Guido's artistic malaise is used to reflect the cultural caesura that Italy's postwar economic miracle created in the national narrative. In *Italian National Cinema* (1996), Pierre Sorlin summarises the cultural effect of Italy's postwar economic boom:

> From the middle of the 1950s to the middle of the 1970s, structural transformations, namely greater applied scientific knowledge, a market-based industrial economy, and the rise of an urban society, triggered a sustained expansion in the retailing of consumer goods. With modernization, the economic benefits of domestic self-sufficiency and the saving of money vanished, but for people to recognize this and act accordingly required a radical change in attitudes. Family self-sufficiency, which was a necessity, especially on farms, was ideologically justified by traditional values supported by religion, the kinship system and gender roles. For this to evolve, a new cultural environment, dominated by secular, individualistic rationality, had to arise.[40]

Although the rapid transformation brought about by the postwar boom was by no means peculiar to Italy, in Fellini's cinema it is negotiated specifically in relation to its Italian context. For instance, take the famous opening of *La dolce vita* (1960), where a statue of Christ flies over modern-day Rome. The numerous partially constructed high-rise buildings it traverses illustrate the growing wealth and population of postwar Italy.

The airborne Jesus illustrates how Italy's Catholic heritage has been, quite literally, ungrounded by this rapid modernisation. The past that informed national identity previously is suddenly not necessarily true, as the shift from a religious to a secular culture created a discontinuity in the national narrative.

In *8½* this same examination of the impact of modernisation on the nation's Catholic heritage (with its commitment to 'family', 'traditional values' and 'gender roles'), is provided by the protagonist's travels within his childhood past. Guido searches the past for a way of understanding his inability to act in the present. He discovers that the values into which he was educated no longer apply to his current situation, 'secular' and 'individualistic' as it is. With the past unable to inform the present he begins to search for a new past (a new, selective image of the past that was) with which to regain his sensory-motor continuity. I have shown how, unable to do so, he creates instead an infinitely deferring memory of the future. Through film director Guido, then, the film demonstrates how the dislocated generation of the Italian economic miracle unsuccessfully searched the past that is, for an informing past that was.

Indeed, this technique of using an individual to explore the national past is a common occurrence in Fellini's cinema. In *8½* character memory is equated with the national past by focusing on layers of the past where Catholicism played a starring role. In various films that followed Fellini focused on layers of the past that starred, the capital in *Roma* (1972), fascism in *Amarcord* (1973), the impact of American culture in *Ginger e Fred* (1986) and the golden age of Italian cinema in *Intervista* (1987). Thus, although *8½* is usually considered to be more of an examination of art than society, its use of character memory to explore questions of national identity actually expresses Peter Bondanella's contention, that 'Fellini's works have provided audiences with significant images of Italian society in the course of representing the director's own artistic concerns.'[41]

I will explain in more detail. In the opening scene of *8½*, Guido dreams that he is trapped in a traffic jam. Most obviously the symbolism represents his artistic block. However, the components of the image illustrate the link between this block and the context of Italy of the economic miracle. The row upon row of identical-looking cars (a Fiat window sticker is prominently displayed in the car in front) represent the mass-produced homogeneity of the rapidly industrialising society. As Guido struggles to escape his car the smoke that pours in suggests the new levels of pollution experienced by this society, as seen in contemporary films like Antonioni's *Il deserto rosso* (1964). The traffic jam is situated in a tunnel, Guido's artistic block being equated with his sexual (or, at least, emotional) block, which we see mirrored in his dysfunctional marriage. These factors, plus the expensive clothes of the other drivers, and the seduction of Guido's mistress Carla (which he sees occurring in another car), all combine to illustrate how the new, 'decadent' consumerism has left Catholic-educated Guido suspended in the interval. Thus, Italy's rapid modernisation is shown to be the cause of Guido's emotional and artistic incapability. It is the cultural caesura created by this new society, especially the break it necessitated from the traditions in which Guido was brought up, that has rendered him immobile. For this reason he can only escape his car in a fantasy of flying, an impossible action which does not rely on organic, sensory-motor continuity. Also for this reason when we first see Guido in 'reality' he is convalescing in bed. Our first glimpse of him, as his hand reaches upwards into the frame and grasps at air, epitomises the unrequited nature of his sensory-motor condition.

This scene also acknowledges the role of the artist in commenting on the cultural malaise, and in realigning the national narrative. Guido's feeling of entrapment is exacerbated by the deadpan faces of the other commuters, who surround him and stare as he struggles to escape the car. Their gaze expresses the public desire for a social commentary from the director, which exacerbated his artistic block in the first place. In general, then, the opening scene expresses the pressure that Guido feels to create under the new individualistic culture that imprisons its populace in mass-produced, automotive monads.

In the travels in his past that follow, Guido's emotional and artistic block are shown to be due to his Catholic education, which provided him with a world view which no longer matches (or informs) that of the present. Specifically he struggles because of the religious and familial hierarchies instilled in him by his upbringing. As Bondanella has exhaustively shown, these reappear in his dreams, as feelings of guilt over his inability to satisfy the memory of his deceased parents and in his memories through the binary roles attributed to women by the Catholic Church.[42] For instance, during the La Saraghina memory sequence Guido is taught that women are either virgins (which in his adult world translate into ideal figures like Claudia and his wife), or whores, like La Saraghina in the past, who is replaced by Carla in the present.

Finding that this past does not inform his present in any meaningful way, Guido searches for a past that will make this one not necessarily true. However, unlike Scottie in *Vertigo*, he cannot find one that works for him. This is mainly due to his inability to construct an image in the present that can retroactively reinvigorate a previously occluded aspect of the past. Guido is caught in the moment of repetition in which the national narrative should be reborn through performance in the present. Unable to perform, however, he is trapped in a self-defeating cycle. Ultimately this cycle is broken in the present after his meeting with Claudia, in which he discovers her to be a human rather than an ideal type. This realisation enables him to acknowledge that the people he has been taught to consider as types are also actually people. Yet in his past there is no match for this realisation. Instead, he discovers that all pasts are equally falsifying, and that he exists on a transformative plane on which the present is forever coming into being.

All the myriad layers of the past that he has visited are now seen as equally informing of his identity. The entirety of the past that is is finally illustrated in the carousel ending. The circling figures of the cast descend from the scaffolding and are displayed on the same level, emphasising that the hierarchies of Church and family of the prewar era have been destroyed. Thus we see the Cardinal along with Guido's deceased parents, his wife, mistress, La Saraghina and so on, all dancing in the circle together. Their perpetual rotation illustrates the infinite deferral of the action of translation-rotation through which Scottie was able to actualise his past as a recollection-image. Rather than rotation–translation we simply have rotation. Here the carousel visualises the circling void of the virtual past that is, evoking once again the cone seen from above of Saul Bass's title sequence to *Vertigo*. Thus it is that Guido realises that he is a 'confusion' of past selves, and that we see his simultaneous existence as both adult male and young boy.[43]

Guido's ability to create a memory of the future on the transformative plane that traverses the past that is, is the condition of the national narrative that the film illustrates in its narrative and demonstrates in its formal construction. Not content to simply show the confusion that exists in Guido's mind between the different layers of the past that is, the film also takes the spectator through this disorienting confusion in its nonlinear construction of narrative time. Moreover, the character's search within time demonstrates the nation's search, at that time, for a new memory with which to reterritorialise the national narrative. However, the film does not provide an answer to this in its narrative, it just visualises the time lag in the double time of the nation.

Yet the role of the artist in the creation of the national narrative remains central to *8½*'s construction of national identity. Whilst *8½* deliberately leaves the role of the past in the present unresolved, and its protagonist accepting of the virtual existence of the past that is (without the need to reterritorialise it into a past that was), the film is ultimately reterritorialised through the agency that it provides Fellini the *auteur*. As I demonstrated in Chapter 1, in postwar Italian cinema, movement-images such as the *peplum* created images in the present that selectively matched images of the past. By so doing they realigned the national narrative. As a time-image, however, *8½* demonstrates the 'impossibility' of this action. Even so, much as the French national narrative reconciled itself to the new wave by virtue of the movement's artistic merit, Fellini's film is similarly reterritorialised through its celebration of the agency of the Italian *auteur*. In effect, the *auteur* (celebrated precisely because he is 'secular' and 'individualistic') connects the film to an informing past that was, to reestablish an apparently continuous national narrative.

The diegetic world offers the briefest glimpse of a solution to Guido's problem, in his return to action as he directs the cast onto the carousel. In his job as director Guido is returned to sensory-motor continuity, even if this action is then immediately disavowed as he inserts himself onto the carousel. Fellini's much rehearsed story of his own failure of self-confidence just prior to making the film is well known. In brief, he claims to have modelled Guido's artistic block on his own experiences, ensuring that *8½* exists as the visual proof of his return to agency as director. In this possibly apocryphal story (Fellini was always the great dissembler) lies the clue to understanding *8½*'s reterritorialisation of the national narrative, for it was through Fellini's international success as an *auteur* that *8½* (a film which posits the impossibility of reterritorialising the national narrative), paradoxically contributed to its reterritorialisation.

In Italy during the 1960s, Sorlin notes, certain films were embraced by the then fashionable Cine-forums as belonging to high culture, 'together with classical music, opera and literature'.[44] Much critical analysis of Fellini's films performs the same function, specifically by relating his films to older Italian artists and artistic traditions. Mira Liehm, for instance, notes the comparisons that have been made between his work and that of Dante,[45] whilst Bondanella makes the perhaps more obvious comparison with the works of playwright Luigi Pirandello.[46] Such comparisons position Fellini in the national pantheon, based on his artistic merit.

This recourse to the *auteur* illustrates the completion of the reterritorialisation of national identity through the evocation of individual agency that typified the period. As the debates around *auteur* theory have shown, celebrating individual authorship was a last-ditch return to Enlightenment individualism in the face of an incipient postmodernity.[47] It is perhaps no coincidence that the international dominance of *auteurs* such as Fellini, Michelangelo Antonioni, Pier Paolo Pasolini and Luchino Visconti corresponded with the peak of modernisation in Italy. The *auteur* expressed the triumph of the 'new' Italy, whilst his correlation with previous Italian artists ensured that he also expressed continuity with the 'old'. When a nation produces as many *auteurs* as Italy did at that time, much as the then-burgeoning French new wave did, they express the new face of the nation as at once a departure from and a reinvigoration of the old national past. Through comparisons with Dante and Pirandello, Fellini is used to create a national timeline that somehow manages to match both an artist searching for a secular meaning within modernity (Fellini) with an artist whose work was inextricably linked to a religious context (Dante), not to mention the theatrical tradition with cinema through Pirandello. Through the figure of the artist, then, what is genealogically speaking a discontinuous history can be reterritorialised as continuity.

That this national narrative is created in a performance that faces outwards to the international festival circuit, and, from thence, the world, illustrates how the national narrative entered into negotiation with a new global marketplace after the Second World War. Paradoxically, films like *8½* suggest that an Italian artist has 'transcended' the national narrative by capturing its point of deterritorialisation, thereby making this the perfect 'universal' film. This apparent universalism is, however, immediately disavowed when its director is heralded internationally (even if not always domestically) as a representative face of Italian national cinema. Fellini's modernist films, like many time-images, self-consciously examine their own existence.[48] Yet for this very reason their introspective take on the performance of identity in time, and the role of cinema in creating this identity, enables them to be seen as demonstrative of the way national narratives are constructed.

Conclusion

In this chapter I have shown how the two different images use character memory to help demonstrate the construction of the national narrative. *Vertigo* illustrates how the movement-image renders the straight line and the labyrinth of time as binary oppositions, here seen as the law versus the 'insanity' of the Mexican other. This process is shown to reterritorialise any potentially ungrounding histories that threaten the dominant view of national history. At points *Vertigo* uses the recollection-image to demonstrate the process through which a match is made between an image selected from the past and one constructed in the present. Yet the film does not go very far in deterritorialising the national narrative in its formal construction, even though it does critique it in its narrative by illustrating the symbolic murder upon which it is predicated. As the subject found in this film is organic and continuous, and is able to act to overcome the sensory-motor interval into which the occluded past threatens to reemerge, so the time lag in the national narrative is also reterritorialised by the film.

In the time-image, by contrast, the labyrinth is seen to be immanent to the construction of the straight line of time and reterritorialisation is therefore indefinitely postponed. Here the national narrative is directly shown to be malfunctioning. The process of time travel through which the protagonist leads the spectator into the past that is demonstrates the process of national searching for an informing past undertaken at the time. As the subject found in this film is crystalline and discontinuous and unable to perpetuate perception into action and actualise a past that was it creates a memory of the future instead. This initially appears to suggest that the national narrative has been similarly deterritorialised. However, in *8½* the national narrative is ultimately reterritorialised through the figure of the *auteur*.

As the brief examples of *Vertigo* and *8½* show, focusing on national contexts enables a rethinking of Deleuze's stance in the cinema texts, especially of his assumption that the shift from the movement- to the time-image expressed an epistemic shift in Western thought after the Second World War. Rather, my analysis shows, each film (be it movement- or time-image) is engaged with the renegotiation of the narrative of national identity of its respective nation. In the chapters that follow I will examine in more detail how recent films that contain aspects of both movement- and time-image formally demonstrate (through their jumbled, multiple or reversed narratives) the struggle between the re- and deterritorialising forces of the two images, as these films renegotiate national identity during periods of historical transformation.

Notes

1. Henri Bergson, *Matter and Memory* (New York: Zone Books, [1896] 1991), p. 79.
2. Ibid. p. 162.
3. Ibid. p. 96.
4. Marcel Proust, *Remembrance of Things Past* (London: Penguin, [1913–27] 1989).
5. Bergson, *Matter and Memory*, p. 102.
6. Ibid. p. 104.
7. Ibid. pp. 168–9.
8. Ibid. p. 134.
9. Ibid. p. 162.
10. Ibid. p. 103.
11. Gilles Deleuze, *Cinema 2: The Time-Image* (London: The Athlone Press, [1985] 1989), p. 54.
12. Ibid. p. 48.

13. François Truffaut, *Hitchcock* (New York: Simon & Schuster, 1983), p. 246.
14. Patricia Pisters, *The Matrix of Visual Culture* (California: Stanford University Press, 2003), p. 37.
15. Deleuze, *Cinema 2*, p. 6.
16. Ibid. p. 54.
17. Ibid. p. 55.
18. Ibid. p. 79. Deleuze states that 'Bergson calls the virtual image "pure recollection", the better to distinguish it from mental images – recollection images, dream or dreaming – with which it might be readily confused.'
19. Gilles Deleuze, *Difference and Repetition* (London: The Athlone Press, [1968] 1997), p. 88.
20. Gilles Deleuze, *Kant's Critical Philosophy* (London: The Athlone Press, [1963] 1984), pp. viii–ix.
21. Deleuze, *Difference and Repetition*, p. 79.
22. Ibid. p. 83.
23. The three syntheses of time are a problematic aspect of Deleuze's work. For some critics the three syntheses are all passive. Ronald Bogue, for instance, is content to define them as simply 'the three passive syntheses of time'. Indeed, Keith Ansell Pearson would seem to largely concur with this reading. He draws a distinction between Deleuze's 'material' and 'spiritual' repetitions. Material repetitions do allow for an active synthesis of time to be seen, but this occurs at the level of representation and does not detract from the essentially passive nature of the three syntheses. The quotation which he takes from Deleuze's *Difference and Repetition* should help to make this distinction slightly clearer: 'What we live empirically as a succession of different presents from the point of view of active synthesis is *also the ever-increasing coexistence of levels of the past within passive synthesis*'. Although all three syntheses are passive, certain of them do, or at least *can*, have an active manifestation. I have drawn upon the way in which the passive synthesis becomes active in the second and static in the third synthesis – as critics as diverse as Dorothea Olkowski and Timothy S. Murphy have done previously – in order to help clarify how these syntheses relate to the different ways in which the subject is formulated differently in the movement-image (active, second synthesis) and the time-image (static, third synthesis). See, Ronald Bogue, *Deleuze and Guattari* (London: Routledge, 1989), p. 65, Keith Ansell Pearson, *Germinal Life: The Difference and Repetition of Deleuze* (London: Routledge, 1999), p. 102, Dorothea Olkowski, *Gilles Deleuze and the Ruin of Representation* (Berkeley: University of California Press, 1999), Chapter 6, and Timothy S. Murphy, 'Quantum ontology: a virtual mechanics of becoming', in Eleanor Kaufman and Kevin Jon Heller, *Deleuze & Guattari: New Mappings in Politics, Philosophy and Culture* (Minneapolis: University of Minnesota Press, 1998), pp. 211–29, p. 218.
24. Deleuze, *Difference and Repetition*, p. 91.
25. Ibid. p. 297.

26. This idea was developed most fully by Deleuze in the conclusion to *Foucault*, where he describes subjectivity as a *superfold* that ungrounds the Man form of the Modern episteme. Gilles Deleuze, *Foucault* (London: The Athlone Press, [1986] 1988), p. 131.
27. Deleuze, *Cinema 2*, p. 98.
28. Deleuze, *Difference and Repetition*, p. 136.
29. Deleuze, *Cinema 2*, p. 7.
30. Deleuze, *Cinema 2*, p. 123.
31. Robert J. Corber, '"You wanna check my thumbprints?": *Vertigo*, the trope of invisibility and cold war nationalism', in Richard Allen (ed.), *Alfred Hitchcock: Centenary Essays* (London: British Film Institute, 1999), pp. 301–14, p. 308.
32. Ibid. p. 307.
33. Anna Powell, *Deleuze and Horror Film* (Edinburgh: Edinburgh University Press, 2005), p. 154.
34. Corber, '"You wanna check my thumbprints?"', p. 302.
35. Ibid. p. 304.
36. Ibid. p. 304.
37. Ibid. p. 306.
38. Ibid. p. 304.
39. Ibid. p. 307.
40. Pierre Sorlin, *Italian National Cinema, 1896–1996* (London: Routledge, 1996), p. 115.
41. Peter Bondanella, *The Cinema of Federico Fellini* (Princeton: Princeton University Press, 1992), p. 265.
42. Ibid. p. 166–8.
43. Deleuze, *Cinema 2*, p. 92.
44. Sorlin, *Italian National Cinema*, p. 121.
45. Mira Liehm, *Passion and Defiance* (Berkeley: University of California Press, 1984), p. 221.
46. Bondanella, *The Cinema of Federico Fellini*, p. 175.
47. For an introduction to this discussion see: Helen Stoddart, 'Auteurism and film authorship', in Joanne Hollows and Mark Jancovich (eds), *Approaches to Popular Film* (Manchester: Manchester University Press, 1995), pp. 37–58.
48. Sorlin, *Italian National Cinema*, pp. 132–3.

Part II

Movement-/Time-Image Films

CHAPTER 3

National Identity in the Global City

Sliding Doors (1997) and *Run Lola Run* (1998) were two of the most formally distinctive narratives to emerge in European cinema in the late 1990s. *Sliding Doors* is a British film that portrays events in its dual narrative as though they are taking place simultaneously in two parallel universes. To facilitate audience comprehension it episodically cuts between the two in a clear and pointed fashion. For its part, *Run Lola Run* replays its narrative three times, each time slightly differently. At first glance both films could be said to express the labyrinthine conception of time characteristic of the time-image. However, on closer analysis it is apparent that these time-images 'caught in the act' of becoming movement-images bear testament to the reterritorialising power of the movement-image.

Both films play with the labyrinth, momentarily allowing it to appear and thereby acknowledging a moment of national transformation. Their multiple narratives demonstrate the time lag during which an 'old' version of national identity is replaced by a 'new' one. However, they both firmly reterritorialise the labyrinth, thereby asserting that this transformation is now over and that the national narrative has been resumed. Thus, although they use a labyrinthine narrative to negotiate a transformation in national identity, they do not deterritorialise the major voice of national identity. Despite their initial acknowledgement of the recent transformation in national identity caused by globalisation, they ultimately reterritorialise the myriad possibilities for change opened up by the double time of the nation with one unifying image of national identity. Here national identity is refigured as a nexus of the global and the local, whilst the new international aspect of the nation is refigured to suggest a continuation of an aspect of its old identity.

Film Futures/National Futures (*It's a Wonderful Life*)

Before examining the two films individually, I will briefly discuss their structural similarities with respect to Deleuze's categories of the movement- and the time-image, and use David Bordwell's article, 'Film Futures' (2002)[1] to demonstrate how the overriding narrative logic that they manifest is that of the movement-image. Building on Bordwell's findings enables a fuller understanding of how these films use their multiple narratives to reterritorialise national identity.

Firstly, how do they manifest characteristics of the time-image? Although they are not labyrinthine in quite the same way that time-images such as *8½*, or Alain Resnais' *L'année dernière à Marienbad* (1961) are, both films formally construct narrative time in a labyrinthine fashion. In *Sliding Doors* this is most obvious because the intercutting between the two parallel narratives emphasises their simultaneity. The existence of these parallel universes suggests that we are in a temporal labyrinth. In *Run Lola Run*, however, the three narratives are played in sequence and cannot be mistaken for simultaneous parallel universes. Yet at the end of the first and second playing out of the narratives the two lead characters appear, lying in bed together and discussing their reactions to events. The three narratives are their joint fantasies, suggesting that the future is not decided and several possible outcomes could exist – again much as they could in the labyrinth of time.

Yet these films are also unmistakably structured by the logic of the movement-image. Most obviously they both use the bodies of their protagonists to create coherency across their multiple narratives as we would expect of the action-image. The recurring image of Lola running, for instance, or the use of the deliberately contrasted blonde and brunette versions of Helen, are entirely consistent with the movement-image. Moreover, through their protagonists' reactions to circumstances, they both maintain a sensory-motor continuum. Turning to Bordwell at this point enables a greater understanding of their existence as time-images caught in the act of becoming movement-images.

Bordwell begins by pointing out that the seemingly labyrinthine narratives of films like *Sliding Doors* and *Run Lola Run* are not particularly labyrinthine at all. Rather, he notes, drawing parallels with literary works such as Charles Dickens' *A Christmas Carol*, and O. Henry's short story *Roads of Destiny*, the number of different possible paths through time open to characters in such narratives are usually portrayed as a simple binary, or choice between three possible futures.[2] These labyrinthine narratives are thus reduced from an infinite set of potentially incomprehensible narrative possibilities to a 'more cognitively manageable conception of what forking paths would be like in our own lives.'[3] For Bordwell, it is 'folk psychology, the ordinary processes we use to make sense of the world' that determines the simplified nature of these labyrinthine narratives.[4]

Bordwell then proceeds to outline seven of the 'strategies characteristic of certain traditions of cinematic storytelling' that have been used to shape the narratives of such films.[5] These include: an overriding adherence to a linear, causal narrative progression across the dual or triple narratives; the signposting of forks in time; the use of recurring characters in different parallel universes and the application of classical narrative devices (such as the appointment or the deadline).[6] In Deleuzean terms, Bordwell is observing how classical narrative devices are used to order the multiple narratives of these films into the coherent, linear schema we expect of a movement-image. Thus their labyrinthine visions of time are mapped in a user-friendly way, once reterritorialised within the parameters of the movement-image.

However, the major omission in Bordwell's treatment of these narratives is any recognition of the way in which these films have deployed their labyrinthine narratives with context specific aims in mind. Bordwell is content to operate at the level of narrative structure, with these European films (and, for instance, the Hong Kong film which I discuss in Chapter 6, *Too Many Ways to be Number One* (1997)) being greatly homogenised as a result. Indeed, his recourse to 'folk psychology' is extremely general and ignores the differences between the various European and Asian cinemas from which these films emerged. An extra dimension can be appended to his study by considering how they use narrative time to negotiate a transformation in national identity. The strategy most relevant to this study is his fifth category: 'Forking Paths will often run parallel'.[7] Bordwell notes that the conventional use of parallel plots is brought to the fore in these multiple narrative films, to offer the simplified choice between 'right' and 'wrong' endings. Yet it actually offers solutions that are 'right' and 'wrong' in relation to the film's construction of national identity. This device is really only a variation on classical narratives such as *It's a Wonderful Life* (1946). As Frank Krutnik has shown, in Capra's film a specifically weighted choice was offered to American servicemen returning from the Second World War.[8] National identity was allowed two possible routes, either a return to the small-town values of Bedford Falls (the 'right' outcome), or the soulless *noir* landscape of Pottersville (the 'wrong' outcome). In these two films the choice on offer is between 'right' and 'wrong' ways to live in the global city.

Bordwell's rather ahistorical conclusions replicate the difficulties that arose from his homogenising study of European art cinema, 'Art Cinema as Mode of Film Practice'.[9] As I discussed in the Introduction and Chapter 1, Steve Neale's subsequent work showed that, when discussing the way an aesthetic has taken shape it is essential to consider the national context from which it emerged.[10] It is not enough to posit Hollywood's classical narrative as a tacitly accepted norm and to group the aesthetic of every other national cinema together as its homogenous other. In this case, the national contexts from which these multiple narrative films emerge, and the different images of national identity that they construct, ensure that they are more different than Bordwell allows. Admittedly they are similar in their use of multiple narratives to confront the shift to a new form of national identity (represented as a global/local hybrid) under the economic conditions produced by globalisation. Just as importantly, however, their context specific differences must also be highlighted. I will examine these films, then, as similar in global intent, and yet as different at a local level. Globally, they both use similar devices to appeal to international markets and to reimagine previous conceptions of national identity in line with the emergence of their national capitals as global cities. Locally, however, they are products of distinct national cinemas, sharing concerns also evident in other British or German films.

I conclude that these films are not so much concerned with demonstrating the way national identity could be constructed as they are with pronouncing a verdict on how it should be (and indeed, supposedly already has been) reconstructed. Although both films formally demonstrate the construction of national identity in their labyrinthine plots, they do not deterritorialise this process in the manner of time-images like *8½*. Despite their time-image characteristics these variations on the classical model are both heavily reterritorialised by the movement-image. By extension, it will be seen, rather than deterritorialising the dominant view of national identity, they merely propagate it.

Sliding Doors

This section examines how *Sliding Doors* uses its labyrinthine narrative structure to construct an image of national identity that corresponds to that of several other British films of the late 1990s. Using flashback, montage sequences, music, star persona and alternative genre styles, *Sliding Doors* depicts an either/or image of the two possible lives available in London, the global city. Despite its initial exploration of a labyrinthine model of time, the way in which this is simplified in binary terms and the one 'right' narrative that it advocates finally return the film to a linear model of time and a singular viewpoint on national identity. In this binary its reterritorialisation by the movement-image is most evident.

A brief plot synopsis is in order. *Sliding Doors* is the story of Helen (Gwyneth Paltrow), a young woman living in London whose identity splits into two separate paths through time. After arriving at work one morning to discover that she has been fired from her job in public relations Helen attempts to return home on the London Underground. In one story she catches the train, but in the other she misses it. The rest of the film is concerned with her two simultaneous existences. In one incarnation the Helen that catches the train returns home to find that her boyfriend, Jerry (John Lynch), has been cheating on her. She leaves him, and rebuilds her life aided by James (John Hannah) her new love interest. Helen meets James on the underground train which her other self failed to catch. After an initial makeover, in which she has her hair cut short and dyed blonde, this Helen becomes a successful business woman running her own PR company. It is clear that this upbeat version of Helen's life is the 'right' narrative, that advocated by the film. In her other incarnation the Helen who misses the train remains ignorant of Jerry's infidelity and is forced to work in two rather menial jobs, as sandwich deliverer and waitress. She remains completely unaware of the existence of James. This comparatively more dreary narrative illustrates the 'wrong' way to live in contemporary London. For brevity I shall refer to the two incarnations as those of blonde and brunette Helen.

Flashback

Like *Vertigo* and *8½*, *Sliding Doors* explores national identity through character memory. Its use of flashback is integral to this process. Although Helen's two incarnations are kept separate throughout the majority of its narrative they are finally brought into contact at the end as both arrive in hospital after serious accidents. Blonde Helen dies, and brunette Helen survives. As blonde Helen dies, brunette Helen has a 'flashback' (I use scare quotes here as the flashback is not her own) in which she sees three distinct images of the city. These are: the bridge on which she, in her blonde Helen incarnation, made up with James just prior to the accident; the American style diner where they first went on a date and, finally, the train on which they first met. The existence of blonde Helen's displaced memories within the universe of brunette Helen suggests a Deleuzean view of identity in time.

As I demonstrated in Chapter 1, Deleuze's labyrinth metaphysically underpins Judith Butler's work on performative identity, in which a change of identity in the present can question the 'truth' of a person's past. It is in the individual's power to falsify their previous identity and to break out of the various constraints on identity imposed by normative repetitions. Should an individual attempt to change their identity in the present a different path through the labyrinth of time will open up before them. Simultaneously, their past will become not necessarily true.

This labyrinthine sense of self can be applied to the curious happenings of the film's ending. The memories of blonde Helen's life that brunette Helen experiences in her flashback are a representation of the past that she might have had. The appearance of these 'memories' allows her to make decisions for her future based upon a past which now becomes not necessarily true. Significantly, on awakening in hospital with these new memories, brunette Helen sends Jerry away. Armed with a new resolve based upon memories from the past of her blonde self she becomes determined to make the past a different story. These events suggest a labyrinthine realigning of time for brunette Helen, from the present, backwards. This is evident in the order in which the places occur in the flashback she receives (from bridge, to diner, to train) as though blonde Helen's story line was running backwards to the point at which they initially split when boarding the tube. Thus brunette Helen's past is realigned with that of blonde Helen with the arrival of her memories. Brunette Helen, realising that the past which she has lived is not necessarily true, acknowledges through her actions in the present that many possible pasts exist, and that she is one of many incarnations of her labyrinthine self.

This labyrinthine self is further reinforced by the events that accompany brunette Helen's departure from the hospital. As she meets James for the first time in her brunette incarnation, she correctly finishes his Monty Python catchphrase for him. In her blonde incarnation she had incorrectly presumed it would be 'Always look on the bright side of life'. However, it turned out to be 'Nobody expects the Spanish Inquisition'. Her knowledge of James' quirk illustrates that she is now fully in touch with her other past, and has the ability to manufacture a future for herself that will make the past that was, not necessarily true.

It would initially appear that the labyrinth of time provides the magical quality necessary for brunette Helen to learn from the memories she receives from her dying blonde counterpart. It is therefore tempting to argue that the deterritorialising power of the time-image is dominant in the film. However, taking into account the politics behind the two incarnations of Helen, the both/and of her identity begins to appear much more of an either/or. In the construction of national identity, then, the reterritorialising dominance of the movement-image comes to the fore.

In fact the flashback at the end of the film has a very obvious intent. It is not solely an exploration of the possibility of self-creation offered by the labyrinth of time. Rather, the bridge, diner and tube station of blonde Helen's memory (all of which are images of London's wealthier aspect) are the film's most direct expression of the map of London that it advocates for a successful life in the global city. I will now show this in more detail, and in doing so, place the film within the broader context of British cinema of the 1990s.

London: Global City

Sliding Doors has already begun to attract critical attention amongst those working on British cinema. In 2000 two edited collections, *British Cinema in the 90s* (2000) and *British Cinema Past and Present* (2000), were published containing a number of chapters discussing British cinema's renegotiation of national identity in post-Thatcherite/Blairite Britain.[11] Several theorists emphasise how the changing face of the British economy (from an industrial-manufacturing, to a services base) has been negotiated in cinema. Subsequently, numerous films of the 1990s are explored in order to uncover exactly what has happened to national identity in this context. As *Sliding Doors* is typical in this respect, it does not pass without comment. For instance, Moya Luckett states that:

> *Sliding Doors* indicates that national identity requires some 'authenticity', despite its ultimate endorsement of glamour, the superficial and the magical. After all, Gwyneth Paltrow is American, and despite her appearance in films like *Emma* . . . and *Shakespeare in Love* as the 'quintessentially British' heroine, her star image undermines her authenticity. Consequently, *Sliding Doors*' attempts to find the truth of the nation rest on supporting characters who all have strong regional identities (James is Scottish; Helen's best friend Anna is Irish; and her two-timing fiancé, Jerry, is played by Irishman, John Lynch). This leaves a vacuum at the centre of the nation: in a London where there are no native Londoners. This suggests that national identity is always elsewhere, a paradox that seems to be echoed in the current efforts of audiences to find the nation in the images of British cinema.[12]

According to Luckett, in films like *Sliding Doors* any sense of a unified nation has dissipated into the image of a regional assembly of identities, apparently constructing a national identity so far 'elsewhere' that it encompasses nearly all of the United Kingdom, and even the Republic of Ireland! If we are looking for a traditional sense of 'British' identity in *Sliding Doors*, Luckett's work suggests, it is unlikely that we will find it. Nor is the influence of globalisation on this recasting of the nation lost on these contemporary writers. Claire Monk, for instance, points out that many British films of the 1990s aim to 'promote a global perception of Britain as a competitive and innovative enterprise economy, thus enhancing its industrial prospects in a global capitalist free market'.[13] The reason for the lack of Londoners in the London of *Sliding Doors* then, can be seen to be primarily due to the swing from an industrial–manufacturing to a services based economy, and to the nation's subsequent attempts to sell itself anew in the global marketplace.

However, whilst the above is certainly true to a large degree, the 'vacuum at the centre of the nation' observed in recent writings on British cinema is also indicative of a slightly different view of London contained in *Sliding Doors*. This apparent absence is only seen as such if we persist in searching for images of a recognisable, British national identity. By altering our focus and engaging with the film's portrayal of London as a global city, a different type of identity emerges. The film's multiple narrative structure is crucial in negotiating this changing conception of national identity.

As a film based in London, *Sliding Doors* exists in relation to a great many other films set in the capital. It has particular resonance when viewed in relation to a small number of films, mostly produced since the late 1970s, that represent London's role in the global economy. Perhaps the most well known precedent is *The Long Good Friday* (1979). Here plans to redevelop London's Docklands with the help of financial investment from America (plans that went ahead under the Conservative government during the 1980s) are represented in the form of an allegorical gangster thriller. In this case, the troubles in Ireland are seen as the major barrier to such a development of the capital, with the American *mafioso* backers pulling out because of the IRA bombing campaign. Flash forward to the late 1990s, however, and the echoes of IRA bomb blasts have been replaced in films like *Sliding Doors* by the gentrified splendour of post-Thatcherite London. Here the changes immanent in *The Long Good Friday* have been implemented, the services economy is in full swing and British foreign policy in Ireland takes a back seat to the selling of a Blairite vision of London.

In fact, *Sliding Doors* is not alone in its focus on London as the physical realisation of the nation's identity. Since the 1990s several British films have depicted London's services industry as the answer to the decline of communities in various parts of the north of England. *Billy Elliott* (2000), for instance, illustrates the move from one to the other in extremely unproblematic terms. The future of its protagonist is assured, despite the ruination brought to his northern community by the closure of its coal mine, in his move to London to study ballet. Coming as it does after the rather more critical stance on London of two of its immediate predecessors, *Trainspotting* (1995) and *Brassed Off* (1996), the upbeat ending of *Billy Elliott* has much in common with the late 1990s, New Labour-styled spin on centralised, British national identity that is also seen in films like *Sliding Doors* and *Notting Hill* (1999).

In this context the dual narrative of *Sliding Doors* is particularly telling. Its two stories illustrate the right and the wrong ways to live in this new global city. It maps the spaces of London, providing two alternate routes to a successful, and an unsuccessful, life. The new do's and don'ts of national identity are played out as a choice between two different, economically defined classes rendered as lifestyles. This can be seen in more detail with reference to some sociological evidence.

In *The Global City* (1991), Saskia Sassen describes the economic situation facing the inhabitant of the global city as one polarised by the emergence of the services industry. She states:

> Major growth industries show a greater incidence of jobs at the high- and low-paying ends of the scale than do the older industries now in decline. Almost half the jobs in the producer services are lower-income jobs, and half are in the two highest earnings classes . . . other developments in global cities have also contributed to economic polarization. One is the vast supply of low-wage jobs required by high income gentrification in both its residential and commercial settings. The increase in the number of expensive restaurants, luxury housing, luxury hotels, gourmet shops, boutiques, French hand laundries, and special cleaners that ornament the new urban landscape illustrates this trend.[14]

This is exactly the polarity between the high- and the low-paid sectors of the producer services economy which is explored in the double narrative structure of *Sliding Doors*. On the one hand, blonde Helen maintains her position within the higher end of the income bracket. With a start-up loan from the National Westminster bank she sets up her own PR consultancy firm and establishes herself as a self-employed member of the global city's elite. Working in public relations she provides a lucrative producer service, one of several that is increasingly common due to the centralisation of the service industry in London.[15] Moreover, her first major contract is the opening of James' best friend, Clive's, gentrified, riverside, 'expensive restaurant'. This choice of location is used to illustrate both the opportunities available to service industry workers such as blonde Helen, and the possibilities that exist for the high-income workers of the global city to establish their identity through the demonstration (or more accurately, the purchasing) of good taste.[16] In the global city, we are shown, the right economic choices lead almost inevitably to the consumption of the lifestyle enjoyed by blonde Helen.

Brunette Helen, by contrast, is reduced to a position of subservience to the more highly paid end of the producer services industry. Unable to find a job for which she is qualified her only option is to take a lower level wage, as a waitress. Thus the film locates her in one of the many low-wage jobs that the proliferation of expensive restaurants necessitates. In order to make ends meet, moreover, she finds that she needs two jobs as the cost of living in the global city is so high. To this end she takes the position of sandwich deliverer. This is another type of occupation on the increase in the global city, again due to the increase in demand brought about by population-intensive, high-income 'residential and commercial gentrification'.[17] The film rubs home its message that this need not be so and that brunette Helen could enjoy another lifestyle altogether if she so desired, by situating her in the same sandwich shop that she used to frequent when she was herself employed in the commercial business district.

The film's split narrative creates a binary that represents the division between the haves and have-nots that now exists in the global city. This is a situation, the parallel suggests, in which it is just as easy to be one as it is the other. Nowhere is this more apparent than in the montage sequence that intercuts between blonde Helen overseeing the opening of Clive's restaurant and brunette Helen waitressing in a different, but comparable, restaurant. The crosscutting between these locations is accompanied by Jamiroquai's 'Use the Force', the upbeat lyrics of which include the lines, 'I must believe . . . I can be anyone' and, 'I know I'm gonna get myself ahead'.[18] Identity in the global city is what you make it, the film stresses, the financial support structures are in place for anyone wishing to be their own boss, and the services industry provides sufficient opportunity for a wealthy, glamorous lifestyle.

Regarding the map introduced by the flashback, this potentially deterritorialising aspect of the film now appears to have a particularly reterritorialising effect. Although this flashback suggests a labyrinthine view of time consistent with the time-image, it is actually used to ensure that blonde Helen's narrative is promoted as the route to success in the global city. Thus, an aspect of the film which, when viewed ahistorically, appeared labyrinthine, now appears much more linear in its construction of one, 'right' version of national identity.

Star Maps

This map is aimed at the two different audience demographics present in the cast of this Anglo-American coproduction. These are both the devolved Britons of the late 1990s, and the international, but specifically, East Coast, transatlantic viewer. Through the characters it portrays and the audiences it targets, the film is able to refigure national identity in late 1990s Britain as a meeting of the global and the local. The role of its star, Gwyneth Paltrow, is central to this project.

In its recourse to the regional cast of characters, the ensemble that led Luckett to conclude that the nation was 'elsewhere', *Sliding Doors* appeals to Britain's devolved provincials, be they from the beleaguered ex-manufacturing communities of the north of England, Scotland and Wales, or even from the neighbouring Irish Republic whose independence was secured in 1921. If you wish to enjoy life in the global city, it illustrates, your identity does not have to be established through interaction with an English, or even a British, national past. According to *Sliding Doors*, identity in London is no longer determined by its status as national capital but, rather, as it is a city with external links, London enables the creation of an identity, that hails from 'elsewhere'. As the transfer of memories from blonde to brunette Helen shows, this is a space in which the past (be it individual or national) can be recreated almost at will. As the Irish and Scottish characters show through their interaction with the American star, Paltrow, the global city is a hyperreal fantasy space in which all national pasts can be forgotten, for English national identity is now 'elsewhere'.

Through Paltrow the film's Blairite vision of London also aims at the American market. Her star presence is used to court an international viewer who may be persuaded to visit, or even to relocate, to London. *Sliding Doors* firmly locates blonde Helen's narrative in certain newly gentrified parts of London. These settings perform both as advertising for the lucrative tourist market and as a sales pitch to the transnational worker. Tourism has been one of London's 'fastest growing service industries'[19] since the early 1980s, increasing the demand for such services as the expensive riverside restaurant, and, consequently, increasing the number of people in part-time, semi-permanent jobs at the lower end of the income scale (for example, those waitressing in these restaurants). The film illustrates both the opportunities to capitalise on tourist revenue that would-be global city workers can expect and simultaneously illustrates exactly what is on offer to the holidaymaker in London. Thus to capitalise on film's ability to advertise London in this manner, 'as a shop window', Film London was recently established.[20]

However, the tourist images in *Sliding Doors* are not those we have come to expect of London-based films, even though these images are still prevalent in several other contemporary films. For instance, the establishing shots of Trafalgar Square and the merry pearly kings and queens so beautifully satirised in *Trainspotting* are noticeably absent. In this case, the film does not aim to sell what is specifically different about London – its culturally specific tourist attractions, its history or its heritage – rather, it focuses on those aspects that establish London as comparable with other global cities. What is sold is not cultural specificity, not a national identity peculiar to England. Rather, we are offered the lifestyle of the young, *transnational* professional of the global city. For this reason the film goes out of its way to choose locations that demonstrate the overhaul that occurred in London during the 1980s and 1990s. From its expensive restaurants to its converted waterfront warehouse bars, the film reassures the international viewer that there are as many amenities here as in any other global city. Again for this reason native Londoners are 'elsewhere', their authenticity being contrary to the image of 'anywhereness' that a global city needs to represent.

The two different views of Gwyneth Paltrow's star persona that the film offers are also used to illustrate the changing face of 'national' identity in transnational London. Whilst entirely accurate, Luckett's point that Paltrow's star status undermines any sense of authenticity she might bring to her role as a young Englishwoman is actually not in any way detrimental to the film's aims. In fact, as Christine Geraghty has shown, the multiple narrative of *Sliding Doors* can be viewed as an expression of the added qualities Paltrow's star status enables her to bring to her performance of an Englishwoman. Geraghty notes that as brunette Helen Paltrow conforms to the 'manners, restraint and control'[21] we would expect of an English lady in a heritage film. However, as blonde Helen she brings her star status to the role as well, adding a touch of what is conventionally thought to be American glamour. The difference between the two performances can similarly be seen to represent the difference between a pre- and a post-Thatcherite sense of identity in London.

As Geraghty points out, Paltrow's transformation is most evident in the montage sequences where 'we are invited to look [at] rather than listen'[22] to Helen. Although Geraghty does not examine it in detail, for this discussion the decoration of her new office is the most pertinent for its selling of the city's spaces through Paltrow's star status. In this elliptical sequence, blonde Helen is depicted painting the walls of her office in a series of sweaters (grey-green and blue) that match the emerging decor. Thus Paltrow's transformation, from dowdy Englishwoman to glamorous American star is reflected back at her from the very walls of the city. This interaction suggests at once the transformation that has occurred in London since the 1980s with the influx of American money,[23] and once again the possibilities of self-creation that the city makes possible. Paltrow's transformation serves as an allegory for the transformation of London, from dowdy English lady to the American style 'dame'[24] of the global city.

Paltrow's star persona is also a direct draw because it has become associated with London's nearest neighbouring global city. Owing to her New York upbringing and her portrayal of several New York-based characters, she is rapidly becoming synonymous with a certain, elite, East Coast breed of American. For instance, around the same time as *Sliding Doors* Paltrow played characters in several films set in New York, including *Great Expectations* (1997) and *A Perfect Murder* (1998). Since *Sliding Doors* the link between her own cultured New York upbringing and the characters she seems best suited to playing has become more explicit. In *The Talented Mr Ripley* (1999), for instance, she plays wealthy Park Avenue socialite on extended vacation in Europe, Marge Sherwood. Similarly, in *The Royal Tenenbaums* (2001) she plays languid Upper East Side intellectual, Margot. Finally, Paltrow's recent marriage to British pop singer Chris Martin of Coldplay, and their choice of Belsize Park in London as a British home, further strengthens the link drawn by her filmic roles between the British moneyed classes and the New York elite.

The multiple narrative of *Sliding Doors* is used to show that the correct way to live in the global city is to follow the entrepreneurial life led by blonde Helen. Hers is the lifestyle that matches that of Paltrow's star persona. The incorrect way to live, by contrast, is the dowdy life of unhappy, brunette Helen, whose aspect clearly clashes with Paltrow's star persona. In the 'right' narrative, Paltrow most clearly fits in with the film's view of London. In the 'wrong' one, as Geraghty's work suggests, brunette Helen represents a more traditionally 'English' sense of identity, and is out of touch with the glamour of the new global city.

Melodrama versus Romantic Comedy

The fact that the corporate video package of blonde Helen's successful narrative is sold as a romantic comedy (as opposed to, Bordwell notes,[25] the melodrama of the dowdier story of brunette Helen) only serves to make it all the more seductive. The presence of James in blonde Helen's narrative ensures that her transformation into a successful businesswoman conflates entrepreneurial success with a successful romance. Thus the final flashback portrays not only the economic route to blonde Helen's success, but also the narrative of her romance with James. The images recap their meeting on the train, their first date in the diner and both their first kiss in the shadow of, and James' declaration of love on, the bridge. James, in fact, is the catalyst behind most of the life-changing decisions made by blonde Helen. He first suggests she start her own company, shows her how the leisured lifestyle provided by London's new, gentrified, riverside pubs and restaurants can be enjoyed, and introduces her to Clive, whose restaurant opening furnishes her first contract. Without James' influence, brunette Helen, the control version of this lifestyle experiment, remains a relative nobody.

Figure 3.1 Helen grasps her opportunity in London, the global city (Source: Paramount/Miramax/Intermedia/The Kobal Collection/Bailey, Alex)

This story of a woman's makeover falls within a tradition that includes such films as *Sabrina* (1954) and *Pretty Woman* (1990). In these films the power behind the makeover is the financially astute man lurking in the background. Whilst this is also true of *Sliding Doors*, its representation of gender roles further illustrates the national specificity of its context. As Dina M Smith[26] demonstrates of *Sabrina*, the romance plot of many Cinderella films function as thinly veiled political allegories. In the case of *Sabrina*, the love affair between lowly Sabrina (Audrey Hepburn) and corporate tycoon Linus Larabee (Humphrey Bogart) stands in for Europe's makeover by American investment in the postwar period. In *Sliding Doors*, by contrast, the extra dimension to the rom-com narrative is added by the gendered representation of London's services economy as the blonde and brunette incarnations of Helen.

With Britain's manufacturing industry previously coded as masculine in such iconic British films as *Saturday Night and Sunday Morning* (1960), it was little wonder that the emergent services industry, with its emphasis on administrative and clerical professions, would come to be represented as feminine. After all, it was to address the crisis of traditional notions of masculinity caused by this shift in emphasis that so many British films of the 1990s dealt with men adapting to this new environment (for example, *Brassed Off*, *The Full Monty* (1997) and *Billy Elliott*). For this reason, whilst films like *Billy Elliott* go out of their way to reassure the audience of its protagonist's masculinity as he enters the feminising environment of the services industry, *Sliding Doors* deliberately foregrounds the femininity of the young professional in the global city. Here the female protagonist represents not only the growing number of women working in the services industry, but also the services industry itself. Admittedly blonde Helen shares the same reliance on her man as the female leads of Cinderella films like *Sabrina* and *Pretty Woman*. However, as a representative of the services-based economy the film uses the influence exerted on her by James to stress that the power behind this industry is, whilst still patriarchal, not as interfering as it was previously.

Noticeably, blonde Helen's romance with James only really blossoms once they are on level terms career-wise. In new London, their romance illustrates, the entrepreneur may want to be prompted in the direction of the small business venture, as Helen is by James, and they may want to make use of their contacts in the services industry, as Helen does of James' friend Clive. However, they do not have to act unless it is in their own interest. Thus the ideal man in *Sliding Doors* acts as a metaphor for the style of government under which the global city of London has emerged since the 1980s. He is a supportive, but not commanding influence over the independent businesswoman.

It is worth remembering however, that the image of national identity offered by the 'right' narrative of *Sliding Doors* is not unique amongst British films of the late 1990s. For instance, the casting of *Sliding Doors* depicts a whitewashed London, portraying the same racially suspect gentrification of the population as *Notting Hill*. As though taking its cue from *Sliding Doors*, *Notting Hill*'s depiction of the nation through its regional characters (the benevolent English shopkeeper, the Irish thief and the Welsh dimwit) again speaks of a nationless identity in the global city. The numerous national histories of London's diasporic populations are noticeably absent from this reterritorialised either/or labyrinth of identity. Moreover, through its vision of a London in which even the most fusty of travel bookstores is fully equipped with the latest security cameras, and where all parks have been transformed into locked, private gardens,[27] *Notting Hill* also represents a very similarly gentrified London to that of *Sliding Doors*. Indeed, its final image – of a contented, pregnant Julia Roberts relaxing in her private park – illustrates much the same use of the star as draw which *Sliding Doors* creates through Paltrow. What sets *Sliding Doors* apart from its British contemporaries, however, is the way its multiple narrative structure appears to offer this view of national identity as though it were a choice that viewers have come to of their own accord.

The film's ending ensures that the spectacle of the labyrinth which we have witnessed is resolved in the image of brunette Helen meeting James in the lift as she leaves hospital. This replaying of their initial meeting ensures that, as in a classical narrative, the end responds to the beginning. It is as though the intervening events had never happened, and blonde Helen's narrative is wiped out of existence. All we are left with is the linear progression of brunette Helen's narrative, whose future will now proceed in a predetermined fashion, due to the map passed on to her by blonde Helen. The labyrinth was but a passing spectacle, a way of envisaging the possible others of national identity. However, it was so heavily constrained by binary logic in its inception that it never offered anything other than an illusory dichotomy. Thus, in *Sliding Doors* we see how the movement-image's plane of organisation takes the both/and of the time-image and reterritorialises it into an either/or, along with the labyrinthine possibilities for national identity that it could conceivably enable.

Run Lola Run

So far I have shown how *Sliding Doors* utilises and reterritorialises aspects of the time-image (specifically the labyrinth) in order to aid the construction of one particular image of national identity. A similar effect is created in *Run Lola Run*, although the model of time used to evoke the labyrinth is slightly different. Here the film deploys a model of time which appears to be based on deterministic chaos. It then reterritorialises this within a view of time closer to that of Einstein's, ensuring that the triple narrative creates an either/either/or, through which the linearity of the movement-image retains its dominance.

Again a brief plot synopsis is helpful. *Run Lola Run* replays a basic narrative idea three times, each time with a slightly different conclusion. At the start of the film, Lola (Franka Potente) receives a phone call from her boyfriend Manni (Moritz Bleibtreu) a small-time courier for a violent gangster, Ronni. Whilst on an errand for his boss, Manni managed to successfully deliver his cargo, but on his return he lost the payment. With no way of knowing where the money is Lola has to find a replacement DM100,000 and get it to Manni in twenty minutes. The three stories that follow chart her slightly different attempts to get the money from her father. The first ends in the police's capture of her and Manni, and in the accidental shooting of Lola. The second ends with the accidental death of Manni after Lola has successfully managed to obtain the money by robbing the Deutsche Transfer Bank where her father works; the third with Manni recovering his own money, Lola winning the same amount at roulette and with both characters alive at the end. The film focuses exclusively on the present moment and does so to offer three possible futures for recently reunified Germany.

In order to examine how this film functions in a manner similar to *Sliding Doors* I will first examine the context of the national cinema from which it emerged. The critical attention paid to *Sliding Doors* has not been as great as that given to *Run Lola Run* on which several articles and chapters have been written closely examining the film and referring to its depiction of Berlin in a global context. In order to avoid repeating these works I will briefly engage with aspects of them, isolating certain points raised by Eric Rentschler, Claudia Mesch, Ian Garwood and Christine Haase and using them as jumping off points for my own discussion. This material will then be discussed in conjunction with the film's depiction of time.

Berlin: Global City

The post-wall German cinema of consensus has been described by several critics as willfully ignorant of questions of national identity in contemporary Germany. This case is often made through negative comparisons with the more politically engaged, New German Cinema of the 1970s. As Rentschler has it:

> Journalists, cineastes and intellectuals at large have frequently rebuked German filmmakers for ignoring the nation's social problems and political debates. Contemporary productions, they tell us, studiously and systematically skirt the 'large' topics and hot issues: the messy complications of post-wall reality, thematics like right-wing radicalism, chronic unemployment, or the uneasy integration of the former GDR into the Federal Republic.[28]

In this sense, *Run Lola Run* can be said to provide equally as gentrified an image of Berlin as *Sliding Doors* does of London. Just as the British film ignores the social conditions of the capital's less-well-off inhabitants to explore the lifestyle issues of its young professionals, so too does *Run Lola Run*, with its focus on the fantastical problem faced by an upper middle-class, twenty-something cyber-punk and her partner. This characteristic is also shared by many other post-wall films. Again, Rentschler notes that:

> In representative features like *Makin' Up* (*Abgeschminkt*), *Talk of the Town* (*Stadtgespräch*), and *Super-woman* (*Das Superweib*), we find young upscale urbanites working in a sector of the culture industry. The protagonists – attractive, successful and around thirty – run up against the reality principle and confront the responsibilities of the adult world. The narratives occupy a liminal space between a bohemian everyday and a bourgeois existence . . .[29]

Taking the first of these as a typical example, in *Makin' Up* (1990) graphic artist, Frenzy (Katja Riemann) lives a bohemian lifestyle in a converted warehouse apartment, but is equally at home in art galleries, various up-market bars, restaurants and clubs. She shares the same liminal lifestyle as Lola, whose revealing clothing, tattoos and bright hair remain constant as she runs effortlessly between her parents' expensive flat, her father's bank, the casino whose dress code she so easily violates and so on.

In contrast to the art cinema classics of New German Cinema, then, post-wall films such as *Run Lola Run* do indeed ignore more recognisable conceptions of nationality in their representation of identity in contemporary Berlin. However, *Run Lola Run* does so in order to foreground the different type of identity it now offers as a global city. There are a number of ways in which this replacement of the old with the new is achieved.

Haase points out that '*Run Lola Run* consistently points to a growing global trend of transnational movements in terms of culture and capital'.[30] Referring to Lola's final roulette win in the casino she argues that the film demonstrates how money acts as the unifying principle in the film's image of Berlin. It illustrates how, like cyber-punk Lola making a fortune amongst the well-dressed global elite, 'you don't have to be like them to participate in what they are doing'.[31] Much as *Sliding Doors* uses its contrasting Helens to illustrate that life in the global city is what you make of it, *Run Lola Run* uses its three contrasting versions of Lola to the same effect. This time, however, there are two 'wrong' narratives and one 'right' one.

For her part, Mesch[32] argues – in a manner that seems initially to be very much in line with Rentschler's critique of the cinema of consensus – that, in contrast to previous films set in Berlin, *Run Lola Run* does not specifically address contemporary issues surrounding the city's, or the nation's past. However, her take on what the film does actually depict is slightly different from Rentschler's.

> Berlin has often been represented, in visual art and in cinematic imagery, as the modern metropolis: the Expressionist and Dadaist painters, Walter Ruttman, Fritz Lang and Rainer Werner Fassbinder all depicted it as the modernising city. Since the '60s artists have staged artworks and performances in the public space of the city which critiqued the cold war order of that space, its institutions, and the hysterical attempt by German government to erase a divided past after 1990. *Run Lola Run* depicts its setting, Berlin, as a cyberspace obstacle course or environment usually associated with interactive video and computer games. The eerie emptiness of the Berlin of *Run Lola Run* – a fantasy projected onto a city which has been called the single biggest construction site in Europe – is necessary to keep the protagonist Lola moving at high speed from the West to the East part of town and back again – another fantasy which is only possible when the city is recast as a virtual environment.[33]

Encapsulated in the image of the unifying figure of the running Lola, Tykwer's film represents an already reconstructed post-wall Berlin. For Mesch, its recent past as a divided city is thus eradicated by the image of the city through which Lola runs, 'from the West to the East part of town and back again'. In fact, although Mesch does not mention it, the supposed interchangeability of spaces in the east and west of the city is flagged up as early on as the set up to the story. After her moped is stolen, Lola takes a taxi to meet Manni. She is late because the taxi driver takes her to the wrong part of town. The reason she gives for this is that there is a Grunewaldstrasse in the East that has the same name as that where she was to meet Manni in the West. East and West Berlin, this incident suggests, are so easily confusable that even locals and taxi drivers cannot always tell them apart. The physical body of Lola, then, acts in the manner we would expect of a protagonist in a movement-image, to unify incommensurable spaces through which it passes. In this instance this is done in the service of the creation of the image of Berlin as a reunified, fully functioning global city.

The film's depiction of the apparent completion of the process of post-wall reconstruction is further emphasised by its strategic choice of locations. For instance, there is the recurring establishing shot of the Friedrichstrasse U-Bahn stop at the start of each replaying of the narrative. This is a location 'near the Brandenburg Gate in the former East Berlin which has undergone extensive reconstruction since 1990'.[34] As with the gentrified Thames-side locations chosen for *Sliding Doors*, the Berlin depicted in *Run Lola Run* is a global city apparently on a par with those that, like London, enjoyed their makeovers during the 1980s and 1990s. The film does indeed contain a marked absence of images of contemporary difference, and it also seems to deny its division prior to 1989, yet this is specifically so that it can offer a depiction of Berlin as a fully developed global city. Although it fails to critique the nation in the way that previous art works have done, its lack of acknowledgement of the reality of life in contemporary Berlin is actually a product of a larger, global aim of the film.

In line with this view of the film, the city's makeover is seen by Mesch to be envisaged as a 'rewiring' of Berlin, into the 'global broadband digital telecommunications network'.[35] Berlin is shown not only to be physically rebuilt, but also economically ready to reintegrate itself within the global economy. Emphasising this readiness, and doubling this virtual network of global telecommunications, is the city's status as part of a larger network of global cities. This is seen through the recurring motif of the grid in the film's *mise-en-scène*. Mesch notes its appearance in various guises, most pertinently for this discussion in the movements of the city's transport networks, its bikes, trains and planes depicting the city as 'an idealised nexus of local, national and global lines of mobility and communication'.[36] Again as in *Sliding Doors*, the national capital is depicted in such a way as to appeal to a twin demographic, both potential migratory workers from the nation's disparate regions and also from foreign audiences. The film's decision to aim at a youth market through its use of Lola and Manni as protagonists is particularly astute in this respect, stressing the city's international status by focusing on the section of the national population most likely, as Mesch points out, to enjoy its annual techno festival, as well as, I would add, the hordes of overseas attendees.

The supposedly arbitrary choice of Berlin as a setting is also evoked by Mesch. She reiterates Tykwer's contention that the film could just as well have been shot in New York or Beijing.[37] I do not entirely agree with this statement for reasons I shall elaborate in the conclusion to this chapter. After all, the reunified, reconstructed city it depicts would certainly portray different meanings if it were anywhere other than Berlin. However, it does reiterate the homogenising intent of global city films like *Sliding Doors* and *Run Lola Run*. In fact, it would be more accurate to state not that the film could have been set in any other city, but rather that, if it had been, it could have been made to look pretty much the same. Thus an international audience is courted by the film in an attempt to increase migration into the city's expanding economy. Once again this is created through the lure of a gentrified city of opportunity, an 'anywhere' that is recognisably similar to its comparable aspect in corresponding areas of cities like New York, London and so on. It is for this reason that we see the concerns of cultural specificity and 'national' identity ignored in this particular example of the cinema of consensus. Again their absence does not signify a lack of the depth often associated with New German Cinema so much as it does a difference of intent. If certain works of New German Cinema sold well abroad because they showed how unique Berlin was, *Run Lola Run* does so because it shows how similar Berlin supposedly is to other global cities.

Finally, Garwood draws out the international aim of Tykwer's film further through a comparison of the aesthetic of *Run Lola Run* with that of *Wings of Desire* (1987).[38] Again his analysis strengthens my reading of the film. As part of a larger discussion of the various similarities and differences between the two films, Garwood illustrates several ways in which *Run Lola Run* is not engaged with the question of national identity as *Wings of Desire* clearly was. Two of the most relevant of these ways to the thesis of this current work are, its 'non-geographically specific minimising [of] its use of landmark Berlin locations'[39] and its apparent emphasis on apolitical questions of memory within the text, rather than of memories of the national past.[40] However, for Garwood, despite its post-wall apoliticism the film's combination of different types of image (footage shot on 35 mm colour stock, black-and-white film, video, animation, still photographs, computer game iconography and so on) is seen to have a slightly more 'positive' intent. Viewed in relation to its appeal to a younger audience this is seen as, 'a practice not dissimilar to that most internationally mass-marketable of audio-visual phenomena, the music video'.[41] Although the film may seem disinterested in the reality of life in contemporary Berlin when compared with a work of New German Cinema, Garwood concludes that it still attempts to reach a contemporary domestic audience. Whilst it does not engage with the question of national identity in the same way as *Wings of Desire*, it is not entirely apolitical. Rather, academics looking for recognisable elements found in New German Cinema have missed its call to audiences now 'literate in the forms of global multi-media'.[42]

Garwood's study raises several points of note. Firstly, in its decided lack of the expected, landmark images of the German capital *Run Lola Run* does indeed appear to ignore, or erase, its national past. However, it can be seen as a film that avoids recourse to culturally specific landmarks in order to focus instead on Berlin's comparability with other global cities, just as *Sliding Doors* depicts London without the cultural identifier of pearly kings and queens. Hence, as Mesch notes, there is still a specific aspect of Berlin deployed by the film, only it deliberately denies the need to define the city by its national heritage. Indeed, Garwood acknowledges that several historical locations are depicted in the film, but points out that 'their historical significance is not dwelt upon', and, rather, that they act as 'a kind of visual support for Lola's constantly moving body'.[43] As I showed using *Sliding Doors*, this disengaging of identity from a national setting is exactly the relationship created in a global city between the city and its non-national residents. In *Sliding Doors* the potential migratory worker is lured by the promise that being English is not a prerequisite of life in London. Similarly in *Run Lola Run* there are no lingering, establishing shots on Berlin landmarks to alienate the uninitiated viewer from the film's vision of the city. Instead, the nationally specific is deliberately backgrounded, suggesting that identity in contemporary Berlin has been released from the specifics of a national past.

More importantly, my reading can enhance Garwood's argument concerning the film's integration of various 'global multi-media'. Its seamless integration of different media aesthetically depicts several similar integrations that occur at the level of the narrative. The most obvious of these is the integration between East and West and the possibilities that offers for international trade. The Berlin through which Lola runs is indeed a city in which it is possible to integrate many different media. However the types of media are played off against each other in a way that stresses their relative ages and sophistications. Both old and new (black-and-white and colour) and higher and lower quality (film and video) are present. Their commingling suggests that nothing is incompatible in the new, rewired Berlin. This is a city, the aesthetic analogy shows, which stands as a gateway between the old, scratchy, low quality East, and the new, hip, cyber-punk West. The global city of Berlin is the point at which the two worlds meet, a border territory across which deals are made. This is most clearly mirrored in the narrative when Manni delivers several Mercedes cars across the border into Poland and smuggles back a payment in diamonds that he then effortlessly converts to cash. Berlin appears as a frontier trading post between the established West and the newly opened market of the East where the seamless integration of the two ensures the transformation of goods into currency and of illicit iron-curtain wealth into acceptable Western currencies. It is an image of the city meant to encourage Eastern and Western European investment, secure in the city's power to seamlessly translate one style of business into another.

In fact, Berlin's global interconnected status is pointedly emphasised, suggesting that it makes worldwide trade a relatively simple matter. For instance, when Manni tells Lola about the hobo who took the bag of money a matter of minutes before, he speculates that by now he could be anywhere in the world. As he speaks we see brief postcard-image flashes of the places he names, including such global cities as: New York, Hong Kong and Tokyo. These images illustrate how rewired Berlin can connect Eastern and Western Europe, and Europe and the rest of the world. As a global city it exists as the nodal point between the nation and the opportunities offered by the global economy.

The annual techno festival evoked by the presence of cyber-punks Lola and Manni and the film's techno soundtrack adds to this image of the internationally connected city. It appeals to a subcultural global network that situates Berlin as part of an entertainment scene stretching to Goa and the beaches of Thailand. Here the global trade in entertainment is evoked to illustrate the growth of the services industry in 1990s Berlin. It also links the lifestyle of these party goers and the global city of Berlin. Places such as Goa and Thailand after all, are the party locales where many wealthy twenty-somethings temporarily convene before commencing their careers in the world's global cities. Lola and Manni's appearance demonstrates an astute marketing decision in its appeal to a youth market looking for a city in which to mix career and leisure, an arena in which to be a punk and still make money. That the three stories are interspersed by shots of Lola and Manni discussing their future together reinforces this, suggesting that Berlin is a city in which they can live out, and control, their fantasies. Here the upbeat accompaniment provided by Jamiroquai in *Sliding Doors* is echoed by Franka Potente's voice, on the soundtrack, wishing herself into myriad incarnations as she runs to Manni's aid:

> I wish I was a stranger who wanders down the sky
> I wish I was a starship in silence flying by
> I wish I was . . . etc.

As Mesch rightly notes, then, the film's grid motif does illustrate that Berlin is a city that exists as a nodal point between the local, the national and the global, but this is a connection that is also explicitly figured in the narrative, in terms of various international flows of people and trade. Rather like the global cities they depict, both *Run Lola Run* and *Sliding Doors* attempt to replace more traditional notions of national identity with an image of a new, outward-facing, globally oriented national identity based in the global city. Thus in their attempt to link the regionally diverse space of the nation and the rest of the globe through the creation of an apparently 'anywhere' space in the global city they appeal to a regional and a transnational viewer.

The film's view of Berlin as a global city may well have been partially determined by the criteria of one of its funding bodies, Filmboard Berlin-Brandenburg. Dedicated to 'the constant and sustained professionalisation of the industry in the Berlin-Brandenburg region'[44] its regionally specific selection criteria stipulates that films applying for funding will be judged on the 'expected regional effect' the production will have on 'the economy of the region', specifically in terms of 'investment . . . jobs and training'.[45] Not surprisingly, their official website lists *Run Lola Run* as one of their major successes.[46] Like *Sliding Doors,* then, *Run Lola Run* also exists as an advert for the national capital created by a growing design industry whose very existence is itself a sign of an emergent global city.

Finally, it is no coincidence that the parity of gender roles evident in the narrative of blonde Helen is also present in the third and final narrative of *Run Lola Run*. Lola and Manni having gained economic parity, the film ends with a freeze frame of Lola's face as the young entrepreneur decides what to do with her money. Similarly, whilst the film's rejection of the traditional patriarchal figure (Lola's banker father) in favour of the one-off gamble could also be seen as yet another example of post-wall apoliticism, there is also a financial message behind this narrative gambit. The global city, we are again shown, favours those who take charge of their own destiny. When the father/nation (shot on 'old' grainy video) has disowned you, and the national bank will no longer support you in the deregulated marketplace, what do you do? In Lola's unlikely roulette victory, the film's answer is, 'take a chance'. Thus, whilst critics like Maurice Yacowar can be forgiven for interpreting the film as a 'contemporary individualist's *Triumph of the Will*',[47] there is more to it than this. Admittedly this is a film that depicts a post-wall generation who do not wish to be determined by their national history. It is also a film about a Berlin in which there are so many amazing opportunities that even a homeless person can become rich overnight! However, rather than failing to represent national identity, post-wall films like *Makin' Up* and *Run Lola Run* represent a new type of national identity situated in the global city that Berlin wills itself to be.

From Chaos Theory to Einstein

To conclude this section I will examine how *Run Lola Run* uses its temporal dimension to reinforce its message of the entrepreneur's ability to determine their future in Berlin. Once again what initially appears to be a labyrinthine model of time indicative of the time-image is actually a reterritorialised version of this model. Like *Sliding Doors*, *Run Lola Run* uses its different narratives to offer choices between 'right' and 'wrong' versions of national identity. This time, however, a view of time close to that of Einstein's creates three versions of the same narrative, each of which is *relatively* more or less 'right'.

Initially the narratives appear to be three alternative universes in a temporal environment structured by the logic of 'deterministic chaos'.[48] Although I will not delve too deeply into chaos theory here, it is useful to understand how *Run Lola Run* initially appears to illustrate its basic principles. In *Who's Afraid of Schrödinger's Cat?* (1997) Ian Marshall and Danah Zohar note of situations such as that of the stock market where the logic of deterministic chaos is evident, that

> such systems are balanced on a knife edge where the slightest deviation one way or the other will have huge effects later on, as in the butterfly effect. The cumulative result of these small differences is that two initial conditions, almost exactly the same at their starting point, will diverge more and more.[49]

In *Run Lola Run* the global city is depicted as such a system, one where the slightest change in input of its entrepreneurial inhabitants can have huge (primarily financial) ramifications. This slight change in input is shown in Lola's initial sprint down the stairs of her apartment building with which each retelling of the narrative starts. Each time she runs past a young boy loitering on the stairs with his dog. The first time she passes the growling dog without incident and runs straight on. The second time she passes the boy trips her, the resulting fall down the stairs causing her to limp and slowing her run. On the third pass she leaps over the approaching dog, thus gaining a few moments on both of her previous incarnations.

The butterfly effect of this different output is shown almost immediately as Lola runs past a lady with a pushchair. With each pass a different photo montage appears which summarises the lady's life. The still photographs express three vastly different outcomes to the minor character's life caused by the slight temporal variance in the point at which they intersect with Lola. The different outcomes are three tidal waves caused by the beatings of Lola's butterfly's wings. The film thus appears to have a 'fractal'[50] structure, generated by the many iterations of its story from the same starting point.

Indeed, this structure sits very comfortably with Deleuze's philosophy. After all, each time the story is replayed its previous existence is rendered not necessarily true. The three narratives could therefore be seen as an illustration of Deleuze's notion of a repetition in difference that comes from the eternal return. Indeed, without wishing to invoke the scorn of Sokal and Bricmont,[51] it could be argued that Deleuze's philosophy shares much common ground with the quantum theories of the 'new physics'.[52] Just as whenever Schrödinger's Cat is conceived at a quantum level it is always at once '*both* alive *and* dead at the same time'[53] so too does each fork in the virtual labyrinth of time produce two possible both/and realities. For this reason it would be tempting to argue that the structure of *Run Lola Run* demonstrates the ungrounding power of the labyrinth to render various possible futures simultaneously possible.

Following this reading, the film appears to use chaos theory to allegorise the huge chances of success that are available in the global city. It offers a metaphysical justification for its depiction of the one-off gamble as the right way to live in the global city. It reinforces the message that Berlin is a place in which an ability to take your chances can greatly enhance your future irrespective of your, or the city's, national past. However, the film is very obviously linear in its progression ('wrong', 'wrong', 'right') towards the correct version of national identity. This progression suggests that the system can actually be controlled by practise, a notion further emphasised in its computer-game-like scenario. Across the three playings of the narrative we see Lola learn new skills. These enable her to progress towards the 'right' outcome. This linearity suggests that the change in initial input does not have quite the huge knock on effect that chaos theory suggests. Instead, the continuous actions of the character within the system are needed to create a tidal wave from the flapping of its wings.

As Lola leaps over the growling dog in the third sprint down the stairs, the 'right' story, she silences it with her trademark scream. This is the same scream she uses later in the same story to influence the fall of the ball on the roulette wheel. In Lola's screams we could detect the individual's ability to use their small input to influence the huge outcome of events. Yet using the scream to influence events is actually a skill that Lola hones across the three narratives. This suggests that the film is much more linear than previously thought. After all, Lola is only able to know which actions can control the system's output because she has been present during the previous two iterations of the same process. Her existence across the three narratives thus provides a linear direction, her physical presence providing the linkage between its incommensurable spaces. Seen from this viewpoint, the reterritorialising effect of the movement-image on the film is apparent. In the course of the film's 'three-act classical narrative structure',[54] Lola looks for a positive response to her situation. Only in the third retelling does she complete the game by making her actions equal to her perception, thereby completing the progression from situation through action to changed situation.

Furthermore, through Lola's learning process the spectator is also provided with the ability to weigh the relative merits of the different narratives. This progression exposes the fact that the conception of time that underpins *Run Lola Run*'s apparent evocation of chaos theory is actually closer to Einstein's view of time (or at least, Bergson's interpretation of it) than to chaos theory. Again without going into too much depth, during the early 1920s Bergson and Einstein entered into a brief debate over Bergson's interpretation of Einstein's special theory of relativity. The debate concluded with Bergson's ideas being discredited, at least with many within the scientific community. However, it is worth briefly revisiting Bergson's argument in order to understand the manner in which *Run Lola Run* reterritorialises as a movement-image.

In *Duration and Simultaneity* (1921) Bergson sought to ascertain 'to what extent . . . [his] conception of duration was compatible with Einstein's views on time.'[55] He hoped to provide a metaphysics for this new physics. Bergson was not antagonistic towards Einstein's theory, but rather, saw the special theory of relativity as an opportunity to complete his own theory of 'duration', which I briefly introduced in Chapter 1.

Einstein's theory broke from the Newtonian model of the universe. This was a universe existing within an absolute, homogenous, and reversible time. He theorised instead the existence of many local times, relative to the observer within them. As Robin Durie has it, Einstein's theory: 'famously recasts the physical universe as a multiplicity of physical systems of reference in motion relative to each other without absolute frame of reference. Yet it maintains a fundamental role for observation and measurement.'[56] The sticking point between philosophy and science concerned the manner in which time was measured in the special theory of relativity. For Einstein this was a matter of using clocks for recording the passing of time. Therefore, the relative passing of time in different places could be accurately measured. Bergson objected, however, that the passing of time was experienced by consciousness and, to cut a long story short, concluded that the only way to measure the relative passing of time for another was to arbitrarily fix the position of the observer measuring the passing of time, as a stationary point of reference. As Durie summarises:

> Bergson . . . concludes that there is in fact just one single time, namely, the time that is 'lived or able to be lived'. The relative time ascribed to the other . . . but which is not actually lived through by the observer, is a mere fiction, an imaginary time.[57]

As I mentioned, Bergson was ultimately shown to be mistaken in his reading of certain aspects of the special theory of relativity, so this conclusion did not in any way dent its armour. Yet, as Durie also notes, it paved the way for Deleuze's conceptualisation of time as a '*virtual multiplicity*'.[58] Although duration is one, singular virtual whole, it contains within it the many different times of Einstein's special theory of relativity, but without any one of them being privileged as a fixed point of reference against which others could be judged. Duration is a virtual multiplicity within which there exists the potential for many times to become actualised, and it is the concept that Deleuze eventually develops into the labyrinthine model of time in *Cinema 2*.

Bergson reasoned that space was not the fourth dimension of time but, rather, the deposit left behind by the passing of time. Einstein's space-time, then, was but another example of the measurement of time in spatial terms. Ironically, for Bergson, Einstein's special theory of relativity – which is usually heralded as enabling the break from the Newtonian model of the universe – was really an abortive reterritorialisation of the almost glimpsed existence of duration. Bergson's duration, the model of time with which Deleuze developed the model of the labyrinth, was therefore restratified by Einstein's space-time. In the movement-image, a similar reterritorialisation occurs when the labyrinthine model of time found in the time-image is constrained within a linear view of time. For instance, when the labyrinth is incorporated into the movement-image a fixed, or originary, narrative is often used against which the observer can judge the relative merits of the others. As I demonstrate below, *Run Lola Run* is a case in point. Moreover, Deleuze argued that movement-images are 'blocs of space-time',[59] mobile sections, or indirect images, of time's virtual whole. It is perhaps no surprise, then, to see a metaphysical commonality in their subordination of time to a character's movement through space and Einstein's conception of space-time, as we do in *Run Lola Run*.

The correlation between *Run Lola Run*'s conception of time and Bergson's interpretation of Einstein is most noticeable in the three-way split screen that emerges as Lola runs to meet Manni towards the end of the first narrative. In this shot the spectator is given the illusion of objective, spectatorial mastery over the relative experiences of time lived by the characters. On one side of the screen, as Manni waits on his fate, time passes slowly for him; on the other, for Lola running to beat the clock, time passes almost too quickly. For the spectator, however, their relative movements appear to be seen objectively, due to the presence as measure of time of the hands of the clock that appears at the top of the screen. This image positions us as the Einsteinian observer theorised by Bergson, who believes himself able to judge the relative passing of time for others against his own measure of time's passing. This single image thereby encapsulates the rationale behind the film's linear sequencing of its narratives.

It is also apparent in Lola's three flights down the stairs of her apartment building. Lola's relative speed is seen to account for the different knock-on effects experienced by the woman with the baby. However, it is only through the privileged perspective on events we are offered by the fixing of the first story as the originary model that we view the effects on the others as due to Lola's relatively faster or slower flight. Only because we have privileged foreknowledge of events can we say that Lola's arrival is relatively sooner, or relatively later, in each retelling of the story. The film thus uses the three replayings of its narrative to provide the spectator with a privileged viewpoint from which to observe its four-dimensional map of the route to success in the global city. It realigns time in a very classical way each time, by returning to the origin and positing a slight difference to explain the conclusions that will be reached in the present. In this case, entrepreneurial success is achieved, we see in the honed scream that Lola employs in the third retelling, by the individual who observes the *relative* merits of her actions and learns to control them. Despite its apparent use of deterministic chaos, then, the labyrinthine possibilities this model offers are actually restrained by the linearity of a much more classical view of time. Unlike previous films such as *L'année dernière à Marienbad* (1961), which sacrificed the clarity of a classical narrative in order to experiment with a labyrinthine view of time, *Run Lola Run* – for entirely understandable, commercial reasons – owes its financial success to a reterritorialised representation of chaos within fairly classical (both narrative and time) parameters.

In both *Run Lola Run* and *Sliding Doors* the labyrinthine possibilities offered by the time-image are caught in the process of reterritorialisation as movement-images. By realigning time to one 'right' conclusion, all other possibilities are rendered 'wrong' and the reterritorialising power of the movement-image retains its dominance in the construction of a coherent image of national identity. As we shall further see in following chapters, these films express the same reterritorialisation of the labyrinth that has long existed in movement-images such as *It's a Wonderful Life*.

Global Labyrinth (*You've Got Mail*)

Both *Sliding Doors* and *Run Lola Run* fall within a much broader tradition of films. Their conflation of the identity of a female protagonist with the labyrinthine model of time strengthens the convention of representing the labyrinth as the female defining other of the normative, 'masculine', straight line of time. Here, attempts by women to change their past are typically exposed as fraudulent and are eventually punished by their reterritorialisation within the straight line of time. A classic example of this type of film would be Alfred Hitchcock's *Marnie* (1964). In terms of the possibility performance offers for recreating national identity this is a very retrograde tradition. It suggests that performances that attempt to deviate from the linear norm are unlawful, by coding them as female, and as films like *Vertigo* and *Marnie* demonstrate, 'insane', racially other and so on.

Even in these contemporary films, which deal much more positively with female performativity, it is seen as a magical fantasy in *Sliding Doors* (through the use of a slow motion rewind of Helen's run down the subway stairs, the presence of a little girl playing with her doll and a magic wand sound effect) and a game-like fantasy in *Run Lola Run*. Both films reduplicate the binary distinction that only enables an expression of female performativity under the guise (!) of a game, magical fantasy, or dream. Thus the reterritorialisation of the woman that we expect of these films is used to justify the 'right' version of the narrative of national identity with which they eventually leave us.

As a comparison that illustrates how strongly reterritorialised these narratives are, take their American contemporary *You've Got Mail* (1998). This New York based romantic comedy retains the classical narrative device of keeping two parallel narratives (those of Meg Ryan and Tom Hanks) separate throughout the film. Thus it prolongs the anticipated moment of narrative resolution and enables the film to simultaneously resolve both its romantic and its economic plot lines. The way the two characters' narratives are eventually brought together through the romance plot paints a friendly face onto the corporate takeover of the local bookstore (Ryan) by the global giant (Hanks). Although it is not creating parallel universes in its parallel narratives, this film also uses its classical parallelism to renegotiate national identity as the friendly coupling of the global and the local. The two European global city films, then, although they initially appear to be unusual in their narrative structures, are, in actual fact, variations on standard classical narrative patterns that we find in movement-images elsewhere. When the labyrinth appears it does so as an other against which the straight line can ultimately by reaffirmed. It serves a fleeting purpose only and is disavowed at the moment of its appearance by its restructuring as an either/or.

Yet despite the bad press usually associated with the labyrinth, in these films it is also evoked to serve a slightly unusual purpose. The labyrinth perfectly describes the experiences of an emergent demographic, the new global city elite. These are the young professionals whose identities are no longer tied to any one national past. As a deterritorialised flow of labour, the transnational professional's ability to move within the global economy is best illustrated by a labyrinthine model which demonstrates how a discontinuity of identity can occur when a person is transplanted to work in another country. The labyrinth enables the global elite to realign their past at any time as a financial, rather than a specifically national, self-recreation. Hence life in the global city is also coded as virtual by the labyrinth, expressing both the virtual interconnectedness of a global existence that relies increasingly on hyperspace for communication, and the 'virtual' existence of this elite class above the dirty reality of the global underclass. For instance, in *Sliding Doors* brunette Helen gentrifies the existence of London's global underclass, omitting the starker realities of low pay, poor housing, sweatshop labour and financial exploitation. In blonde Helen the global elite transcend this reality in a virtual realm of transnational wealth and status.

The labyrinth has further resonances with the global elite. By borrowing the labyrinthine model of time from art cinema, these popular genre films become hybrids that appeal to several different markets. Generically *Sliding Doors* belongs to both the romantic comedy and the melodrama and *Run Lola Run* to the action genre.[60] However, their formal experimentation with narrative time also situates them within the art cinema mould. Their market appeal is therefore broad, with a major target audience being precisely the new global elite. Like them it crosses boundaries between

European and American traditions, expressing for Anne Jäckel, both 'the traditions of European art/*auteur* cinema and Hollywood entertainment values'.[61] This high/middlebrow mixing of art and popular suggests exactly the lifestyle purchasing of the global elite. These films brand, or define their consumers, as both hip to popular culture, and yet in need of intellectual stimulus. As such they are gentrified popular genre films, which appeal precisely to the 'anywhereness' of their target audience.

Yet as I have shown above the labyrinth is often evoked, but also always reterritorialised. Admittedly in these films its status as dream or fantasy reaffirms the aspirational nature of the identities on sale. However, such a dream does not reflect the reality of many people's lives in the global city. It is escapist at best, and as I will show in Chapter 5 using *Family Man* (2000), for this reason this dream is not always seen in a positive light. Thus, despite this new, upbeat spin on the labyrinth, these films ultimately return their respective narratives to a single view of national identity in their binary of 'right' and 'wrong' choices. The pastless, rootless nature of the labyrinth is therefore disavowed by the specifics of the national narrative that these films seek to realign. Although they reconfigure identity as a meeting of the global and the local, this is still an image of *national* identity.

Conclusion: The Old and the New

The final question that must be answered is how these two films, which so obviously stress a new form of national identity over the old, retain the linearity of the national narrative? What aspects of the past are used to suture over the national transformation they evidence in their multiple narratives? The answer is different in each case. In *Run Lola Run* a link to the nation's cultural past is maintained through its cinematic aspect, in spite of the erasure of the national past that its narrative enacts. In *Sliding Doors* a previous image of imperial Britain is maintained in a slightly modified 'Cool Britannia' format. This image necessitates the disavowal of the separate identity of England, in order to maintain an image of a unified Britain. In these different ways both films reconcile their respective depictions of an apparently absent nation in the 'anywhereness' of the global city, with the seemingly continuous presence of the particular nation in which each global city exists.

In *Run Lola Run* the film's art/popular genre hybridity is crucial in this respect. As Haase argues it provides 'Hollywood pleasure without giving up its Heimat identity'.[62] Although creating an aesthetic 'anywhere' that matches its vision of global-city Berlin, it is also recognisably German.

This is not simply because of the language spoken and the specific cultural aspects peculiar to Berlin (such as its globally renowned underground rave scene) that it evokes. As was the case with Fellini, here again continuity with previous German cinema movements is maintained through the *auteur* status attributed to Tykwer. Therefore, despite the differences Rentschler notes between the post-wall cinema and its New German predecessor, *Run Lola Run* is often viewed as continuing the same tradition. For instance, although Haase, Garwood and Mesch variously point out the differences between Tykwer and his predecessors (Lang, von Sternberg, Wenders, Fassbinder and so on) his international acceptance as *auteur* confirms his continuation of their legacy. The new *auteur*'s work may appear more 'American' due to the influence of globalisation, but he is still a German *auteur*. Through Tykwer, national identity is at once shown to have been disrupted by the influence of America, and yet also to continue. Witness Tykwer's existence as the international face of German cinema.

Furthermore, Germany's cinematic past is also evoked in the historical 'anywhereness' of the film's hyperreal Berlin. As Haase, Garwood and Mesch point out, Tykwer mixes together intertextual references from various films by the aforementioned *auteurs*. Through all the virtual layers of the cinematic past that they evoke runs Lola. As Mesch[63] notes her name recalls Marlene Dietrich's character from von Sternberg's *The Blue Angel* (1930), and the Fassbinder remake, *Lola* (1981). A continuous national narrative is retained, then, both within the text and in its *auteur*, in their evocation of the nation's cinematic past. Both may appear very different from their predecessors, but their new faces suggest a cultural continuity to German identity, just as their narratives demonstrate the supposed end of national identity.

This cultural referencing is used to very political ends. Major historical events of the twentieth century are sutured over by the cultural reconnection between Tykwer, Lola and their cinematic predecessors. As noted above, the nation's recently divided past is replaced in the film by an image of Berlin whose East and West aspects are now supposedly equally redeveloped. Moreover, the absence of recognisable national landmarks enables a complete avoidance of the National Socialist past. Thus the film's spatial and historical 'anywhereness' and its evocation of the falsifying power of the labyrinth, suggest that the national past has been wiped clear by globalisation, and that what remains are jumbled fragments of an apparently ahistorical but artistically informing cultural past.

In *Sliding Doors* an Anglo-centric view of British identity is created to erase the reality of Britain's post-imperial status. Emerging in the same year as the New Labour party's electoral victory, it reproduces the same view of Britain (as a number of united regions that gravitate towards the English centre) that was propagated by their rhetoric of 'Cool Britannia'. This is seen most obviously in the regional cast of characters, and particularly in the romance between Anglicised-Scot, James (witness his rowing on the Thames and incessant quoting of Monty Python), and 'English' Helen. Like *Notting Hill*, *Sliding Doors* also excludes the postcolonial other, those primarily Afro-Caribbean, African and Asian diasporas most commonly found in the low-wage jobs that brunette Helen performs. Thus, in the face of the various ungrounding histories that reemerged with devolution and the postcolonial era, the film retains an image of a unified Britain whose major transformation, it suggests, has been brought about by the impact of globalisation.

Paradoxically, at the centre of Britain is an absent England, whose identity (we see in American star Paltrow) has been made-over with American finance. Yet this made-over England still maintains an 'English' identity through its continuation of certain Anglo-centric, British cinematic traditions. Firstly Paltrow's plummy Home Counties accent evokes the use of this particular region of England to represent the totality of Britain during the First World War.[64] Moreover, its upbeat representation of London resonates with famous images of swinging 1960s London, a cultural origin that itself relates back to a Victorian conception of imperial Britain. It is not surprising, then, that *Austin Powers: The Spy Who Shagged Me* – a film which drew upon exactly this nostalgic, Anglo-centric vision of Britain – appeared only two years later in 1999. As Michael Gardiner puts it: 'In popular culture, Cool Britannia connoted a high Britishness of familiarly 1960s, and (therefore) neo-Victorian charm.'[65] Again, as in *Run Lola Run*, the continuation of national identity is evoked by the continuation of previous cinematic conceptualisations of the nation. A similar effect is achieved by Hugh Grant's performance of Englishness in *Notting Hill*. His stereotypically bumbling, neo-Victorian Englishman is most obviously undermined by the physical reality of his much-publicised liaison with Divine Brown in 1995. 'Essential' Englishness, then, has been eradicated by the seductive 'glamour' (in Paltrow/Helen's case) or indeed, notorious celebrity in Grant's, of America. Yet it is still performed, as a mannered attitude in British cinema.

In fact, *Sliding Door*'s use of England as a structuring absence actually aids its disavowal of the break up of Britain. As both Tom Nairn and Gardiner point out, after devolution it is England that has the most to lose (specifically its position at the heart of Britain) by officially redefining itself as an independent nation.[66] Thus it refuses to give up its Anglo-centric view of Britain in these global city films. Instead, *Sliding Doors* literally gives

England's voice to an American representative, to shift the focus from local considerations to more global ones. In this way the film retains an aspect of its previous imperial definition (of a regional state that pulls towards the centre) but also represents this centre as having been made-over by American finance. The fact that this 'elsewhere' at the heart of the Britain is both global and local, retains continuity with previous definitions of Britishness created when England was the centre of an international empire. The different, potentially deterritorialising, labyrinthine pasts submerged by the imperial British past (be they postcolonial or post-devolutionary), remain pointedly absent.

Notes

1. David Bordwell, 'Film futures', *Substance: A Review of Theory and Literary Criticism*, Issue 97, 31:1 (2002), pp. 88–104.
2. Ibid. p. 89.
3. Ibid. p. 90.
4. Ibid. p. 90.
5. Ibid. p. 91.
6. Ibid. pp. 92–103.
7. Ibid. pp. 96–7.
8. Frank Krutnik, 'Something more than night', in David B. Clarke (ed.), *The Cinematic City* (London: Routledge, 1997), pp. 83–109.
9. David Bordwell, 'Art cinema as mode of film practice', *Film Criticism*, 4:1 (1979), pp. 56–64.
10. Steve Neale, 'Art cinema as institution', *Screen*, 22:1 (1981), pp. 11–39.
11. See, amongst others, Moya Luckett, 'Image and nation in 1990s British cinema', pp. 88–99; Robert Murphy, 'A path through the moral maze', pp. 1–16 and Claire Monk, 'Men in the 90s', pp. 156–86, in Robert Murphy (ed.), *British Cinema in the 90s* (London: BFI, 2000); also Julia Hallam, 'Film, class and national identity', pp. 261–73, in Justine Ashby and Andrew Higson (eds), *British Cinema Past and Present* (London: Routledge, 2000).
12. Moya Luckett, 'Image and nation in 1990s British cinema', pp. 88–99, p. 98.
13. Claire Monk, 'Underbelly UK: The 1990s underclass films, masculinity and the ideologies of "new" Britain', in Justine Ashby and Andrew Higson (eds), *British Cinema Past and Present* (London: Routledge, 2000), pp. 274–87, p. 284.
14. Saskia Sassen, *The Global City* (Princeton: Princeton University Press, 1991), p. 9.
15. Ibid. p. 12.
16. Ibid. p. 267. Sassen makes this point by drawing on Nigel Thrift and Peter Williams (eds), *Class and Space* (London: Macmillan, 1987).
17. Ibid. p. 281.

18. Jamiroquai, 'Use the force', from, *Travelling Without Moving* (S2: September 1996).
19. Anthony D. King, *Global Cities* (London: Routledge, 1990), p. 124.
20. Charles Whitehouse, 'Capital Co-ordinates', *Sight and Sound*, 14:6 (2004), p. 6.
21. Christine Geraghty, 'Crossing over: performing as a lady and a dame', *Screen*, 43:1 (2002), pp. 41–56, p. 53.
22. Ibid. p. 55.
23. Saskia Sassen, *The Global City*, p. 265.
24. Christine Geraghty, 'Crossing over: performing as a lady and a dame', p. 54.
25. David Bordwell, 'Film futures', p. 101.
26. Dina M. Smith, 'Global cinderella: *Sabrina* (1954), Hollywood, and postwar internationalism', *Cinema Journal*, 41: 4 (2002), pp. 27–51.
27. For a much fuller analysis of this film and its depiction of London, see Charlotte Brunsdon, 'London films: from private gardens to utopian moments', *Cineaste*, 26:4 (2001), pp. 43–6.
28. Eric Rentschler, 'New German cinema to post-wall cinema', in Scott MacKenzie and Mette Hjort (eds), *Cinema and Nation* (London: Routledge, 2000), pp. 260–77, p. 262.
29. Ibid. p. 262–3.
30. Christine Haase, 'You can run, but you can't hide: transcultural filmmaking in *Run Lola Run*', in Randall Halle and Margaret McCarthy (eds), *Light Motives: German Popular Film in Perspective* (Detroit: Wayne State University Press, 2003), pp. 395–415, p. 402.
31. Ibid. p. 403.
32. Claudia Mesch, 'Racing Berlin: the games of *Run Lola Run*', in *M/C: A Journal of Media and Culture*, 3:3 (2000). http://journal.media-culture.org.au/0006/berlin.php (06/07/05).
33. Ibid. p. 1.
34. Ibid. p. 3.
35. Ibid. p. 5.
36. Ibid. p. 2.
37. Ibid. pp. 2–3.
38. Ian Garwood, 'The autorenfilm in contemporary German cinema', in Tim Bergfelder, Erica Carter and Deniz Gö (eds), *The German Cinema Book* (London: BFI, 2002), pp. 202–10.
39. Ibid. p. 208.
40. Ibid. pp. 206–8.
41. Ibid. p. 208.
42. Ibid. p. 209.
43. Ibid. p. 210, n. 19.
44. Filmboard Filmförderung in Berlin-Brandenburg. http://www.filmboard.de/english/fbb_e.htm (05/07/03).
45. Ibid.

46. Ibid.
47. Maurice Yacowar, '*Run Lola Run*: *Renn* for your Life', *Queen's Quarterly*, 109:4 (1999), pp. 557–67.
48. Ian Stewart, *Does God Play Dice?* (London: Penguin, 1989), p. 2.
49. Ian Marshall and Danah Zohar, *Who's Afraid of Schrödinger's Cat?* (London: Bloomsbury, 1997), p. 84.
50. Ibid. p. 212.
51. Alan Sokal and Jean Bricmont, *Intellectual Impostures* (London: Profile, 1988).
52. Marshall and Zohar, p. xiii.
53. Ibid.
54. Anne Jäckel, *European Film Industries* (London: BFI, 2003), p. 33.
55. Henri Bergson, *Duration and Simultaneity* (Manchester: Clinamen Press, [1921] 1999), p. xxvii.
56. Robin Durie in his introduction to Henri Bergson, *Duration and Simultaneity* (Manchester: Clinamen Press, [1921] 1999), p. vi.
57. Ibid. p. xii.
58. Ibid. p. xxi.
59. Gilles Deleuze, *Cinema 1*, p. 59.
60. Christine Haase, 'You can run, but you can't hide', p. 397.
61. Anne Jäckel, *European Film Industries*, p. 33.
62. Christine Haase, 'You can run, but you can't hide', p. 397.
63. Claudia Mesch, 'Racing Berlin: The games of *Run Lola Run*', p. 2.
64. Michael Gardiner, *The Cultural Roots of British Devolution* (Edinburgh: Edinburgh University Press, 2004), p. 106.
65. Ibid. p. 108.
66. Tom Nairn, *After Britain* (London: Granta Books, 2000), p. 109, and Gardiner, pp. 156–83.

CHAPTER 4

American Triumphalism and the First Gulf War

This chapter examines how certain American films that emerged after the First Gulf War manipulated narrative time in order to construct national identity. It begins with a discussion of triumphalism, arguably the dominant national narrative of the USA in the nineteenth and twentieth centuries. Triumphalism is a mythical inversion of colonial reality that has existed in American cinema since (at least) *The Birth of a Nation* (1915). *Saving Private Ryan* (1998) is then analysed, especially its use of flashback in conjunction with character memory, to determine how this contemporary movement-image facilitates the construction of a triumphal national narrative. Its use of narrative time to negotiate the recent transformation of America – from cold warrior to small-scale interventionist global police force – provides a clear contrast against which to then measure *Memento*'s (2000) deterritorialisation of triumphalism.

Like the hybrid films discussed in the previous chapter, *Memento* is a time-image 'caught in the act' of becoming a movement-image. In contrast to *Saving Private Ryan*, this independent film offers a critique of the national narrative, using character memory, a fragmented narrative structure and national allegory to deterritorialise the triumphal narrative that dominates many American action-images. Although it does not depart from the classical narrative structure to the extent that films discussed in later chapters do, the deterritorialising force of the time-image is clearly evident in this film.

Triumph of the Past (*Birth of a Nation*)

There are a range of convergent critical perspectives on triumphalism's manifestation in American cinema of the 1990s. In a special issue of *The Journal of Popular Film and Television* (2002), Albert Auster and John Hodgkins examine its existence across the range of movies set during the Second World War, which emerged during the 1990s. Auster argues that in films like *Saving Private Ryan*, the Second World War provided 'anodyne' subject matter with which America could represent its return to triumphant ways.[1] This was necessary because the ambiguous victories 'won' in the Cold War and the First Gulf War only really enabled a partial valorisation of American triumph. *Three Kings* (1999), for instance, celebrates the 'moral victory'[2] of the three protagonists as they aid oppressed Shiites in their flight into Iran. However, this moral victory is screened in lieu of the less clear-cut military 'victory' achieved in the Persian Gulf by the superpower's vastly superior military hardware. Instead, Auster notes, Spielberg's film uses the Second World War to create a mythical origin for the nation's present, victorious state.

> Just as the Civil War served as a touchstone for those same patriotic values in the last half of the nineteenth century and the early part of the twentieth, World War II has become for Americans that mythic, edenic moment when the entire nation bent itself to victory over evil and barbarism.[3]

As I demonstrated in Chapter 2, this positing of a mythical origin is precisely the historical alignment we would expect when a movement-image constructs a single, linear timeline of national identity. By choosing an originary moment from the past that can be said to match the present, it establishes a linear continuity between then and now.

John Hodgkins goes much further in this respect, albeit without directly mentioning triumphalism. He also notes how the Second World War is used in films like *Saving Private Ryan* as a battlefield in which to imagine America's military victory in the Gulf. His analysis of the similarities between its famous opening and the televisual ground-level reporting of the First Gulf War is instructive in this respect. Hodgkins argues that the victory *Saving Private Ryan* imagines in the battlefields of the Second World War effectively sutures over the defeat in Vietnam. Noting the film's ideological equation with the rhetoric of George Bush Sr ('By God, we've kicked the Vietnam Syndrome once and for all'), Hodgkins argues that if 'the Gulf War was a military and political attempt to atone for the conflict in Vietnam, then *Saving Private Ryan* is a filmic one.'[4] In Deleuzean terms, the film creates a recollection-image between an aspect of the past and the present in order to erase the difference (particularly the American military loss) that occurred in the interim.

The slight drawback with Auster's use of the term 'triumphalism' is that he effectively defines it as the celebration of American military triumph. Indeed, whilst Hodgkins never outwardly claims to be discussing triumphalism, he takes a similar line. However, in his book on the subject, *The End of Victory Culture* (1995), Tom Engelhardt provides a more considered definition. Engelhardt argues that the triumphal narrative asserts that American military triumph is inevitable because it is America's destiny. This notion is drawn from the nineteenth century idea of Manifest Destiny, in which the supposed right of the Europeans to conquer the New World was coded as inevitable, thereby eliding the reality of their colonial actions. Moreover, in the triumphal narrative American military victory is coded as righteous, as an action only committed once provoked. Engelhardt demonstrates how in early captivity narratives victory was typically seen as an act of justified vengeance perpetrated by European settlers against the wild and savage inhabitants of the lands they innocently traversed.[5] Thus, for this particular narrative of national identity, the nation reluctant to arm itself will always be victorious when forced to fight, secure in its moral righteousness as the aggrieved party.

Engelhardt's work has already been incorporated into the Film Studies canon. As Robert Stam and Louise Spence famously argued, in cinema this type of inversion is typical of colonial narratives.[6] Such films revise history by positioning the spectator along with the colonial power, for instance as hemmed in within the ambushed 'wagon circle' iconography of the western. This conflation of point of view with the outnumbered, courageous heroes ensures that the colonial other is only ever viewed through a gun sight. Thus: 'Hundreds of Hollywood westerns turned history on its head by making the Native Americans appear to be intruders on what was originally their land, and provided a paradigmatic perspective through which to view the whole of the non-white world.'[7]

In generic terms the triumphal narrative shares the same pattern as a rape–revenge drama, but with an added national dimension that justifies colonial conquest. The historical moments on which the American national narrative was initially constructed are well known. In the nineteenth century dramatic losses such as the battles of the Little Big Horn and the Alamo were used to justify morally sanctioned bloodletting in the name of Manifest Destiny.[8] They became the 'rape' origins that the triumphal national narrative avenged. Indeed, the narrative continued to function in the same fashion into the twentieth century. In 1941, for instance, it was the Japanese attack on Pearl Harbor that acted as just cause for America's entry into the Second World War. As I will demonstrate in the next chapter, 9/11 has since been used in much the same way.

Yet in the twentieth century the triumphal narrative has not always been dominant. Most obviously it suffered when America lost the war in Vietnam. Engelhardt points to the use of cinema to reassert triumphalism after this shock, citing *Star Wars* (1977) as the type of film that 'returned history to its previous owners'.[9] This film is a very useful example of the creation of a mythical origin from which to generate a recollection-image in the present. The narrative is a loose, allegorical retelling of the American

War of Independence, with American rebels victorious over the technically superior British Empire. By introducing the film with the pedagogical title, 'A long time ago . . .' the film mythically asserts the historical origin it uses to disavow the recent American loss of its national narrative. *Star Wars* reassures the viewer that just as things were in the past, with the underdog Americans triumphant at the national origin, so apparently they are now. Thus the recent loss in Vietnam is eradicated, and the triumphal narrative reasserted.

In fact, the regeneration of the triumphalist narrative after Vietnam was strongest under President Reagan. As Douglas Kellner has shown, films like *Rambo: First Blood Part II* (1985) represented 'a mythic redemption of the U.S. defeat in Vietnam by heroic action'.[10] However, prior to a significant military victory, it was always going to be a struggle for the national narrative to wipe out the memory of defeat in Vietnam. Hence, after the First Gulf War the triumphal narrative was resurgent in the 1990s. Returning to *Saving Private Ryan*, in a piece which defines triumphalism much more in line with Engelhardt's work, Frank P. Tomasulo notes how the opening battle represents the Second World War from the viewpoint of the 'underdog' American soldiers as they land on Omaha Beach. The initial American victory against the odds is rendered as a 'counteroffensive' as opposed to an invasion.[11] For Tomasulo the Second World War is used as a context 'in order to renew and revivify America's mythic rightness as a nation, particularly as U.S. and NATO forces bombed Serbia and ground troops were sent into Kosovo'.[12]

Indeed, it is not surprising that triumphalism was resurgent after the first major land conflict since Vietnam. John Storey argues that under Reagan, loss in Vietnam was renegotiated through the myth that the nation of America had been 'ambushed' by governmental failings.[13] America lost in Vietnam, because the government did not allow the military to use their full capabilities to win. Under Bush Sr, then, the First Gulf War became the retaliatory action through which these feelings of national betrayal could be assuaged. America's triumph in the Persian Gulf could be constructed as a retaliatory gesture against the previous, albeit apocryphal, political ambush of the military. As films like *Apocalypse Now* (1979), *Platoon* (1986) and *Hamburger Hill* (1987) previously suggested, America had not been allowed to fulfil its Manifest Destiny in Vietnam, not because of the tactics and resilience of the Vietnamese, but because of the nation's preoccupation with fighting itself. Through victory in the Persian Gulf it could return to triumphal ways, an opinion expressed in several films of the 1990s.

All A-Ryan, All American

Now, it would be a little reductive to categorise all American cinema in this way. I am obviously not suggesting that all American films of the 1990s were directly concerned with the First Gulf War or with reconstructing triumphalism. After all, as Robert Burgoyne demonstrates in *Film Nation: Hollywood Looks at U.S. History* (1997), a number of films in the 1990s expressly challenged the 'dominant fiction'.[14] Films like *Glory* (1989), *Thunderheart* (1992), and *Born on the Fourth of July* (1999) illustrated 'that there are potentially many histories embedded in a given historical moment, histories that may be plural and conflicting, and that require different constructions of the national past'.[15] Yet whilst some of these were successful films, their desire to challenge the accepted face of the national narrative was unusual. As Burgoyne himself notes in a slightly later work that returns to his previous position on *Forrest Gump* (1994), the film actually 'rewrites the social and historical past in a way that dovetailed with conservative and reactionary political movements in the mid-1990s'.[16]

Certain American films of the 1990s did deterritorialise the national narrative. They illustrate, as Burgoyne argues, Bhabha's 'hybrid national narrative'.[17] Yet there were just as many – including notable successes such as *Forrest Gump* and *Saving Private Ryan* – that reterritorialised the national narrative into its singular form. To examine the roots of this phenomenon I will now turn to *The Birth of a Nation*.

In a now much quoted statement, Jacques Ranciere claimed that the 'dominant fiction' in American cinema was that of the 'birth of a nation'.[18] It is through this narrative, this 'privileged mode of representation by which the image of the social consensus is offered to members of the social formation',[19] that the major voice of national identity makes itself heard. Thus American cinema, in its perpetual need to reestablish an origin (a 'this is where we come from'),[20] has a long standing relationship with the linear model of time. Without wishing to posit a straw man in the action-image, there is no denying its normative status as the 'privileged mode of representation' through which American national identity is constructed. This narrative structure is closely tied to triumphalism, a connection that is most apparent in *The Birth of a Nation*.

Griffith's film draws heavily on the generic roots of the frontier Indian captivity story, substituting 'the black man's rape of the white woman for the red man's capture of the white woman'.[21] In its concluding sequences the ambush narrative is evident in a number of forms. The town is at the mercy of a lawless African-American mob, Elsie Stoneman's (Lilian Gish) virtue is in danger from the predatory Silas Lynch (George Siegmann), assorted representative Anglos are encircled in the rustic log cabin, and Ben Cameron's (Henry B. Walthall) Klansmen are motivated by the 'courageous' suicide of his little sister, Flora (Mae Marsh) when lustfully pursued by Gus (Walter Long). Triumphant over all these adversities are the Klan cavalry.

As we would expect of a triumphal narrative, an encircling force is needed over which the forces of righteousness can triumph, apparently justifying castration, lynching and other forms of physical violence. In a typical colonial inversion, this negative force is provided by the film's racist representation of African Americans. What is important about the film for this discussion is the much analysed way in which its closing sequence uses cross cutting to unify the spaces through which the Klan ride, as the editing reduces the space of the nation to one unified domain of Klan rule. Through this process the physical actions of the Klan members become sufficient to change the situation in the manner we expect of the action-image. Moreover, these sequences illustrate the return of a singular history that controls and subdues the chaotic resurgence of America's occluded, colonial pasts during the Reconstruction and post-Reconstruction eras.

Michele Faith Wallace recently argued that *The Birth of a Nation* asserts the dominant 'Confederate myth' of African-American failure that emerged during the Reconstruction period. This myth – which held that the African-American population was too uneducated to succeed once freed – obliterated the reality of active African-American participation in civil society[22] and public office[23] during the Reconstruction era. Moreover, the film obfuscated the possibility that 'violence by whites against blacks, not the ignorance of the former slaves, was the chief problem of the postwar decade'.[24] The film attempted to use this myth to 'make sense' of the present.

In the years following the end of Reconstruction, and especially in the thirty years immediately preceding the making of the film, racial violence had once again flared in America.

> When Reconstruction ended, former Confederates managed to resume local power in the South. Between 1890 and 1907, every southern and border state 'legally' disenfranchised the vast majority of its African American citizens. Lynchings rose to an all-time high.[25]

Reflecting this context, Wallace's work demonstrates how the film's depiction of the 'righteous' lynching of Gus for his sexually motivated pursuit of Flora Cameron,[26] and the Klan's policing of the African-Americans on polling day, replayed negative aspects of the post-Reconstruction era in a triumphal light. In this way, origins were constructed in a fictional past for events occurring in the present, and once again the dominant myth of triumphalism was perpetrated. The past provided an aspect (the Confederate myth of the Reconstruction) with which the racial violence of the recent present could be matched. Thus, in *The Birth of a Nation* the historical revisionism of the American dominant fiction ('this is where we came from') and the structure of the action-image are inextricably entwined in the construction of a triumphal narrative. As Michael Paul Rogin notes, the film itself gave birth to the nation, in that it created a 'screen memory . . . through which Americans were to understand their collective past and enact their future'.[27] This same process is also evident in *Saving Private Ryan*.

Saving Private Ryan

Saving Private Ryan follows the fortunes of an eight-man squad of US Rangers during the Second World War. They are led by Captain John Miller (Tom Hanks). After surviving the slaughter of the D-Day landings, they embark on a 'Boy's Own' adventure through Indian Territory. The squad is sent to retrieve James Francis Ryan (Matt Damon) whose three brothers have recently been killed in combat. When Ryan is finally found, however, he refuses to be sent home to his mother, preferring to stay and defend a tactically vital bridge. Although he survives, all but two of the squad are killed.

As the critics listed above have noted, *Saving Private Ryan* illustrates the colonial reversion of triumphalism that is evident in *The Birth of a Nation*. Redefining an invasion as an act of self-defence is simply a matter of framing and point of view. Accordingly, the film uses the squad's quest for Ryan to create the illusion that their narrative is one of salvation rather than colonisation. Moreover, through the brief scenes set in the vast cornfields of Iowa the film conflates the saving of Ryan with the saving of the future of the nation. In these scenes the nation is equated with his mother, who crumples to the ground as she receives the news that three of her sons are dead. It is to triumph over this 'attack' on the heartlands of America that the squad act. Ryan's appearance at the beginning and end of the film, still alive in the 1990s with his extended family, confirms their victory.

Significantly, the squad that triumphs is ethnically diverse, but not racially integrated. Admittedly this is both entirely historically accurate, as well as reminiscent of many Second World War movies of the 1950s. [28] However, the effect of this is that the film creates what Peter Canning calls, drawing on Serge Daney, a 'warrior theater', where the lives of a small group of people (usually 'white' people), come to represent the official view of history.[29] In *Saving Private Ryan*, America's European diasporas are unified, the squad suggests, in their quest to save America. However, America's significant racial insiders are nowhere to be seen. In this way the film's triumphal narrative also tacitly validates white supremacy.

In the triumphal myths of the nineteenth century, the conquest of America was depicted after the fact as a triumph of a select handful of heroes against the overwhelming odds of multitudinous savages. Here the 'liberation' of twentieth-century Europe is portrayed in much the same way. It is no coincidence that the squad are US Rangers, troops with a history that stretches back to the frontier Indian wars of the seventeenth and eighteenth centuries. Furthermore, what appears to be a narrative depicting the saving of America actually disguises a narrative of colonialism that illustrates America's postwar infiltration of Western Europe. Thomas Doherty rightly points out that Spielberg's film is unusual in its choice of General George C. Marshall as the heroic individual who takes the decision to save Ryan. 'Marshall has been almost erased from the popular memory of World War II, never granted the big-screen recognition of Generals Patton or Eisenhower.'[30] Yet his appearance makes complete sense if we consider the film's depiction of the conquest of Fortress Europe, a fractured land across which its pioneering warrior heroes write the national narrative of triumphalism. Every time the troops seize a position, salty Sergeant Mike Horrack (Tom Sizemore) bellows: 'We're in business.' His mercantile attitude prefigures the imposition of the American, capitalist, free-market narrative upon the postwar world that would follow with the Marshall Plan. Through this scheme, authored by George C. Marshall, America assisted in the rebuilding of Europe, and in so doing created the expanded market for American goods that bolstered the American economy during the postwar years.

What none of these critics note, however, is that in this process the film simultaneously depicts the reterritorialisation of the time-image by the movement-image. Typically for a triumphal narrative it represents the squad's journey through the battlefields of France as a pioneering action that defends America. However, it also renders visible the reterritorialisation of the 'any-space whatevers' (the unidentifiable spaces of postwar Europe) which Deleuze saw as characteristic of European time-images. Rather than a setting for the aimless wanderings of 'seers' of time-images, like the characters in Rossellini's *Paisà* (1946) and *Germany Year Zero* (1947), here the rubble of Europe's cities are mapped and secured by the American soldiers. As men of action these 'doers' impose a colonial order upon Europe's liminal spaces, just as the movement-image does on the deterritorialising lines of flight of the time-image. To demonstrate this

Figure 4.1 The squad triumph over Europe's any-space-whatevers. (Source: Dreamworks LLC/The Kobal Collection/James, David)

process I will examine how a triumphal narrative is constructed in a manner that also illustrates the reterritorialising force of the movement-image. First, however, it is necessary to sketch in the film's triumphal narrative in a little more detail. The potential for deterritorialisation apparent on the plane of consistency is figured in the destruction of all forms (buildings, machinery, people) on the French battlefields. Across this unformed land the squad travels, bringing a linear order that reestablishes the movement-image's plane of organisation, just as it reterritorialises the triumphal narrative of American national identity.

Shaking Hands

There are a number of ways in which this triumphal narrative correlates with the film's existence as a movement-image. One of the most obvious is the way in which character identity is used to represent national identity. As the opening battle for the beachhead illustrates, the film considers France to be a deadly, duplicitous other world in which the narrative of American identity must constantly battle for supremacy. The any-space-whatevers of war-torn France that the squad negotiate threaten to unground their pioneering American narrative, just as the labyrinth constantly threatens to unground the straight line of time. Thus the film plays with notions of identity on several levels, acknowledging Butler's theory of performative identity as it simultaneously reterritorialises the potential for difference that it offers. This is most clearly seen in the opposition the film establishes between the real Ryan and a different private, James Ryan, that the squad encounters early on in the film. This fake version of Ryan is feminised, predominantly through his tears on hearing the news of his brothers' deaths. In sensory-motor terms, he 'breaks down'. This Ryan emphasises the dangers American national identity faces once it leaves its own shores. In the authentic Ryan, however (who reacts stoically to news of his brothers' deaths), the squad discover the heroic subject of the national narrative. Through his decision to stay and fight to avenge their deaths, the triumphal narrative is restored. In short, then, saving the identity of Ryan saves American national identity and reasserts the dominance of the triumphal myth. Ryan's courage ensures that the narrative's sensory-motor drive does not 'break down', and thus, along with the triumphal national narrative emerges the action-image.

The role of Captain Miller is similarly integral to the construction of both the triumphal national narrative and the action-image. He is a reluctant hero who understands his job as one of necessity, performed solely in the desire to return to his wife in America. He therefore rationalises the loss of men under his command as justifiable, due to the greater number of lives he saves with their sacrifice. Through Miller the invasion of Europe is further coded as a triumphal defence of homeland and family. Moreover, through his physical form the film asserts the authority of the action-image in the construction of a triumphal narrative.

The struggle to maintain the triumphal national narrative is most clearly played out when Miller refuses to execute a German prisoner of war, 'Steamboat Willie'. The squad threaten to mutiny, their pioneering narrative unravelling when triumphal duties are not paid. After all, the German machine gun nest previously ambushed an American patrol, and in the course of subduing it, Miller's own squad lost medic Lieutenant Wade (Giovanni Ribisi). The squad argue their right to kill the POW, using the inexorable logic of triumphalism. To quell the mutiny, Miller reveals that behind the mask he wears in war there exists a sensitive high-school teacher. Reminded of the 'essential' American identity that they are fighting to save, the squad relent. Yet, in what initially appears to be a paradox, Miller's own death is caused by this inability to follow through with the triumphal narrative when he is shot by the German soldier whose life Miller previously saved. This paradox is resolved by the film's validation of his essential, organic identity and the Miller/Ryan father/son relationship.

At several points during the film, Miller's essential self shows through in the uncontrollable motor actions of his shaky right hand. Most obviously these shakes iterate the difficulty that this cultured man has, extending perception into action during wartime. However, they also have an allegorical function. Whereas films like *Sliding Doors* and *Run Lola Run* use multiple versions of the same body to demonstrate transformations of national identity, *Saving Private Ryan* uses Miller's uncontrollable shakes to illustrate national identity under threat. Miller's shakes are most evident during his tearful breakdown over the death of Wade. His shaking hand reassures us that there is an essential American identity that the warrior theatre is performed in order to protect, even if this warrior theatre necessarily works against the essential grain. The paradox raised by this is that somehow America's essential identity must be overcome in order for triumphalism to proceed, even though American triumph could be considered a supposedly essential attribute of Manifest Destiny. However, this paradox is disavowed by the film's Cartesian division of Miller. His body and mind are all American, as he reveals through his knowledge of Emerson (mind) and his role as coach of the baseball team (body). His body has been brutalised by war, as we see in his shaky hand, and yet he continues to fight due to the strength of his character. By asserting the power of mind over body and continuing in his quest for Ryan, Miller demonstrates that he is able to overcome physical difficulty in order to reassert the national narrative. This is exactly what we would expect of the protagonist of the action-image, the ability to progress from situation, through action, to a better situation.

In *8½*, Guido first enters the frame as a close-up of a grasping hand that cannot extend into action. In *Saving Private Ryan*, Miller is introduced as a close-up of a shaking hand that struggles to act. Both characters represent an interruption in the sensory-motor continuum that, as I demonstrated in Chapter 2, also gives literal form to a rupture in the national narrative. The difference is that, whilst in the time-image Guido remains within the malaise of the past that is, in the action-image Miller is able to extend his legacy, of the All-American past that was, into the present. This is clearly illustrated at the end of the film, when Miller's death is followed by a close-up on his now stilled hand. The American national narrative has faced a crisis, but in Miller's founding sacrifice it has been saved from potential dissolution. Its survival is figured in his successor, Ryan, who is constructed as Miller's son or pupil. By finally cutting from Miller's death to Ryan in the present, the film suggests that the next generation inherits the triumphal myth that soldier/teachers like Miller died to save.

It is also instructive to note how the greenhorn interpreter, Corporal Timothy Upham (Jeremy Davies), is used to position the audience within the film's triumphal narrative and to posit the cure for Miller's shaky physique. Like Ryan he is also figured as a pupil of schoolteacher Miller. Through Upham ('I make maps and I translate') the audience is positioned to witness the actions of the squad. Following Tomasulo's idea, he is a way into the action for the audience, much as some war reporters were during the First Gulf War. I find this most evident in the scene where the squad overruns the machine-gun nest, an action presented from Upham's point of view, through a telescopic rifle sight. The physical mapping of France that the film depicts, then, is reflected in the ideological mapping of the triumphal narrative onto Upham's psyche. Unlike the battle-hardened squad, Upham is initially incapable of action. At the end of the film, however, he learns to act, significantly mastering his sensory-motor continuity through the revenge killing of Steamboat Willie that validates the triumphal narrative. It was Upham's reasoning that persuaded Miller to release Willie, thereby enabling him to reappear in the final battle and shoot Miller. Realising this, when Upham finally captures Willie he shoots him in cold blood. Thus is Miller's failure to complete the triumphal narrative avenged by his pupil, Upham, and the action-image restored by Upham's decisive action.

Finally, alongside this focus on character identity is the physical progress of the squad through France. This provides both a physical performance of the triumphal narrative and a literal rendering of the movement-image's power of reterritorialisation. The squad's movement mirrors the invasion itself, a colonial narrative of mapping discussed as military strategy by Miller and 'Pathfinders' Captain Hamill (Ted Danson).

Hamill: You gotta take Caen so you can take St Lô.
Miller: You gotta take St Lô to take Boulogne.
Hamill: Boulogne you got Cherbourg.
Miller: Cherbourg, you got Paris.
Hamill: Paris, you got Berlin.

The military conquest of space is an enforced mapping that utilises the squad's well trained sensory-motor skills. Through the unfolding of their action-image the American national narrative of triumphalism is also writ large upon Europe. The narrative's progress is inexorably linear – 'Cherbourg, you got Paris', Paris, you got Berlin' – and for this reason the bridge that the squad finally defend is of such strategic importance. Without it the whole invasion could fizzle out, and with it the linear trajectory of the triumphal national narrative.

Flashback

Adding an extra dimension to the narrative's focus on character identity the triumphal narrative is also constructed in conjunction with the formal structure of the action-image. In *Flashbacks in Cinema* (1989) Maureen Turim charts the evolution of the flashback as it developed in European and American cinema. For Turim, American cinema's use of flashback emerges around the time of D. W. Griffith, and uses a subjective memory to stand in for that of a nation; she argues,

> flashbacks are central to Griffith's version of history, saturated with emotional identification and symbolism. We can see his films as one of the formative stages of the massive effort in American films to subjectivize history . . . The theme of collective memory as determinant of history and individuals as exemplars of collective memories in their most personalized and subjective form is developed in *Birth of a Nation* (1915) through the use of one of Griffith's melodramatic strategies, the interweaving of personal tragedy and love stories with epic narratives of major historical events.[31]

As an example of the process whereby a subjective flashback masquerades as a national truth, Turim describes the incident in *The Birth of a Nation* in which Southern Belle Margaret Cameron (Miriam Cooper) is amorously pursued by Yankee Phil Stoneman (Elmer Clifton). Just when she seems about to succumb to his advances the intertitles declare: 'Bitter memories will not allow the Poor Bruised South to forget.' The film then cuts from Margaret's face, to a shot of her brother dying during the Civil War, an image which – in some prints – is tinted an emotive red. This image, which had previously been seen as part of the film's narrative development, was not one to which Margaret was privileged. What appears to be a personal recollection, then, due to the cut from her face to the image of the dead, is in fact an image of a 'collective' past through which the film attempts to 'subjectivize' history. It illustrates, as Turim contends, the conflation of historical events with personal tragedies in order to raise an emotional response in the viewer. This process recurs in *Saving Private Ryan*, as it too uses character memory to construct national identity.

The events depicted in wartime France take place during a single flashback. Initially we are led to believe that the narrative is recounted from the point of view of the elderly Ryan. The flashback begins with a very conventional close-up on his aging face as he visits a cemetery in Normandy. Over this close-up the sound of the sea is heard, creating the audio overlap that situates us in the past to which we immediately cut, to witness the landings on Omaha Beach. However, it cannot be Ryan's memory that we are seeing, as he parachuted into France and did not witness the bloody landing. Rather, an ideologically biased account of the national past is passed off as a veteran's account of real events. Rather like Margaret Cameron's supposed flashback in *Birth of a Nation*, here, again, a collective memory is shown as though it were personal. Thus this piece of warrior theatre illustrates 'the interweaving of personal tragedy' with an epic narrative of 'major historical events' that is typical of much American cinema.

The ending of *Saving Private Ryan* provides closure by returning to Ryan in the present. By starting at the end and then flashing back to the beginning of Ryan's story it posits its own first cause retroactively. In this is takes a device found in innumerable American films, although perhaps most memorably in *Double Indemnity* (1944) and *Sunset Boulevard* (1950). Here the images that bookend the narrative are literally 'flagged' as being of national significance. They are close-ups of the stars and stripes, waving in the breeze over the cemetery in Normandy. These images are accompanied by the soft, mournful tones of trumpets. The flashback's narrative, then, has an inevitable ending already inscribed in history, which is used to seemingly legitimise the fictional representation of events that then follows. If ever there was an origin to America's contemporary triumphal identity, the film argues, this war is it.

As the camera moves in on Ryan's face just prior to the flashback, we focus in on his blue eyes, shining, wet with tears. Although the colour blue and the salt-water image function primarily as a graphic match with which to transport us back in time to the coastal waters off France in 1944, it also codes the 'history' which follows as one of white supremacy. Finally, the use of washed-out colours to depict this history lesson ensures that, as Michael Hammond argues, 'the images are double coded in the narrative, as well as in the faded colours of the image, as a memory and as memorial'.[32] Through the linearity created by this flashback structure it is evident that the action-image's structure – especially in its positing of a mythical origin to contemporary history – is integral to the construction of the triumphal narrative.

'Alamo Alamo!'

In fact, *Saving Private Ryan* is extremely blatant in its evocation of historical origins. The final battle sequence conflates the defence of a bridge in the Second World War with several battles that were instrumental in the construction of American national identity. It also reterritorialises the past to suggest the continuity of American triumphalism from these historical points of origin.

In many ways reminiscent of an episode of *The A-Team*, the squad's final victory against the odds is obtained through the use of guerrilla tactics. Typically, then, the role reversal found in frontier ambush narratives is again in evidence, with the white colonials positioned as the outnumbered guerrillas from whose point of view the action is shown. Even though this is actually an ambush set by the American troops it is refigured as an heroic last stand.

As the squad falls back to blow up the bridge, they repeatedly shout the name of their final refuge, 'The Alamo'. In this version of the 1836 defence of the Texas Mission, however, reinforcements arrive in time, and The Alamo does not fall. As a result, the bridge, symbol of the continuous sensory-motor mapping of the American national narrative onto postwar Europe, is saved. Spielberg's historically revisionist narrative 'remembers the Alamo' as the originary ambush that must be avenged if triumphalism is to be retained.

Moreover, as was the case with George Lucas's *Star Wars* (1977), the film's finale also replays the American War of Independence in miniature. The film focuses on a band of plucky scavengers who miraculously defeat the might of a previously all-conquering military empire. This focus ensures that we do not dwell on images of America's mighty war machine rolling through the streets of Europe. The last minute arrival of the cavalry to save The Alamo (the Air Force's P51 'Tank Busters') thus appears not as a symbol of US expansionism, but rather as the heavenly sanctioned, 'Angels on our shoulders' that Miller dubs them. As was the case in *The Birth of a Nation*, the cavalry arrive in the final scene to reunify both the physical space through which the film's narrative passes, and the temporal longevity of the national narrative. In Miller's dying words to Ryan (that he must 'earn' the sacrifices of the Rangers), this new origin of American triumphalism is shown to be something that can only be reconfirmed in retrospect – like any recollection-image – by making the present match the past. This has been achieved, the film suggests, through Ryan's progeny, as the film brackets the flashback with shots of his extended family in the Normandy cemetery. In this way the righteousness of events in the Gulf are suggested, as though they are his generation's contribution to the continuation of the postwar era and its retrospective 'earning' of the American victory in Europe.

This mingling of American military history is completed by General Marshall's reading of a letter from 'Honest' Abe Lincoln. Lincoln's letter to the mother of five brothers lost during the American Civil War positions the film's Second World War context on a level of national importance comparable with that of the war which unified the North and the South.

Civil War and Second World War are equated through this voiceover with the birth of the nation. Lincoln's presence as divine logos, the word of the nation's deceased father, also legitimises America's postwar colonial ambitions. His abolitionist stance gives credence to both the US expansionism which followed the war, and also the film's narrative, in which black servicemen are conspicuously absent even as extras. The white narrative of the nation's history is thus given a sense of continuity, from the War of Independence, through the Alamo, the Civil War, and finally, to the Second World War.

The mythical nature of this narrative is summed up by the historically contested content of Lincoln's letter. In fact it is very unlikely that the events it depicts (a mother's loss of five sons during the Civil War) ever actually happened. Like *The Birth of a Nation*, *Saving Private Ryan* also constructs national history along mythical lines:

> *Saving Private Ryan* . . . essentially works as another opportunity to embrace a story which signals that the contemporary era should be proud and grateful for the preservation of the principle of democracy in itself, rather than evaluate its systematic abuse in the postwar era.[33]

It is altogether unsurprising that this myth was created using the Second World War as a primal scene to match the salvation of democracy recently enacted in the Persian Gulf. During the First Gulf War, comparisons with the Second World War were manifold. As Douglas Kellner notes in *The Persian Gulf TV War* (1992), the American media equated Saddam Hussein with Hitler,[34] the Iraqi invasion of Kuwait was dubbed a 'blitzkrieg',[35] and the US-led coalition referred to as the 'allies'.[36] Moreover, the country was mobilised to war in the knowledge that the 'allies' were in Kuwait to revenge its 'rape', a term variously deployed by the media, President Bush Sr and General Schwarzkopf.[37] As we would expect from a triumphal narrative, its justification is rape, its revenge military victory. The return to mythical origins evoked by *Saving Private Ryan*'s narrative trajectory, moreover, equates the salvation of the nation (the maintenance of triumphalism) with the construction of the recollection-image.

'Forget the Alamo' (*Family Man, Lone Star*)

In many ways *Saving Private Ryan* is typical of a number of American films of the 1990s. For instance, *Courage Under Fire* (1996) deployed its *Rashomon* (1951)-inspired narrative structure to clear American troops of accusations of cowardice during the First Gulf War. Although it illustrates the process through which the past is rewritten to reconstruct a triumphal narrative, this process is not critiqued, not deterritorialised in any fashion. Rather it is used to exonerate the military. *Rules of Engagement* (2000) also focuses on clearing the US military, especially those now involved in post-Cold War policing actions in the Middle East, of any failings when ambushed in Vietnam. It even reiterates, through its treacherous National Security Advisor Bill Sokal (Bruce Greenwood), the Reagan-era myth that the military only fails to perform when hindered by meddling politicians. Sokal destroys the video evidence that would clear Colonel Childers (Samuel L. Jackson) of accusations of murder, thereby attempting to obscure the triumphal 'truth' that Childers acted in self defence when ambushed by terrorists in Yemen. In this post-Gulf War movie, however, the politicians ultimately fail to ambush the military. After all, victory in the Gulf had shown that the military are triumphant once again.

This trend was not only true of war films. Consider, for instance, the science fiction film. *Stargate* (1994) provides a particularly obvious allegory for US involvement in Kuwait, as an elite squad of US troops travel to a desert planet to save a community of 'Arabian'-costumed mineral miners from an alien dictator and his evil empire! Indeed, other science fiction films not specifically focused on the military also reconstructed the past to create recollection-images that explained the national present. *Blast From the Past* (1998) and *Frequency* (2000), for instance, variously posit origins for America's pre-millennium computer boom in the 1950s and 1960s. They are all part of a more general trend in American cinema that negotiates historical transformations by returning to the past, and reasserting a singular, mythical timeline that stems from a fictional origin. As John Davies and Paul Wells argue:

> The deep theme of much American cinema is still the simultaneous longing to acknowledge the profound effects of late industrial capitalism and technological innovation, yet also for a nostalgic desire to look back upon our past in the spirit of loss for supposedly better times. It was always thus. Whilst sustaining a model of progress, the United States has always been anxious about the values and achievements it may have left behind.[38]

This process of national identity formation is most obvious in American films that, using a similar technique to *Sliding Doors* and *Run Lola Run*, offer two or more different versions of the same national present. As I noted previously, these films follow the same pattern as *It's a Wonderful Life*. In Capra's film a conservative, nostalgic view of national identity is ultimately coded as the 'right' one on offer. Despite the transformations that the nation had undergone during the Second World War, in Bedford Falls a prewar vision of small-town, community-oriented values was offered. As

Kaja Silverman argues in *Male Subjectivity at the Margins* (1992) the film worked to 'neutralise the historical trauma of civilian reentry' for ex-servicemen returning from Europe.[39] It sutured over the period of economic transition of the postwar years, during which they discovered that their previous position of economic authority had been eroded by increased female participation in the workforce. *It's a Wonderful Life*, then, participated in the 'gradual reaffirmation and reconstitution of the dominant fiction' through its focus on a flawed male protagonist who was nevertheless found to be indispensable to both family and community.[40]

Whilst the British and German films examined in the previous chapter celebrate the 'new' national lifestyle offered by an historical transformation, American films usually celebrate a supposed continuation of the 'old' version of national identity. Several American films of the 1990s follow the same narrative pattern as *It's a Wonderful Life* – and conclude in a similar fashion. *Groundhog Day* (1993), *When Time Expires* (1997) and *For All Time* (2000) are all good examples. The way such films deal with the, then contemporary, crises (of family values, masculinity, post-Cold War economic recession and racial segregation) through a narrative which focuses on the heroic white male, has already been examined by several theorists.[41] However, slightly more recent films such as *Family Man* (2000) and its immediate remake *Three Days* (2001) have negotiated the same territory slightly differently. *Family Man* sees Nicholas Cage's Jack Campbell offered a glimpse of the life he could have had, had he settled in Jersey and not become a self-serving career man. In the film's conclusion he renounces his yuppie self and convinces his ex-girlfriend that they should leave their wealthy lives in New York, return to middle America and start a family. As in *It's a Wonderful Life*, the right/old and the wrong/new are starkly contrasted in favour of the ideal vision of small-town America.

Family Man is slightly different from its 1990s predecessors, however, as it also investigates how its protagonist's alternate futures are determined by globalisation. Financially successful career-man Campbell initially earned his stripes working as an intern at Barclays Bank in London. By contrast, the family-man version of Campbell never stayed in New York's neighbouring global city to become 'corrupted' in this way. He immediately returned to his girlfriend in America to become a family man. When Campbell finally renounces his wealth he also convinces Kate not to leave for Paris but to settle with him in America. Through the renunciation of these international links the film contrasts starkly with *Sliding Doors* and *Run Lola Run*, becoming almost the 'anti-*Sabrina*' in its valorisation of the national over the transnational. Rather like *It's a Wonderful Life*, *Groundhog Day*, *When Time Expires* and *For All Time*, this film reassures those who never became successful entrepreneurs that their lives are still indispensable to the nation. Thus the struggle of the majority of middle Americans to maintain the old in the face of the new is triumphant.

In fact, whilst all these films of the 1990s and 2000s 'acknowledge the profound effects of late industrial capitalism and technological innovation', they also reemphasise a nostalgic myth of small-town family values. The origins of this myth are explicitly figured as having been imported from the ranch lifestyle of the frontier pioneers (*When Time Expires*) to the small town (*For All Time*, *Groundhog Day*, *Three Days*) to the middle-class suburb (*Family Man*), thereby creating an apparently linear national narrative. Like *Saving Private Ryan*, these films all construct national history through a return to mythical origins. Indeed, For Thomas Doherty, *Saving Private Ryan* also references Capra's films through Captain Miller, a man who 'embodies the Frank Capra version of the American soldier . . . who wants only to finish his job and get back home to his wife in smalltown Pennsylvania'.[42]

However, in spite of this tendency towards a reterritorialisation of the national narrative, some post-Gulf War films did critique this use of the past to establish false origins for the present. The films Burgoyne discusses in *Film Nation* are good examples of this counter movement. Two further examples are *Lone Star* (1995) and *Memento*, both films that formally demonstrate the deterritorialisation of the movement-image's plane of organisation. I will now turn to examine these independent films, which are both time-images 'caught in the act' of becoming movement-images.

John Sayle's *Lone Star* self-consciously illustrates the existence of the many different national histories (African-American, Anglo-American, Native-American, Mexican-American) held by America's different racial demographics. It also illustrates, through a local sheriff's murder investigation, the many different layers of history that can be unearthed through a genealogical excavation of the past. Despite this, at first glance it appears to be a movement-image, not least because its flashbacks are all truth confirming, and informing of one single linear narrative. However, as Neil Campbell argues in his excellent chapter, 'Forget the Alamo' (2003), its aesthetic is constructed in a rather unusual way to expose the myriad layers of national history.[43] For Campbell the film expresses 'a Deleuzian deterritorialization' of identity.[44] This functions in a number of ways, the most pertinent to this discussion being its refusal to signal when a flashback shifts the narrative to the past. 'In "erasing" the border between past and present cinematically, Sayles shows that history and memory are alive in the present, informing and shaping the choices people make.'[45]

Extrapolating from Campbell's position, it is clear that *Lone Star* engages with the past that is, rather than the past that was. For instance, the blurring of past and present through the use of unsignalled flashbacks exposes the transformative plane of time previously seen in *8½*, this time through the camera's effortless pans across different layers of time. Thus *Lone Star* not only illustrates but also formally demonstrates its deterritorialisation of the national narrative. The film's formal construction of the past deconstructs the use of origins typical of American cinema, as Sayles' film concludes with the words, 'Forget the Alamo', spoken in front of a disused drive-in movie screen. Here, rather than reconstructing the Alamo as an image that actualises to match the present, *Lone Star* avoids confirming the linearity of the past through the construction of a recollection-image. Instead it calls for a Nietzschean forgetting that would realign time in a labyrinthine manner to acknowledge America's multiple histories.

It could conceivably be argued, however, that this is a particularly subtle way of demonstrating a more open view of the past than is usually found in American cinema. Several people working in this field have noted the reasons for this. As Charles Lindholm and John A. Hall state, in American cinema in general 'overtly political films have never been popular'.[46] Accordingly, Davies and Wells assert, political messages are often smuggled into American films, be they reactionary or revolutionary in intent.[47] When it comes to American independent films, this act of smuggling often occurs through a formal deterritorialisation of classical conventions and norms. As Geoff King has it in his book, *American Independent Cinema* (2005),

> the 'artistic' and the 'political' are far from separate categories . . . Formal experimentation and departure from dominant conventions is, potentially, a major resource for the deconstruction of dominant ideologies.[48]

This deconstruction, however, is dependent upon the spectator having previously 'internalised' the normative conventions of the dominant mode, from which these formal departures then become more noticeable.[49] Thus King theorises independent cinema as more interactive than mainstream Hollywood cinema. It engages the spectator, increasing 'consciousness of the process of narration itself'.[50] This recourse to self-conscious narrative distanciation has almost become an aspect by which independent films are defined, and, rather than a disorienting departure from the norm, the multiple, disjointed, jumbled or reversed narratives of many independent films are actually 'anticipated' by spectators.[51]

As I have argued elsewhere in relation to *The Big Lebowski* (1997), this interaction between spectator and film is itself a product of a dual address evident in many independent films since the 1970s.[52] Films such as *The Big*

Lebowski, *Lone Star* and *Memento* address a split audience demographic. They use a technique similar to that noted by Nöel Carroll as the 'two-tiered system of communication' deployed by post-classical Hollywood films since the 1970s/80s to maximise audience figures.[53] The audiences these films reach are both those seeking an entertaining story (complete with all the usual ingredients of murder, drugs, money, sex, violence and so on) and those whose expectations have been trained (often institutionally in American colleges) to construct a political subtext from clues inserted into the film's form and content. As King's work suggests, these clues often take the form of departures from classical conventions and norms. For instance, Campbell's analysis of *Lone Star* shows how the strategic deployment of formal devices such as soundtrack and flashback (coupled with the use of different racial identities amongst its characters and a strategic deployment of various liminal settings) enables Sayles' film to deliberately smuggle politics into what is otherwise a juicy murder investigation.[54] Similarly, in *Memento* this smuggling is evident in its deployment of an aberrant narrative time scheme, used in conjunction with character memory, to deterritorialise the accepted norms through which a triumphal national narrative (and an action-image) is usually constructed.

Memento

In this concluding section I examine how the formal construction of *Memento* illustrates its existence as a time-image 'caught in the act' of becoming a movement-image. I also determine the extent to which this structure deterritorialises the national narrative of triumphalism. It will be seen that its jumbled narrative provides a similar critique, a similar formal demonstration of the ungrounding of the national narrative, as Campbell uncovers in *Lone Star*.

Memento is the story of Leonard Shelby (Guy Pearce), a man obsessed with finding and killing the murderer of his wife. However, Shelby has a chronic case of short-term memory loss. Unable to make any new memories he can only retain information concerning the present for a very brief time. He lives much of his life following clues he has left for himself in the past. His most striking tattoos read: 'John G. raped and murdered my wife' and 'Find him and kill him'.

Like *Saving Private Ryan*, *Memento* examines the link between an essential identity and a violent performance of identity. In this respect it engages with the national narrative through its meditation on vengeance. In her seminal work on horror fiction, *Men, Women and Chain Saws* (1992), Carol J. Glover discusses the rape–revenge film and the way it crosses genre boundaries in American cinema. She puts its ubiquity down to its emphasis on vengeance, stating, 'vengeance may very well be the mainspring of American popular culture, from westerns and *Dirty Harry* to teen comedies and courtroom dramas.'[55] *Memento* engages with this ubiquitous popular tradition, questioning the manner in which national 'vengeance' is justified by a constructed origin. The sanctioned triumphal killings enacted in the 'defence' of national identity seen in *Saving Private Ryan* are thereby deconstructed. *Memento* turns the trajectory of the rape–revenge narrative on its head, illustrating that such killings are tantamount to 'getting away with murder'.

Memento formally deterritorialises the creation of triumphal narratives by demonstrating how the falsifying possibilities of the labyrinth are reterritorialised by the straight line of time. It effects this deterritorialisation by engaging the viewer in the construction of the narrative. *Memento* encourages identification with a character who is lying to himself, by creating a false origin to a rape–revenge narrative, in order to commit murder. In *Saving Private Ryan*, Upham's point of view was used to position the spectator amongst the action, allowing no distance from which to judge events in the narrative. In *Memento* by contrast, the viewer is forced to reconstruct the protagonist's triumphal narrative, and in doing so, becomes aware of the false origins on which it is based.

In this process of critical inversion the interaction between character memory and flashback are of vital importance. *Memento*'s narrative also works within the loose parameters of the flashback structure of *Saving Private Ryan*. By creating confusion within this structure, however, it questions its usual linear progression. Thus as a time-image 'caught in the act' of becoming a movement-image, the film foregrounds how false origins are used to reterritorialise the labyrinth with a triumphant narrative of national identity.

Initially both Shelby's identity and the film's narrative seem to demonstrate a labyrinthine structure. Shelby appears to construct his identity by falsifying the past, and thereby to live his life through the performance of not necessarily true roles. The narrative of the film, moreover, appears to work in the same way. It starts at the narrative's conclusion, and then realigns events backwards to explain how the film's beginning was reached. However, neither the time of the narrative, nor Shelby's identity, are quite what they seem.

Shelby's recurring lapses of concentration ensure that his past appears to be constantly overwritten. In order to cope with his inability to make new memories Shelby leaves a series of messages for himself (notes on paper and the backs of photographs and tattoos on his body) concerning the identities of the people around him and the facts of his investigation into his wife's death. Owing to his constant lapses of attention, every time Shelby reads a note it is as though for the first time, for in effect he has become a different person due to his loss of memory. Initially, then, Shelby seems to correspond to Deleuze's 'forger' of *Cinema 2*. For Deleuze the forger emerged with the time-image's realisation of the powers of the false to become: '*the* character of the cinema.'[56] His power to perform his identity comes directly from the labyrinth. He is 'the man of pure descriptions and the maker of the crystal-image, the indiscernibility of the real and the imaginary . . . he provokes undecidable alternatives and inexplicable differences between the true and the false'.[57] Consequently Shelby's identity initially appears to correspond to that of a character in the time-image.

The film's apparent denial of the existence of an essential self in favour of performative identity is shown in a number of ways. For instance, one of the tattoos on Shelby's arm that contains information about the killer, reads: 'FACT 3: FIRST NAME: JOHN'. However, at some point in the past this seemingly irrefutable fact has been revised, and underneath a homemade tattoo has been added that reads, 'OR JAMES'. In the labyrinthine life of Shelby even facts as irrefutable as someone's name are changeable. Responding to Shelby's repeated attempts to assert the fixity of his identity – 'I'm Leonard Shelby, I'm from San Francisco' – crooked cop Teddy (Joe Pantoliano) replies, 'That's who you *were*. You do not know who you *are*, what you have become.' As Shelby himself realises when he begins to wilfully deceive his future self by dressing in the clothes of the murdered drug dealer Jimmy Grants, identity is in fact a process of becoming-other, of masquerading. In this process, the past (and indeed, the past self) becomes not necessarily true. In *Memento*, as in the time-image, who you are is who you are becoming, not who you were.

The film also uses this bizarre situation to show the impossibility of either recording or representing truth – or historical facts. In the black-and-white sequence that dominates much of the first half of the film we see Shelby tattooing FACT 5 onto his leg. However, during this process he receives a number of misleading phone calls. As a result he changes his initial tattoo of 'Access to drugs', to 'Drug Dealer'. The misinformation which leads him to this conclusion, however, will be forgotten the next time he reads the tattoo, which will seem to be an undeniable historical fact. Thus the film foregrounds that all history is an illusion and can only be legitimised, or falsified, in retrospect. As in the time-image *8½*, here all pasts are not necessarily true.

Furthermore, *Memento*'s narrative construction seems similarly falsifying in intent. The film begins with the fading out of development of the photograph Shelby takes of Teddy's body. Events then begin to play backwards, the photo sliding back into the camera, blood off the walls back into Teddy's head, the bullet back into the gun and Teddy back to life. In this way the opening sequence introduces how the narrative will proceed, playing backwards in a series of colour episodes, each one of which ends with the event that began the previous episode. The narrative thus unfolds before us as a sequence of events played in reverse order. It would seem as though the line of time that the narrative constructs is, as Shelby's memories are, always realigning itself, from the present backwards. Indeed, the film makes the link between its narrative structure and Shelby's memories crystal clear, in its very first image of a photograph fading out of existence. A little later in the film, Shelby describes his own memories in exactly the same way, saying 'I can't make new memories', adding, 'everything just fades'.

However, on closer inspection it is clear that this is not everything that is happening. The film sets up a labyrinthine narrative and sense of self like that found in the time-image, but it then demonstrates the process through which they are reterritorialised by the movement-image. Indeed, by foregrounding this process – and especially by forcing the spectator to take part in it by resembling a jumbled narrative – it deterritorialises the same process of triumphal narrative creation that *Saving Private Ryan* celebrates.

Getting Away With Murder

Memento's novel way of building the narrative is actually only the continual retroactive imposition of a series of causes for the events that have just occurred. In this way the narrative reterritorialises Shelby's labyrinthine performance within a linear schema that is eventually shown to also structure his identity. The narrative gains its consistency from its retroactive linearity, in which the past is definitely that which causes the present that we have already witnessed. For this reason, any possibility of a contingent past to the film's narrative is negated. Like *Saving Private Ryan*, *Memento* demonstrates the process through which the time-image is reterritorialised by the movement-image. The difference is that here the narrative's self-conscious play with this theme also exposes its Machiavellian potential.

Each of the colour narrative episodes is interspersed by a small part of the black-and-white sequence in which Shelby, in his motel room, talks to Teddy on the telephone about Sammy Jankis. This sequence is the originary moment of the narrative, the point at which the story begins. Significantly it is to this point that we first jump immediately after seeing

Shelby kill Teddy in the opening sequence. The motel-room scene in the flashback provides the same origin to the narrative seen in films like *Double Indemnity*, *Sunset Boulevard* and *Saving Private Ryan*, only this time its fragmented format questions its usually truth-confirming state.

The film alternates between sections of the black-and-white sequence and the colour episodes that immediately precede the murder of Teddy. In fact, the colour episodes play backwards until they meet the black-and-white sequence. The point at which they overlap is the murder of Jimmy Grants, the drug dealer whom Teddy has manipulated Shelby into believing to be his wife's killer. Here black and white becomes colour with the developing of the photo Shelby takes of Grants' corpse. When they meet and correspond so exactly in this way, the two directions through time in which the narrative simultaneously moves foregrounds the impossibility of the narrative's deviation from its singular, linear trajectory. The events that led up to and caused the first murder are thus shown, albeit in a fragmented fashion, as though the final event to which they led is inevitable. Whilst this convention is 'obvious' in *Saving Private Ryan* because of the signalling of Ryan's false flashback, here it only reveals itself at the end of the film with the *noir*-ish twist of Shelby's wilful decision to commit murder.

Any hint that the film could be acknowledging a number of different possible pasts is eradicated by the narrative's reterritorialisation within a linear schema. In this way the film invites a questioning of the normative use of this narrative structure. As we might expect from a movement-image, the film's underlying chronological order is clearly signalled. In the black-and-white sequence Shelby is busy tattooing 'FACT 5' onto his body. The colour narrative for its part, that which the black-and-white sequence (literally) 'develops' into, is concerned with what happens as a consequence of the tattoo 'FACT 6'. On one level, then, the film uses clear signals in order to retain continuity across a disorienting narrative. In this sense it is very conventional. On another level, however, the overall linear schema foregrounds that it is developing, quite literally, 'by the numbers'. The fact that the past is shot in black and white, and the present in colour only makes the development of this linearity all the more obvious. For the spectator, the very act of interpreting the film reterritorialises it as a movement-image, a fact to which *Memento* self-consciously draws our attention by involving us in the process.

The linearity that grounds an otherwise labyrinthine narrative is also evident in the film's construction of Shelby's identity. Shelby constructs probable causes for the present situations he finds himself in, thereby establishing a linear origin to his identity. Admittedly this does make his previous identity not necessarily true, but it does so by establishing a series of false origins. For instance, after the murder of drug dealer Jimmy Grants, Shelby adorns himself in Jimmy's clothes and drives away in his Jaguar. Slightly later, when Shelby has lost all memory of killing Grants, Teddy asks him where he thinks he has got the money from for such an expensive lifestyle? Shelby immediately creates a fictional cause: 'I have money . . . from my wife's death, I used to work in insurance, we were well covered.' Shelby creates an unbroken timeline that explains his present situation through the positing of a (false) first cause. As events unfold, however, the spectator comes to understand that Shelby is actually lying to himself to cover up a murder. Through his establishment of false causes, then, the very process of constructing a triumphal linear narrative is laid bare.

The point at which the two narratives meet, the murder of Jimmy Grants, also deconstructs the cinematic sanctioning of triumphal killing. This is an act that, as we see in *Saving Private Ryan*, does not usually detract from the 'essential' goodness of the American protagonist. By contrast, when Shelby takes the photo of Grants' corpse he is busily changing into the dead man's clothes. In *Saving Private Ryan* the concern is that, by killing, the character may lose his essential identity. In *Memento*, by contrast, Shelby embraces this potential loss of self. As he tells Teddy, 'I think I'd rather be mistaken for a dead guy than a killer', a statement which contrasts starkly with Miller's, 'Every man I kill, the farther away from home I feel'. In *Memento*, the warrior theatre of *Saving Private Ryan* is exposed as deliberately disavowing the link between an essential American identity and the act of killing. In Spielberg's film a righteous essential self remains beneath the warrior's mask, as seen in Miller's shaking hand. In *Memento*, however, this process is figured as simply the disguising of a murderer. Shelby therefore acknowledges that to lose your essential identity may make you a 'dead guy', but for the righteousness of the national narrative to be maintained it is apparently better that than to be considered 'a killer.'

Find Him and Kill Him

In fact, much black humour is derived from Shelby's self deceit. By uncovering Shelby's capacity to manipulate himself, *Memento* deconstructs the functioning of the organic form typical of the movement-image's organic regime, especially its favouring of the mind over the body. Shelby's amorality, so beguilingly attractive in its seeming innocence, is ultimately shown to be a hoax. Shelby is deliberately deceiving himself in order to get away with murder. To demonstrate this, the film goes out of its way to emphasise the underlying continuity to Shelby's being. At the end he asks himself: 'Do I lie to myself to be happy? In your case Teddy, yes I will'. At this point he deliberately leaves the clue that the tattoo of 'FACT 6' entails, Teddy's license plate number. This will enable him to later kill Teddy with a clear conscience, acting on what he believes are facts. This statement is interesting because, as in Deleuze's deconstruction of Descartes' *Cogito* that I examined in Chapters 1 and 2, there is a split 'I' in evidence. The I that contemplates (I think) and the I that endures (I am) are here equated with the I that lies (I lie) and the I that is happy (to myself).

This split I is figured as a controlling, lying I that manipulates an enduring I. Following the formula I established in Chapters 1 and 2, the I that endures exists virtually in the past, and the I that lies is the actual I of the present. In *Memento*, the I that endures, the preserved I of the past, is constantly being manipulated by the I that passes in the present. Despite the labyrinthine deceits perpetrated by the passing I of Shelby, there is always an underlying, linear I in existence. Yet this essential I, rather than being protected by a triumphal masquerade, is actually the unknowing dupe of the I that passes. The enduring I commits the murders, but it does so under false pretences. As this unknowing I is equated with the I of the past that is preserved, the film is able to comment on the manipulation of history that occurs when a triumphal narrative is constructed in the present. This manipulation of the self is explained away through most of the film as a consequence of Shelby's condition and his subsequent gullibility. At several points in the film, however, inconsistencies of behaviour uncover Shelby as the culprit of his own deception. Through these slight inconsistencies Nolan's film deconstructs the portrayal of the officially sanctioned masquerade of characters like Captain Miller as the manipulation of the self in order to get away with murder.

For instance, after finding himself in a motel room with Dodd, and unable to remember why this is, Shelby confronts Natalie, and asks her why he has found a note in his pocket telling him to get rid of Dodd. As she explains to him her perspective on the events, Natalie tries to tear up the photograph of Dodd. In a very brief aside Shelby snaps: 'You have to burn them'. How does he know this? As the film further unravels, and we witness his conversation with Teddy just after having killed Grants, we see Shelby burn the photos of his actions. This event preceded the conversation with Natalie, yet if Shelby's memory is constantly being erased, how can he possibly 'remember' that the photos must be burnt?

A number of other like incidents occur, such as Shelby's decision to jump both Dodd (in his motel bathroom) and Teddy (just after killing Grants) even though, for all he knows, they could be his friends. If this were not enough, Nolan has put in a much more obvious clue to Shelby's self-deception in the story of Sammy Jankis, the man with the same memory condition as Shelby. As Shelby recounts the story of Sammy Jankis, for a split second he replaces Jankis in the flashback, suggesting that this perpetually recounted story is actually about Shelby himself. The recurring anecdote foregrounds how the manipulation of the self (here figured as an action of mind over body) is not necessarily the righteous action applauded in *Saving Private Ryan*.

Shelby's assessment of Jankis' condition was that his inability to make new memories was a psychological, rather than a physical condition. Jankis' failure in the series of lab-rat style tests to which he was subjected suggested to Shelby that his condition could not be physical. If it was he would have learned to avoid the electrified objects through conditioning. Believing his own condition to be real (that is to say, physical), however, Shelby reasons that he should be able to live his life through conditioning: 'Habit and routine make my life possible, conditioning, acting on instinct.' Shelby is attempting to live purely as a physical presence, a body that acts according to its conditioning through routines and habits. Indeed, if Shelby's life were purely physical, and controlled by conditioned instinct, this would go a long way towards explaining his violent reaction when surprised by Dodd and Teddy. As we begin to believe that Shelby is actually faking, however, this begins to seem unlikely. If his condition is actually psychological, as the flashback of Shelby-as-Jankis suggests, then this habitual body is actually being manipulated by his mind.

Physical habit is actually manipulated by Shelby in the present to ensure that he never forgets his quest for his wife's killer. The 'remember Sammy Jankis' tattoo on his left hand triggers the false memory that enables him to commit future murders. Each retelling of the Sammy Jankis story in the same way retroactively reposits the false origin that validates his quest for triumphal justice, a fact that the viewer knows to be a manufactured fiction of Shelby's devising. Shelby puts his trust in the organic form, as we would expect of a character in the action-image, but it is not to be trusted. It has been manipulated by the mind, which predicts in advance the future consequences of its actions. As though commenting on the action-image itself, the film posits that through the organic form Shelby can in fact condition himself to make new memories, to 'remember' things that have happened since the incident with his wife, not least of which is the fictional story of Sammy Jankis. Like Guido in *8½*, Shelby finds 'true' and 'false' pasts indiscernible. However, this is not seen to be a deterritorialising, Nietzschean evocation of the eternal return, as it is in the time-image. Rather, this situation is used to illustrate how movement-images like *Saving Private Ryan* posit false causes, enabling one dominant interpretation of history to prevail and excusing bloodshed in the name of the national narrative.

Nodding Donkey

Finally, in addition to this formal critique of the triumphal narrative in mainstream American cinema, how is a national allegory also smuggled into *Memento*'s content? Rather like *Run Lola Run*, which uses gangsters, robberies and international drug smuggling to allegorically represent a new economic situation in post-wall Germany, *Memento* negotiates recent transformations in American identity through a story of murder, revenge, crooked cops and drug dealers. Shelby believes himself to be a righteous avenger. He therefore conditions himself to act upon false evidence, removing pages from his police report in order to create what Teddy calls: 'a puzzle you could never solve'. Living the life of the wounded and vengeful detective, very much in the style of Dave Bannion (Glenn Ford) in Fritz Lang's *The Big Heat* (1953), he describes himself as living: 'only for revenge'. Yet this manipulation of evidence enables Shelby to transform himself in a very specific way. The character we meet at the beginning of the film is wearing Jimmy Grants' expensive suit and driving a Jaguar. We later find out that, because of Grants' occupation as drug dealer, his car boot is also full of money. However, in the black-and-white sequence we find that prior to the murder of Grants, Shelby was actually a much less snappy dresser.

The film's primary allegorical focus is Shelby's body. His physical transformation mirrors America's transformation from Fordist to post-Fordist economy. This is most clearly seen in his change of clothes, from the jeans and chequered shirt of the archetypal blue-collar labourer to the expensive suit of the executive. More importantly, his car changes from a pick-up truck (the automobile that epitomises Fordism) to an expensive foreign import. Finally, his income, once he transforms himself into Jimmy Grants, is money from the drug trade. Through Shelby's transformation, then, we are shown an allegory for the way the American economy transformed itself in the 1980s into a post-Fordist, services-based economy with links to international trade.

Significantly, Shelby's financial transformation is due to a murder committed in an abandoned oil refinery.[58] Although this location was apparently not the crew's first choice (making it difficult to draw any deliberate significance from this setting), its resonance with the rest of the film cannot be ignored. *Saving Private Ryan* uses the Second World War as a context in which to valorise American intervention in the oil rich Persian Gulf, representing it as an act of national defence. By contrast, *Memento*'s use of the abandoned oil refinery suggests that this intervention is an act of murder from which considerable mineral wealth is obtained. After all it is here that, as Shelby changes into Grants' clothes, *Memento* critiques the hypocrisy of American cinema's separation of essential identity and the killer's facade. This murder, moreover, is committed by a body that has been duped by itself in order to misremember the past, although what it believes to be an act of revenge is actually a murder. Shelby's actions, then, are used to foreground how American post-Cold War intervention abroad is recoded in cinema through the triumphal myth. As several of the authors collected in *Beyond the Storm* (1992) pointed out soon after the conflict, in many respects the First Gulf War was a continuation of postwar American foreign policy, whose aims were in large part financial.[59] With domestic oil reserves dwindling (noticeably the oil refinery is abandoned), America's economy required a stable flow of oil. Consequently, intervention was necessary in the Persian Gulf. Michael Tanzer summarises this stance most succinctly, describing the intervention as 'a reassertion of the old Anglo-American oil imperialism which prevailed in the Gulf region for many years',[60] where '[h]istorically, it has always been a U.S. goal to have as much control as possible over non-renewable resources, especially oil'.[61] Thus by setting the murder in a relic of America's past oil wealth, the film demonstrates that the motive behind such 'murderous' intervention is primarily financial.

Admittedly *Memento* cannot be seen to be allegorising in exactly the same manner as *The Big Lebowski*, which, as I have shown elsewhere, humorously flags its allegorical critique of America's intervention in the Persian Gulf through the comical appearance of Saddam Hussein in a surreal dream sequence.[62] However, it is like the Coen Brothers' film in that it also offers a politically engaged subtext for those in the audience trained to interpret meaning from a disrupted narrative structure and a foregrounded meditation on memory, history and identity. It seems no coincidence that the black-and-white becomes colour with the murder of Jimmy Grants. The film here is deliberately punning on the way this change of costume brings colour to Shelby's life, whilst also mixing different film stock to render an economic shift (as Shelby changes identities) in a similar manner to *Run Lola Run*. Thus, in a setting that evokes the financial motivation behind the First Gulf War, Shelby's transformation into post-Fordist man critiques the foreign policy that underpins America's recent economic transformation.

Finally, whereas in *Saving Private Ryan* a flashback is used in the manner described by Turim to pass off a supposedly subjective memory as historical 'fact', in *Memento* this very process is questioned. In the film's final episode, when Teddy begins to question Shelby's memory of what happened to his wife, we are shown that Shelby's real crime is his own complicity in his wife's murder. Teddy suggests that Shelby himself is to blame for her death through his administration of an overdose of insulin. This is an event which Shelby had previously maintained was the fate of Sammy Jankis' wife. At this point the flashback we had previously witnessed of Shelby pinching his wife's thigh is replayed. This time however, we see that her small exclamation of 'Ow!' is not because he pinches her, but because he injects her. Shelby blankly refuses to accept this alternative truth. He reaffirms the pinching memory, which we see as a flashback, to reconfirm his belief in the one unchanged, triumphal past. At this point in the narrative, however, the viewer has lost all belief in Shelby, and consequently the fraudulent nature of this action is foregrounded.

The realisation of the labyrinth of time which brunette Helen used to enact a change of identity in *Sliding Doors* is here immediately reterritorialised by Shelby. He must retain his false origin to continue to live out his vigilante, rape–revenge narrative. However, by once again equating this action with murder, *Memento* deterritorialises the typical use of character memory in American cinema, to construct an origin, to actualise a recollection-image, to return to a mythical past. Shelby's short-term memory enables the film to deterritorialise the normative construction of national identity in America. It shows how the immediate past, especially events such as Vietnam, are constantly 'forgotten' through the perpetual reinstatement of a triumphal narrative that justifies military intervention abroad. In short, the manipulation of the character's mind by his body reflects the manner in which American cinema attempts to similarly dupe the body politic.

Conclusion: Interminable Vengeance

At the very end of *Memento*, Shelby takes the decision to fool his future self into killing Teddy. He closes his eyes at the wheel of his car, and sees himself lying on a bed with his wife. On his chest we see the 'I'VE DONE IT' tattoo, which he previously told Natalie he would have done once he had found and killed his wife's killer. At this point the future is open to him and, as for brunette Helen, there are at least two directions that it could take. Either he could allow himself to forget his false cause, his wife's death and his quest for vengeance, or he could continue on his way and knowingly murder Teddy. It is a choice between two tattoos, either 'I'VE DONE IT' or, 'FACT 6'. He decides to kill Teddy, and gets 'FACT 6'. He denies the labyrinthine powers of the false and opts instead to maintain the linear timeline of his unending quest. His self-falsifying act is a retroactive positing of a first cause, the tattooed 'FACT 6' that will legitimise his future act of murder. Rather like the repetition of the same that is his constructed memory of Sammy Jankis so, too, must his memory of the outcome of his quest be kept the same (he must never allow himself to think that he has done it) if he is to maintain his cover and his capacity to murder. This is a conclusion that, whilst deconstructing American cinema's tendency to valorise the past, also reenacts it. Thus, although the film goes a long way towards deterritorialising the action-image's form – particularly through the way its jumbled narrative demands spectator interaction – it, like *Sliding Doors* and *Run Lola Run*, is far from a time-image.

It is very hard to watch the film without being aware of the conscious effort you must make to construct the narrative. Yet, whilst deconstructing the reterritorialisation that the movement-image typically enacts upon the time-image, the film cannot deterritorialise to the extent that it become a time-image. This is most obviously seen in its use of a variation on the classical flashback structure, which ensures its linearity by flashing back to the beginning (the black-and-white sequence) just after showing us the end of the narrative. Indeed, its self-conscious use of certain rather obvious devices, such as the transformation from black and white to colour and the use of numbered clues, also foregrounds the construction of continuity. Hence *Memento* does not present us with the labyrinth, rather it demonstrates the process through which it is reterritorialised. It is not a time-image, but a time-image 'caught in the act' of becoming a movement-image.

Memento represents the triumphal rape–revenge narrative with a sardonic wink, foregrounding the Machiavellian machinations of its protagonist to deterritorialise its typical manifestation in mainstream American cinema. Like *Lone Star*, it investigates American cinema's tendency to perpetually reconstruct mythical origins, but rather than declaring, 'Forget the Alamo', it foregrounds the murderous intent through which the Alamo comes to be posited as origin. Treading carefully between a split audience demographic, it demonstrates independent film innovation, whilst also providing an attention-grabbing *noir* story of duplicity and murder. In Comolli and Narboni's terms, this could be termed a category c film, whose 'content is not explicitly political, but in some way becomes so through the criticism practised on it through its form'[63]. Yet the film's critique of Shelby is ambiguous. His character, at once likeable dupe and evil genius, is celebrated. After all, he does get away with murder.

I am not claiming then, that in 'opposition' to the mainstream there are independent films that can somehow be homogeneously lumped together as the anti-Hollywood. As I have shown the hybrid nature of these films usually ensures that it is not a simple case of movement- or time-image.

Rather, there are greater or lesser degrees of de- and reterritorialisation visible in each specific film, with examples such as *Lone Star* and *Memento* being the exception rather than the rule. In fact, despite the existence of such films as *Memento*, in which a deterritorialisation of triumphalism is evident, triumphalism was not in any danger in American cinema of the 1990s and 2000s. In spite of the severe knock it took during the 1960s and 1970s, the mythic narrative of triumphalism survived in American cinema through the 1980s and into the 1990s. The next chapter will examine how the cinematic constitution of this narrative was effected by the events of 11 September 2001.

Notes

1. Albert Auster, '*Saving Private Ryan* and American Triumphalism', *Journal of Popular Film and Television*, 30:2 (2002), pp. 98–104, p. 104.
2. Ibid. p. 100.
3. Ibid. p. 104.
4. John Hodgkins, 'In the wake of Desert Storm', *Journal of Popular Film and Television*, 30:2 (2002), pp. 74–84, p. 77.
5. Tom Engelhardt, *The End of Victory Culture* (New York: Basic Books, 1995), p. 22–8.
6. Robert Stam and Louise Spence, 'Colonialism, racism and representation – an introduction', *Screen*, 24:2 (1983), pp. 2–20.
7. Ibid. p. 6.
8. Engelhardt, *The End of Victory Culture*, p. 4.
9. Ibid. p. 267.
10. Douglas Kellner, 'Film, politics, and ideology: reflections on Hollywood film in the age of reason', *The Velvet Light Trap*, no. 27 (1991), pp. 9–24.
11. Frank P. Tomasulo, 'The empire of the gun', in Jon Lewis (ed.), *The End of Cinema as We Know It* (London: Pluto Press, 2001), pp. 115–30, p. 118.
12. Ibid. p. 127.
13. John Storey, 'The articulation of memory and desire: from Vietnam to the Persian Gulf', in Paul Grainge (ed.), *Memory and Popular Film* (Manchester: Manchester University Press, 2003), pp. 99–119.
14. Robert Burgoyne, *Film Nation* (Minneapolis: University of Minnesota Press, 1997), p. 1.
15. Ibid. p. 10.
16. Robert Burgoyne, 'Memory, history and digital imagery in contemporary film', in Paul Grainge (ed.), *Memory and Popular Film*, pp. 220–36, p. 231.
17. Burgoyne, *Film Nation*, p. 10.
18. Jacques Ranciere, 'Interview: the image of brotherhood', *Edinburgh 77 Magazine*, vol. 2 (1977), pp. 26–31, p. 28.
19. Ibid. p. 28.

20. Ibid. p. 28.
21. Engelhardt, *The End of Victory Culture*, p. 33.
22. Michele Faith Wallace, 'The good lynching and *The Birth of a Nation*', *Cinema Journal*, 43:1 (2003), pp. 85–104, p. 97.
23. Ibid. p. 95.
24. Ibid. p. 95.
25. Ibid. p. 97.
26. Michael Paul Rogin previously argued that the film may have contained a depiction of Gus being castrated that was censored from the final cut. Michael Paul Rogin, *Ronald Reagan, the Movie* (Berkeley: University of California Press, 1987), p. 218.
27. Ibid. p. 192.
28. Albert Auster, '*Saving Private Ryan* and American triumphalism', p. 101.
29. Peter Canning, 'The imagination of immanence: an ethics of cinema', in Gregory Flaxman (ed.), *The Brain is the Screen* (Minneapolis: University of Minnesota Press, 2000), p. 330, n. 6.
30. Thomas Doherty, *Projections of War* (New York: Columbia University Press, 1999), p. 306.
31. Maureen Turim, *Flashbacks in Film* (London: Routledge, 1989), pp. 40–1.
32. Michael Hammond, 'Some smothering dreams', in Steve Neale (ed.), *Genre and Contemporary Hollywood* (London: BFI, 2002), pp. 62–76, 69.
33. Philip John Davies and Paul Wells eds, 'Introduction', in Philip John Davies and Paul Wells (eds), *American Film and Politics from Reagan to Bush Jr* (Manchester: Manchester University Press, 2002), pp. 3–12, pp. 8–9.
34. Douglas Kellner, *The Persian Gulf TV War* (Boulder: Westview Press, 1992), p. 63.
35. Ibid. p. 121.
36. Ibid. p. 287.
37. Ibid. pp. 70 and 121.
38. Philip John Davies and Paul Wells, *American Film and Politics*, p. 3.
39. Kaja Silverman, *Male Subjectivity at the Margins* (London: Routledge, 1992), p. 93.
40. Ibid. p. 64.
41. Susan Jeffords, 'The big switch: Hollywood masculinity in the nineties', in Jim Collins, Hilary Radner and Ava Preacher Collins (eds), *Film Theory Goes to the Movies* (London: Routledge, 1993), pp. 196–208 and Jude Davies, 'Gender, ethnicity and cultural crisis in *Falling Down* and *Groundhog Day*', *Screen*, 36:3 (1995), pp. 214–32.
42. Thomas Doherty, *Projections of War*, pp. 308–9.
43. Neil Campbell, 'Forget the Alamo': history, legend and memory in John Sayles' *Lone Star*', in Paul Grainge (ed.), *Memory and Popular Film* (Manchester: Manchester University Press, 2003), pp. 162–79.
44. Ibid. p. 176.
45. Ibid. pp. 166–7.

46. Charles Lindholm and John A. Hall, 'Frank Capra meets John Doe', in Mette Hjort and Scott MacKenzie (eds), *Cinema and Nation* (London: Routledge, 2000), pp. 32–44, p. 32.
47. Davies and Wells use Michael Bay and David Fincher as examples of these poles. Philip John Davies and Paul Wells (eds), 'Introduction', *American Film and Politics from Reagan to Bush Jr*, pp. 7–9.
48. Geoff King, *American Independent Cinema* (London: I.B. Taurus, 2005), p. 2.
49. Ibid. p. 63.
50. Ibid. p. 84.
51. Ibid. p. 102.
52. David Martin-Jones, 'No literal connection: images of mass commodification, US militarism, and the oil industry, in *The Big Lebowski*', in Stephen Böhm et al. (eds), *Against Automobility* (Oxford: Blackwell, 2006).
53. Nöel Carroll, *Interpreting the Moving Image* (Cambridge: Cambridge University Press, 1998), p. 245.
54. Neil Campbell, 'Forget the Alamo', p. 166.
55. Carol J. Glover, *Men, Women and Chain Saws* (London: BFI, 1992), p. 115.
56. Deleuze, Gilles, *Cinema 2: The Time-Image* (London: The Athlone Press, 1985), p. 132.
57. Ibid. p. 132.
58. James Mottram, *The Making of Memento* (London: Faber & Faber, 2002), p. 156.
59. Phyllis Bennis and Michel Moushabeck (eds), *Beyond the Storm: A Gulf Crisis Reader* (Edinburgh: Canongate, 1992).
60. Michael Tanzer, 'Oil and the Gulf Crisis', in Phyllis Bennis and Michel Moushabeck (eds), *Beyond the Storm*, pp. 263–7, p. 266.
61. Ibid. p. 263.
62. David Martin-Jones, 'No literal connection'.
63. Jean-Luc Comolli and Jean Narboni, 'Cinema/Ideology/Criticism', in Bill Nichols (ed.), *Movies and Methods* (Berkeley: University of California Press, [1969] 1976), pp. 22–30, p. 26.

CHAPTER 5

Renegotiating the National Past after 9/11

After 9/11, North American cinema's construction of national identity took on a slightly different relationship to the past. In many ways the attack enabled American cinema to continue to propagate a triumphal narrative. After all, America was the aggrieved party and could easily justify retaliation. However, the traumatic events of September 2001 also necessitated a reexamination of the recent past. Many films produced or released since 9/11 allegorically relive this trauma in order to work through national loss. Unable to directly represent the attacks themselves, they explore national identity by focusing on an individual's attempts to regain agency after a recent trauma in their personal past (*Anger Management* (2003), *The Butterfly Effect* (2004), *Fifty First Dates* (2004), *The Interpreter* (2005)), to survive an immanent apocalyptic event (*The Sum of All Fears* (2002), *The Day After Tomorrow* (2004), *Terminator 3: The Rise of the Machines* (2003)), or historical event (*Pearl Harbour* (2001), *Black Hawk Down* (2001), *We Were Soldiers* (2002), *The Alamo* (2004)).

Yet this therapeutic use of cinema held a distinct danger for triumphalism. Whilst the past had to be allegorically replayed in order to be worked through, paying too close attention to the root causes of these personal traumas might have suggested the need to interrogate America's own complicated role in the lead up to 9/11. Such an approach would threaten the US's 'ambushed' status. For this reason, many post-9/11 films code the past trauma in an individual's life as inevitable, and emphasise the need to move on. Protagonists are denied the ability to change the past, and thereby alter the future, a conclusion that is directly the opposite of previous films like *Back to the Future* (1985), *Terminator 2: Judgment Day* (1991), *Timecop* (1994) and *Frequency* (2000).

Similarly, in post-9/11 disaster movies the imminent apocalypse is unstoppable (admittedly as the genre demands), with films such as *The Day After Tomorrow* using this situation to rewrite recent history by focusing on the unlikely survivors of a meteorological attack on New York. Whilst *The Sum of All Fears*, *The Day After Tomorrow* and *Terminator 3* all acknowledge in passing America's failure to avert disaster the blame for this is attached to one or two myopic politicians rather than the military–industrial complex or the intelligence services. The message propagated by the major voice of national identity is that, to come to terms with the attack, ordinary Americans must recognise that 'they' could not have saved those who died. National guilt is thus absolved, for if such a disaster was inevitable there was nothing that could have been done to prevent it. Instead of examining the causes of the attacks, the future must justify the sacrifices of those who died. Admittedly this is typical of many similar predecessors, including *Titanic* (1997), *Armageddon* (1998) and *Deep Impact* (1998), yet the concentration of such films in the years immediately following 9/11, and the, at times, rather conspicuous references to the events in New York, suggests the allegorical link. Typically of America's triumphal national narrative, the national loss of the past cannot be saved, only avenged. Thus 9/11 becomes an origin from which triumphalism can flow once more.

Initially this chapter focuses on the movement-image *Terminator 3* to illustrate how this dominant view of national identity is constructed. Reference is also made to other films that express a similar sentiment, particularly *The Butterfly Effect*. As was the case in the last chapter, the second half then explores how certain independent films have deterritorialised this prevailing tendency. Here the primary focus is *Eternal Sunshine of the Spotless Mind* (2004), a film that, like *Memento*, smuggles in a political critique through its use of flashback and character memory.

Eternal Sunshine is a time-image 'caught in the act' of becoming a movement-image. It demonstrates, both in its narrative content and in its jumbled formal construction, the manner in which the national narrative was reterritorialised after 9/11 by movement-images like *Terminator 3*. Critiquing this process, it offers, instead, the possibility of constructing a different future by acknowledging the existence of the labyrinth of time. Rather than being defined by a traumatic loss from their recent past its protagonists decide to rework this loss. Instead of seeking a triumphal revenge over the recent past, they consciously choose to recreate the situation that led up to their trauma, and to reexamine their own role in creating it. They determine that if they can avert the trauma this time they can break out of the vicious cycle of triumphalism, a cycle rendered in the film as the actions of brainwashed automatons.

Terminator 3

Inevitable Apocalypse

In brief the plot of *Terminator 3* is as follows. An outdated T101 Terminator (Arnold Schwarzenegger) is sent back in time to save the lives of John Connor (Nick Stahl) and Kate Brewster (Claire Danes) from a newer model, T-X Terminator (Kristanna Loken). The T-X has been programmed to terminate Connor and Brewster by computers in the future. The T101 has been programmed to save them by Brewster's future self. Although *Terminator 2: Judgment Day* (1991) saw Connor and his mother avert 'Judgment Day' (a global nuclear war), in *Terminator 3* the T101 informs him of its inevitability. Connor did not previously avert Judgment Day, only postpone it. At the end of the film the computer system 'Sky Net' takes charge of America's military capabilities and launches its nuclear missiles. The T-X pursues Connor and Brewster to Crystal Peak, a Cold War nuclear bunker for VIPs. The T-X is killed by the T101, who is also destroyed. Connor, responding to radio distress signals, begins to lead the resistance.

Terminator 3 uses the revitalisation of John Connor's identity into his predestined role as leader of the global resistance to allegorically represent the supposed rebirth of American national identity after 9/11. Judgment Day is equated with 9/11 in the film's opening sequence. The narrative then portrays the hours leading up to this inevitable moment, focusing on Connor's unsuccessful attempts to avert it. Although his actions are shown to be futile and the attack inevitable, in the interim he is remasculinised by the Terminator. In this process he learns the value of national defence previously expounded during the Cold War. Consequently, once the attack gets under way he is able to respond.

The film begins with a lengthy voiceover from Connor that comments on his current existence. Over a black screen we hear him say, 'The future has not been written. There is no fate but what we make for ourselves.' A flying missile then appears, heading rapidly towards an American city. It explodes on impact. Connor continues, 'I wish I could believe that.'

The end of the previous film, *Terminator 2*, is immediately questioned by Connor's persistent, recurring nightmares of the apocalypse. Made in 1991, in the immediate wake of the end of the Cold War, *Terminator 2* suggested that the inevitable nuclear apocalypse imagined during the Cold War (and predicted in *The Terminator* (1984)) had now been averted. In this new context there was, *Terminator 2* repeatedly claimed, 'no fate but what we make'. In *Terminator 2* the end of the Cold War ensured that the apocalypse was no longer imminent. In *Terminator 3*, by contrast, Cold War nightmares are evoked in order to address 9/11.

As we are introduced to Connor by the film's opening montage and accompanying voiceover, one image stands out that is extremely redolent of Ground Zero. Introduced by a close-up of a sledgehammer blow, Connor is shown working with a team of hard hats to clear a demolition site of rubble.

Situated amongst tall skyscrapers, it would be hard for an American audience not to make a link (even if only subconsciously) between this image and that of Ground Zero. The fall of the sledgehammer is accompanied by the words, 'It hasn't happened', by which Connor refers to the Judgment Day that his mother predicted. Although in the diegetic world Connor is discussing a global nuclear attack, this image conflates the imminent arrival of Judgment Day with the attacks of 9/11. It signals that the rest of the film will use Connor's attempts to stop Judgment Day to allegorically examine America's own inability to stop 9/11, the aerial attack evoked in the film's opening shot of a speeding missile.

Connor describes his life since *Terminator 2* in terms which suggest that, although he never truly stopped believing in his destiny, he has ceased to function as a member of the society he is destined to save. He says,

> I should feel safe, but I don't. So I live off the grid. No phone, no address. No one and nothing can find me. I've erased all connections to the past. But as hard as I try, I can't erase my dream, my nightmares.

Connor represents a particular view of post-Cold War American identity, an identity considered disconnected from its Reaganite past by the Clinton years, and consequently almost a nonentity. This view is perhaps most clearly stated by the hard line conservatism of 'The Project for the New American Century' (PNAC), whose signatories include Jeb Bush, Dick Cheney, Francis Fukuyama, Dan Quayle, Donald Rumsfeld and Paul Wolfowitz. Founded in 1997, PNAC promotes itself as an 'educational organisation whose goal is to promote American global leadership'.[1] Its major concern is that, with the end of the Cold War, 'American foreign and defence policy is adrift'.[2] Consequently, America must play a much more active role (particularly militarily) in determining global events. In its 'Statement of Principles', PNAC explicitly harks back to the Reagan years to stress the difference between America's global role then and that which it was pursuing under Clinton.

> We seem to have forgotten the essential elements of the Reagan Administration's success: a military that is strong and ready to meet both present and future challenges; a foreign policy that boldly and purposefully promotes American principles abroad; and national leadership that accepts the United States' global responsibilities.[3]

It is this view of an America no longer fulfilling its global role that Conner initially represents. We know from *Terminator 2* that since his birth in the 1980s Connor has been trained by his mother to be a cold warrior. In *Terminator 3* he returns to represent the generation of Americans who are supposedly hiding from the fulfilment of this destiny, or who, at the very least, have been denied it by the end of the Cold War. As he says, he cannot feel safe in this post-Cold War world, and has retreated from his personal responsibilities much as PNAC believe America has retreated from its global responsibilities.

The film uses its protagonist's attempts to recover agency after the loss of his mother to explore the nation's return to global military prominence. Moreover, as an action-image, *Terminator 3* uses Connor's return to agency to demonstrate how it believes national identity should be reterritorialised after 9/11, offering a reterritorialisation that falls neatly in line with PNAC's principles. Watching Connor come to terms with his destiny is to witness America's return to triumphal ways after what it considers to be an unprovoked attack. The film thus initially paints Connor as a man hiding from his inevitable destiny, and does so in a manner typical of the action-image. On the voiceover Connor states, 'I feel the weight of my future bearing down on me, a future I don't want'. At this point he loses control of his motorcycle, suggesting that the post-Cold War era has disrupted his sensory-motor continuity. To remasculinise Connor, to bring him to the point where he is able to fulfil this destiny (to move him from this situation, through action, to a changed situation), *Terminator 3* deploys Schwarzenegger's star persona. Through his resurrection of his role as the T101, Connor's generation are taught the militarist values of the Reaganite era so precious to PNAC, a process which restores both their sensory-motor continuity and the triumphal narrative of American national identity.

'I'm back'

The film's conflation of 9/11 with a nuclear attack suggests that the aspect of the past that most closely matches the present, is the 'defensive' stance of Cold War America. A recollection-image is created, suggesting that the potential threat of attack from terrorism in the present is equitable to that of the threat of nuclear attack during the Cold War. This is most clearly seen in the use of Arnold Schwarzenegger's star persona, and the route he maps for Connor and Brewster to the film's final scenes in the Cold War command bunker at Crystal Peak.

During the 1980s, Schwarzenegger's star persona was initially constructed as a hard-bodied, white, masculine hero. Various writers have commented on this tendency as it then existed, usually in relation to the physiques and active bodies of such actors as Schwarzenegger, Sylvester Stallone, Mel Gibson and Bruce Willis. For instance, Douglas Kellner discusses the *Rambo* films as military fantasies that both mirrored Reagan's own small-scale interventionist foreign policy, and, indeed, transcoded 'Reaganite anticommunist and pro-militarist discourses'[4] into cinema. Similarly, Richard Dyer points out how the muscular frame of these 1980s heroes was usually depicted in a setting that evoked Western colonial triumph. This was particularly true of Schwarzenegger in films like *Commando* (1985) and *Predator* (1987).[5]

Moreover, as Mark Jancovich argues, *The Terminator* initially critiqued the power of the military industrial complex over the lives of ordinary Americans. [6] This was due in large part, he argued, to the 'new Cold War' context in which it emerged.[7] However, although Jancovich is content to view both films in this way, *Terminator 2* is a little different. It actually sanitised the critique contained in the original, replacing it with a more family-oriented vision of the military industrial complex. Susan Jeffords charts the transformation of Schwarzenegger's T101 from *The Terminator* to *Terminator* 2, where he is reborn as the new man of the 1990s, thereby revising the brutal masculinity of his 1980s action persona.[8] Although Jeffords does not mention it, this alteration of his persona was part of a larger move by Schwarzenegger to reinvent himself as the family-oriented man in films like *Twins* (1988), *Kindergarten Cop* (1990), *Last Action Hero* (1993), *True Lies* (1994) and *Junior* (1994). As Jeffords work shows, the masculine tendency to express emotions physically (which was initially noted by Steve Neale in his seminal piece on masculine spectacle)[9] is here replaced by a more fatherly aspect. This replacement is pushed to such an extreme that a maternal role is denied to Sarah Connor in *Terminator 2*, thus reassuring postindustrial masculinity that, though its position of financial provider was eroded, it still had a role to play as provider of emotional support.

Terminator 3 resurrects Schwarzenegger's T101 in a very specific manner. It uses the connotations of his previous existence as a critique of the Reaganite cold war, military–industrial 'monster'[10] (*The Terminator*) to instruct Connor on how to survive an aerial attack like that of Judgment Day or 9/11. However, this lesson is provided by his caring, post-Cold War, nineties man of *Terminator 2*. The recollection-image created in this process rejuvenates the hard-bodied aspect of Schwarzenegger's star persona from the 1980s, but filters it through his sensitive family-man persona of the early 1990s, in order to match the post-9/11 context. Thus Connor's graduation to agency is conflated with the return of the hard-bodied hero of the 1980s, and, consequently, the Reaganite rejuvenation of the Cold War during that era, but with a slightly more sensitive twist.

Connor's initial lack of agency is apparent from his decision to hide from society and his symbolic motorcycle spill. It is also evident when shortly afterwards he is easily trapped by Kate Brewster in a dog kennel. In fact, during the first half of the film Connor is shown constantly reacting to events or trapped by circumstances. He relies on the Terminator to save him, his passivity emphasising his lack of agency. The most obvious example of this occurs when the Terminator carries him out of danger in a coffin. Without masculine agency he is, quite literally, a dead man. After all, it is his death in the future that facilitated the return of the T101 through time to save him, a return which was facilitated by his wife.

Schwarzenegger's T101 restores Connor's agency by mapping the territory of pre-apocalyptic (pre-9/11) America. After initially saving Connor from the T-X the first place that he takes him to is his mother's arms stash. This is hidden in a crypt in a coffin bearing her name, a stockpile set aside by one of America's more paranoid cold warriors. This relic of Cold War militarism suggests a return of the repressed that speaks both of the action genre films in which Schwarzenegger starred in the 1980s and the militarism of that era. The T101 also takes Connor and Brewster to her father, General Robert Brewster, from whom they receive the entry codes to Crystal Peak. Finally, it is the T101 who enables their access to Crystal Peak, as he quite literally holds the door open for them.

Schwarzenegger's character thus maps the any-space-whatevers of the film (building site, empty back roads, desert, empty interstate, gas station, graveyard, military base, mountain range) showing Connor the way back to the Cold War bunker – complete with its authentic 1960s decor, low-tech equipment and murals of the space race – in which the film ends. In this way the hard-bodied masculinity of the Reaganite era restores the triumphal national narrative to prominence.

After finally acknowledging his role as leader of the resistance, Connor's voiceover returns, musing on the events that led up to his and Brewster's survival:

> Our destiny was never to stop Judgment Day. It was merely to survive it together. The Terminator knew. He tried to tell us, but I didn't wanna hear it. Maybe the future has been written, I don't know. All is know is what the Terminator taught me. Never stop fighting. I never will. The battle has just begun.

On his return to agency, Connor praises the foresight of previous generations of cold warriors, whilst determining to avenge these attacks on the USA. This inevitable future of which he speaks is prefigured at the beginning of the film. During the initial montage a brief flashforward occurs in which Connor imagines himself victorious over the machines, with a battered but defiant US flag waving behind him. Just as *Saving Private Ryan* prefigured its narrative's triumphal conclusion (again with US flag waving) before returning to its inception during the Second World War, so

Terminator 3 suggests that the roots of America's new triumphalism (the film was made before the situation in Iraq became as unflattering for the US military as it subsequently has) can be found in the Cold War. Here the tools necessary for America's survival are to be unearthed in a return to arms stockpiling and bunker culture. This message undoubtedly struck a chord in America at the time of the film's release, where the ' "duct (tape) and cover" ethos'[11] sweeping the nation had even rejuvenated the 1950s craze for the family fallout shelter.[12]

'I'm an obsolete design'

The danger apparent in this use of Schwarzenegger as instructive Cold War father figure is that, in comparison, Connor could appear feminised by his relative lack of agency. The film manoeuvres around this threat by infantilising both Connor and Brewster in relation to Schwarzenegger's caring, nineties man (droid) persona. Representing a post-9/11 generation coming to terms with loss they are rendered childlike to illustrate the lesson they must learn from the Reagan/Bush years. In fact, Connor and Brewster's eventual emotional entanglement, although apparently inevitable if their destiny is to be fulfilled, is only inevitable if the T101 is successful in his mission to protect them. Thus the friendly face of the military–industrial complex is shown to be necessary for the continuation of America's progeniture.

Their reliance on the Terminator is most clearly seen in two scenes, both of which position Connor and Brewster as children talking in the back of vehicles driven by the T101. In the first of these they are locked in the back of Brewster's van, sitting on the floor. They discuss their initial meeting as adolescents in Mike Krypke's basement. In the diegetic world of the trilogy, this moment occurs in *Terminator 2* on the night before the T1000 appeared and killed Connor's foster parents. Had his adventures with the friendly T101 not begun at this point, they realise, they would have become a couple back then. Their relationship was interrupted by Connor's previous success in averting Judgment Day. In the post-Cold War era of *Terminator 2*, they were not destined to be together. However, as *Terminator 3* argues, the second film simply offered a fool's optimism, and the post-Cold War era a short-lived peace. The experience of 9/11 has returned the nation to its previous hard line foreign policy, and for this reason the protagonists are returned to their childhood selves, to remember the path to their inevitable destiny.

The second such scene is much more obvious as it occurs in a family motorhome, with Connor and Brewster busily preparing explosives in the back whilst the T101 drives. It is here that the Terminator informs them of the *fait accompli* that is their future, in which they will be married and have children. Here the 'delegitimization'[13] Jeffords notes of the mother's role in *Terminator 2* is taken to its final extreme. Now the mother is entirely absent and the father creates the family. Whereas in *The Terminator*'s critique of the military–industrial complex the mother was the only alternative, in *Terminator 3* the military–industrial father holds the keys to the future.

Terminator 3 also deploys the 'female' T-X as a negative foil against which to posit the legitimacy of Brewster as Connor's choice of partner. In this way the remasculinisation of Connor is played off in a very traditional manner, as a choice between two women, one right, one wrong. When the T-X arrives in the present she emerges in a boutique window on Rodeo Drive, Beverly Hills. The heat generated by her arrival melts two female mannequins in the window display. Naked, the T-X steps out of the window onto the street. This is an obvious intertextual reference to the original version of *The Time Machine* (1960) in which George (Rod Taylor) notes the speedy passing of time by observing the rapid changes in women's fashion on a mannequin in a shop window.

Here, however, director George Pal's use of an objectifying male gaze and changes in women's fashion to demonstrate time's passing seems to be deconstructed. Most obviously, the T-X is more powerful naked than George ever was in his time machine. Moreover, as her destruction of the mannequins proves, and as her physical superiority over the T101 also shows, she is not there to be objectified by the male gaze. Notably, her nudity is also masked and obscured by the camera. She is shown mostly through head and shoulders shots and close-ups of her feet, and when a full-length view of her is included, it is from behind and partially obscured by dim lighting. Loken's status as a supermodel is not entirely disavowed in this way, however, for she remains a body on display, in tight-fitting leather clothing for most of the film. However, her fragmentation avoids fetishisation, because she remains an active, not an objectified body. Indeed, the film's portrays Loken's naked form in exactly the same way as it does Schwarzenegger's. This parity of cinematic construction initially seeming to place Loken's T-X on a par with the active masculinity of the film's hard-bodied 1980s star.

Furthermore, the use of a Rodeo Drive boutique as location for her arrival suggests that she is not, as Vivian Ward (Julia Roberts) is in *Pretty Woman* (1990), defined by the wealth of the man who buys her clothes. Rather, the T-X self-consciously performs her identity. Not only does she take on the physical appearance of others, but she also alters her appearance to gain an advantage over men. When stopped by the police, for instance, she spies a billboard advert for underwear, which accompanies a shot of a woman in a bra with the question, 'What is Sexy?' The T-X enlarges her breasts to match this image, and uses them to distract the policeman, dispose of him and take his gun. In both her ability to masquerade any number of roles and to rewrite the cinematic past, her identity would appear to be celebrated as a labyrinthine performance, much as blonde Helen's initially appears in *Sliding Doors*.

However, as I showed in the conclusion to Chapter 3, the movement-image is structured by a binary logic that typically constructs labyrinthine female performativity as 'wrong'. *Terminator 3* is no exception. Using a classical device found in any number of American films, from the Bette Davis classics of the 1940s to more recent films such as *Single White Female* (1992), *Terminator 3* plays off a 'right' version of its female lead (Brewster) against her 'wrong' other.

The murderous T-X is dubbed a 'Terminatrix' by Conner, suggesting that her strength is actually that of a dangerous female sexuality. Her name suggests a mechanically enhanced version of her biological definition. Not XX chromosomes, but TX. Her ability to withstand the T101's barrage of blows with a urinal a little later in the film further strengthens this view of her. Brewster, on the other hand, is a plucky but family-oriented young woman (she is engaged at the beginning of the film), a conscientious professional, but without the qualifications of her male superior. A veterinary assistant, she demonstrates the nurturing qualities typically expected of the 'right' woman in American cinema. Although it is dangerous to impose too black-and-white a view upon these characters roles – after all Brewster shoots down a flying terminator and can fly a plane, whilst the T-X's awesome power is often framed with a knowing wink – it is actually their economic power that sets them apart.

After leaving the shop window, the T-X encounters a middle-aged woman. She kills her, taking her leather trouser suit and expensive Lexus convertible. Although the T-X could be championed as a fantasy version of a contemporary career woman taking on the old Cold War male dinosaur T101, she is actually constructed as a usurper of a much older woman's wealth and status. A post-Fordist woman, the film seems to be saying, she is wealthy before her time. As was the case in *Memento*, the aspirational action of taking another's clothes and car is tantamount to getting away with murder. However, whilst *Memento* sets its murder in an abandoned oil refinery, thereby critiquing the fact that much post-Fordist wealth is actually based on the exploitation of other countries (as was seen in America's interference with the global supply of oil in the First and Second

Gulf Wars), here this type of wealth appropriation is seen to be murderous because it is performed by the new career woman. The right and wrong versions of female identity are used to show that, in a milieu in which men are now objectified for money (as the T101's initial encounter with a male strip show illustrates), the post-Fordist woman threatens the continuity of the Cold War sensibilities of the 1950s, those heterosexual family values which the T101 rejuvenates in slacker Connor, and wife to be, Brewster.

Against this mini-drama of female identity the continuity of the masculine authority of the aged T101 is reaffirmed. This is clearly seen in his unlikely victory over his vastly superior female successor. However, he first has to overcome his own hard-bodied prowess in order to be victorious. Defeated by the T-X, the T101's circuitry is contaminated by her nanotechnology. Effectively, he becomes her puppet. Yet, when he is about to kill Connor at her command, he manages to self-terminate instead. Typically of the action-image, this moment is played out as a contest between the T101's mind and his body. As he approaches Connor he warns him verbally to escape, even as his body continues its deadly pursuit. When he self-terminates, then, the T101's mind wins out over its body, reaffirming the Cartesian logic of the movement-image. Indeed, somewhat typically of the Terminator films, with their message of human superiority over machinery, his self-termination in the service of human life preservation also reaffirms the organic regime of the action-image.

The T101's victory suggests that the superiority of the post-Fordist career woman is actually just a failed attempt to control the 'body' of an otherwise continuous, Cold War masculine power. This point was reiterated when, during the Californian recall-election debates, candidate Schwarzenegger gained increased media attention by indirectly comparing his opponent, successful journalist Arianna Huffington, to the T-X. Like Reagan, who, Michael Paul Rogin demonstrated in *Ronald Reagan the Movie* (1987),[14] drew on his filmic roles to perform his role as President, Schwarzenegger used his performance in *Terminator 3* to blur the line between his films and his political position. As Ziauddin Sardar and Merryl Wyn Davies put it, his 'manifesto was his celluloid output'.[15]

Terminator 3's use of Schwarzenegger to construct a recollection-image that matched the new Cold War politics of the Reagan years with the post-9/11 world is most apparent if we consider that Schwarzenegger, alongside his usual gym routine, often spent as many as five or six hours a day in makeup during shooting.[16] Attempting to create the illusion that, like a machine he had not aged, his erasing of the years between *Terminator 3* and the first two movies reflected the film's political realignment (through the construction of a recollection-image), of his past and present incarnations as the new cold warrior.

Preserving the End of History

As a commercial for Scharzenegger's gubernatorial election campaign for Governor of California in 2003, *Terminator 3* strikes a hard-right line that resonates loudly with the principles of right-wing organisations like PNAC. As I will now show, it also reflects Republican policy of the early 2000s. As I have so far demonstrated, *Terminator 3* posits that 9/11, and America's subsequent return to its former 'defensive' Cold War position, was inevitable. To put this message in perspective it is worth briefly considering just a few of the contentious issues it avoids. In terms of American foreign policy, *Terminator 3* reflects the position taken up by the Bush administration in the first weeks in power. As Kellner argues in *Grand Theft 2000* (2001),

> [a] hardright foreign policy reminiscent of Cold War tension at its highest emerged in Bush's first fifty days as president. In the opening weeks, Bush bombed Iraq and heightened tensions in the Middle East, threatened China, told Russia to expect reduced aid, worried much of Europe with his insistent approach to national missile defence (NMD), and made clear that he does not intend to pursue constructive negotiations with North Korea . . . Thus, the world has returned to the hard-line Cold War paranoid universe of the military–industrial complex . . .[17]

Indeed, if we follow Kellner's argument in his follow up book, *From 9/11 to Terror War* (2003), then the film's 'forget the causes' of the past stance also absolves the intelligence services for not providing adequate warning of terrorist build ups, the Bush administration for failing to follow up on the Clinton administration's anti-terrorist measures, and the media for not seriously focusing attention on terrorism.[18]

Of course, America's unacknowledged involvement in the build up to 9/11 obviously goes much further back than this. For Noam Chomsky in *9–11* (2001) it is the last two centuries of American foreign policy that should be considered as contributing factors for the attacks of that day. Most significant is CIA activity in Afghanistan, creating the 'Afghan trap' for the USSR in 1979, and continued American support for Israeli military action against the Palestinians. Moreover, Chomsky repeatedly returns to the World Court's ruling against America over its involvement in Nicaragua in 1986, and America's dismissal of its findings, concluding from this that 'in much of the world the U.S. is regarded as a leading terrorist state'.[19] Yet, when you consider the ambush rhetoric of triumphalism, it is not surprising that these factors are swept under the carpet of history by films like *Terminator 3*. To acknowledge them is to suggest complicity, thereby reducing the moral grounds for retaliatory action.

In its avoidance of such issues *Terminator 3* also reflects the official stance taken by the bipartisan *9/11 Commission Report* (2004) in its attempts to realign the national narrative. The first chapter of the report recreates the events of 11 September 2001. Like the proliferation of films about past traumas that have emerged since the attack, this repeated reiteration of the event is an attempt to gain mastery over the past. It corresponds to the techniques of repetition deciphered in television coverage of catastrophic events by Patricia Mellencamp, whereby repetition and narration of the event enables a sense of mastery over catastrophic loss.[20] The second chapter is entitled, 'The *Foundation* of the New Terrorism' (my italics). It posits the period of 1988–98, during which Bin Laden repeatedly declared war on America, as the origin of the attacks. Thus, in the style of triumphal movement-images such as *Saving Private Ryan*, the report begins with the event itself before flashing back in time to the supposed origin of this event. Although it does actually acknowledge (admittedly without much emphasis) America's anti-Communist influence in Afghanistan prior to this, by fixing the period 1988–98 as the origin of the attacks the report suggests that what came before this was not particularly important. In this way the triumphal narrative of an unprovoked ambush is maintained. Indeed, the 'inevitability' of the attack suggested by *Terminator 3* vindicates the CIA for its inability to uncover the plot. Using one particularly evocative 'ambush' quote, the report notes that:

> There were limits to what the CIA was able to achieve in its energetic worldwide efforts to disrupt terrorist activities or use proxies to capture or kill Bin Laden and his lieutenants. As early as mid-1997, one CIA officer wrote to his supervisor: 'All we're doing is holding the ring until the cavalry gets here.'[21]

Terminator 3 thus resonates with the report's suggestion that, despite the best efforts of America's security agencies, the attack was an inevitability. In fact, the final report on the commission's findings concludes: 'since the plotters were flexible and resourceful, we cannot know whether any single step or series of steps would have defeated them'.[22] It is exactly this manner of reconstructing the triumphal national narrative that *Terminator 3* taps into, constructing a triumphal narrative that begins with an inevitable attack. When events are framed in this way, the only defence appears to be Cold War paranoia.

Furthermore, in its depiction of national events *Terminator 3* also corresponds to political developments in America, especially (although admittedly not exclusively) under the second Bush administration. The concluding montage sequence shows nuclear missiles taking off and destroying Earth's cities on Judgment Day. Thus, although the film initially appears critical of the notion that a computer could be placed in charge of national defence, its evocation of the threat of nuclear attack actually advocates the need for a 'Son of Star Wars' defence programme. Moreover, the film conflates the threat of cyberterrorism and nuclear war in exactly the same manner as does The US Commission on National Security for the 21st Century, which, in 1999, claimed that 'outer space and cyberspace' were the two primary areas in which the US must be watchful of its national defence.[23] It is no surprise that the Bush administration also supports a National Missile Defence shield, further stressing its inheritance of the policies of the Reagan/Bush years. Connor's voiceover accompanies this shot of American missiles taking off from silos hidden in the cornfields of the nation's heartlands. By referring to the missiles as 'weapons they'd [i.e. mankind] built to protect themselves' Connor positions the dominant global superpower as a surrounded nation that stockpiles nuclear arms simply for self defence. This disingenuous stance excuses America's immense military budget, which (according to The Stockholm International Peace Research Institute's Yearbook), in 2003, accounted for almost half of the entire world's military spending![24]

The film's reference to cyberspace is important for another reason. At Crystal Peak, Connor and Brewster finally realise that Sky Net is a computer virus, affecting 'ordinary' computers worldwide, and without an easily destroyable system core. This analogy equates with US conceptions of its new post-Cold War enemies, especially terrorist networks after 9/11. As Renata Salecl convincingly argues in *On Anxiety* (2004), with the end of the Cold War the terrorist has been most commonly figured as a viral infection that is already present within the borders of the nation and which can erupt without warning at any time.[25]

Finally, the film's conclusion also advocates the conflation of American national identity with global identity, reiterating once again the stance of the *9/11 Commission Report*. The answer to the inevitability of attacks like 9/11 is prefigured in the film's opening montage, during which Connor envisages himself triumphally fulfilling his destiny by leading 'what was left of the human race to victory'. As I noted previously, prominent in the image is a battered stars and stripes. The T101 states that Connor is to become the leader of the 'worldwide resistance'. Yet the presence of the American flag along with the phrase 'human race', and later, 'worldwide resistance', creates a conflation typical of many American films, in which the US represents the entire world. As Michael Billig has shown, this is a very common occurrence because 'American political nationalism often presents itself as the universal voice of reason'.[26] According to the *9/11 Commission Report*, however, the spread of international terrorism now justifies American intervention anywhere in the world for, in this new context, 'the American homeland is the planet'.[27]

This image also reiterates the broad thrust of PNAC's 'Statement of Principles', which calls for 'American global leadership'[28] in the post-Cold War world. This is hardly surprising considering one of its prominent signatories is Fukuyama. In his famous article 'The End of History?' (1989), Fukuyama declared that the close of the Cold War represented the ultimate triumph of liberal democracy, the zenith of 'mankind's ideological evolution and the universalization of Western liberal democracy as the final form of human government'![29] From this evolutionary perspective the triumph of American style (or, indeed, American imposed) liberal democracy seems inevitable.

In its triumphal flag-waving scene, *Terminator 3* imagines the eventual triumph of American-style liberal democracy (effectively market capitalism) over the rest of the post-Cold War globe. It is for this reason that Schwarzenegger's star persona is so effective, recalling memories of the white male's conquest in colonial settings in *Commando* and *Predator* and any number of other 1980s films that reflected the American military interventions that were pursued under Reagan and have now reappeared under Bush Jr.

The Butterfly Effect

Obviously not all post-9/11 films have emphasised a militarised, right-wing agenda. However, a noticeable range of films have asserted the inevitability of either a personal trauma or historical disaster, the innocence (that is to say the non-complicity) of those involved, and the need to overcome this trauma in the future. These films stand in stark contrast to several films made before 9/11 that did allow for a past trauma to be rewritten. For instance, *Frequency* (2000), expresses a similar triumphal view of the past as *Saving Private Ryan*, using a time-travel conceit to rewrite the loss in Vietnam allegorically. Here it is the life of a firefighter and father, Frank (Dennis Quaid), that is saved in 1969 by the actions of his son in the present. *Frequency* thus reflects the rewriting of a past loss in the present that was enacted after the First Gulf War. By contrast, these post-9/11 films do something rather different, as can be seen in *The Butterfly Effect*.

The Butterfly Effect follows the life of Evan (Ashton Kutcher), a young man with the ability to travel back in time within his own life. He learns to realign time by altering the past, but, after four attempts, finally gives up. His best efforts cannot create a happy ending for himself and his childhood sweetheart, Kayleigh (Amy Smart). *The Butterfly Effect* is interesting because of its two endings, the theatrical version, and the director's cut on the DVD. Whilst the director's cut suggests that its protagonist would be better off never having lived (in the final scene he returns to his own birth, and chokes himself to death in the womb) in the version released in movie theatres he enters the past through a home movie, returning to a party he attended as a child. There he deliberately alienates Kayleigh so that she leaves town. In this way he saves Kayleigh and her brother, his mother, himself and his best friend, Lenny, from potentially horrendous lives. An independent production (by FilmEngine and BenderSpink), *The Butterfly Effect* was distributed by New Line Cinema, Time Warner's independent cinema arm. I do not wish to valorise director over studio, and leaving aside the potential financial motivation behind the decision to recut the ending (after all, this ensured that there were two movies to sell), the difference between the two endings is very relevant to this discussion.

The theatrical release falls in line with the attitude towards the past evident in *Terminator 3*. Again, the film charts a young man's unsuccessful attempt to regain agency by rewriting a traumatic moment in the past. Although in a sense Evan finally does save the past, he only does so by acknowledging the 'inevitable' loss of Kayleigh. Rather like Connor before him, Evan realises the need to accept loss and move on. This is clearly seen in the final scenes of the theatrical release, which are entirely absent from the director's cut. In this ending Evan burns the journals, photo albums and home movies through which he was previously able to access the past, saying: 'I know who I am, I don't need a bunch of stuff to remind me'. A helicopter shot then establishes a change of location to New York, under the caption, 'eight years later'. In the post-9/11 present Evan passes Kayleigh in the street. She turns and looks back at him, but he keeps his back to her and walks away. On the soundtrack, beginning with the ceremonial burning of Evan's past, Oasis's 'Stop Crying Your Heart Out' is heard. The lyrics punctuate the action, driving home its message.

> Hold up, hold on
> Don't be scared.
> You'll never change what's been and gone. . . .
>
> Take what you need,
> and be on your way,
> and stop crying your heart out. [30]

In these final scenes the film argues that national identity is already known ('I know who I am') and an examination of the causes of the past trauma is no longer needed, hence the past is burned. Moreover, the classical heterosexual closure expected of American cinema is denied in order to illustrate the rupture that has occurred in national identity, Evan and Kayleigh's parting suggesting that the past must be put to rest if the nation is to 'stop crying its heart out'.

This ending changes the message of *The Butterfly Effect* from a self-conscious meditation on exactly how Evan is caught up in the creation of the traumatic events of the past (when he is struggling for memory recall under hypnosis his psychologist tells him to 'think of it like a movie') and suggests instead that he must say goodbye to those lost in the past, and move on. The director's cut actually critiques the notion that by returning to a point of origin time can be realigned in a triumphal manner thereby deterritorialising the simplistic choices offered by films such as *It's a Wonderful Life*. The ending of the theatrical release, however, negates this effect. It stresses the inevitability of the past, and the need to turn your back on loss. Thus, in post-9/11 films the origin of the national narrative is still found in the past, but now there is a loss at the origin (9/11 itself) as opposed to a victory. National history that occurred before this loss is no longer informing, or worthy of consideration, yet this loss cannot be rewritten in the present as the trauma is too close. Rather, it must be rewritten in the future.

In the mainstream, then, the prevailing tendency in American cinema is to offer therapy to the survivors of this national catastrophe, but also to advocate a studied blindness to America's role in causing the attack. Rather than considering what could have been done to alter the past, these films stress the need to 'forget the causes' of the past trauma. However, a critique of this stance has been offered by certain independent films that deterritorialise the dominant version of national identity. Take Spike Lee's *25th Hour* (2002) as one example. As Patricia O'Neill has argued, its protagonists share the guilt of 9/11 in a manner that acknowledges America's role in the build-up to the attacks. Ground Zero is depicted in the film as 'the result on a global scale of the tragic consequences of the nation's unthinking sense of entitlement'.[31] Moreover, like the director's cut of *The Butterfly Effect*, the film's ending critiques the either/or of national identity found in *It's a Wonderful Life*. As Monty Brogan (Edward Norton) drives towards prison his father offers him the possibility of another life out west. However, Brogan rejects this fantasy of a parallel universe and instead goes to jail to pay off his debt. For O'Neill, the film resists 'amnesia for what has happened and nostalgia for a time that never was and never will be'. She adds, 'The circle of globalization has closed; there is no open frontier'.[32] Here the return to the golden past seen in pre 9/11 films like *Family Man* is rejected as is the 'amnesia' over national culpability in the attacks found in *Terminator 3*.

Eternal Sunshine of the Spotless Mind

Eternal Sunshine is also critical of the view put forward by films like *Terminator 3*. It foregrounds the danger that such an approach to the past entails: that by not comprehending the causes of a past trauma people are destined to perpetually repeat it. Although there is no doubting that this independent film is a well marketed niche product, and not iconoclastic in the way that American independent films have been in the past, it still deterritorialises the major voice found in more mainstream post-9/11 films. Formally demonstrating the reterritorialisation of the time-image by the movement-image a map motif is again deployed, this time in conjunction with an analysis of the movement-image's typical depiction of the Cartesian mind/body split. Character memory is again used as an allegorical hook through which to smuggle in a critique of mainstream American cinema's construction of national identity.

Since the 1980s, the American independent film has shifted its territory both financially and in terms of its ideological content. In their acquisition or establishment of an independent unit the major studios have acknowledged the financial gain to be had by targeting a niche market not always satisfied by mainstream genre films and blockbusters. The most famous acquisitions of the 1990s were those of Miramax by Disney and New Line by Time Warner. To these influential players in the independent market I would add Fox's independent arm, Fox Searchlight, and Universal Studio's Focus Features. Together these companies have been responsible for the distribution, if not the production, of a large number of independent films. Focus Features, for example, distributed *Eternal Sunshine*. Financially, then, as Emanuel Levy has it, 'Indies now form an industry that runs not so much against Hollywood as parallel to Hollywood.'[33]

Indeed, this may explain why several independent hits since the late 1990s have followed something of a recognisable formula. Since the cult success of *Being John Malkovich* (1999), and in the style of the Coen brothers, films such as *The Royal Tenenbaums* (2001), *Secretary* (2002), *Adaptation* (2002), *Eternal Sunshine, I Heart Huckabees* (2004), *Garden State* (2004) and *The Life Aquatic with Steve Zissou* (2005) all have similar characteristics. They all cast recognisable stars in quirky character roles, often with their movie-star good looks played down by the addition of bad hair styles and unfashionable costumes. They also foreground their debt to the European art cinema tradition through a self-conscious examination of the cinematic medium not seen in such force since the 1960/70s. They deploy interesting but not obtrusive visual effects, in a manner contrary to that of the contemporary blockbuster, and they focus on issues of interest to a twenty/thirty-something audience demographic. This is illustrated both by the ages of their characters and the ratings/certificates their content necessitated. In America, for instance, the above all received R ratings,[34] and in the UK, all were 15 certificates with the exception of *Secretary*. In contrast to the larger, family-oriented markets, then, these are already niche products.

The formulaic nature of these particular films is partly attributable to the influence of prolific scriptwriter Charlie Kaufman and directors such as Spike Jonze, David O'Russell, Wes Anderson and Michel Gondry. However, their undoubted abilities notwithstanding, it is apparent that a certain type of independent film has been recognised by the studios as marketable to a certain niche audience. Fox Searchlight, for instance, distributed a number of R-rated films since the late 1990s including *Boys Don't Cry* (1999), *Sexy Beast* (2000), *One Hour Photo* (2002), *The Good Girl* (2002), *I Heart Huckabees*, *Garden State*, *Sideways* (2004), and *Kinsey* (2004). Focus Features, for its part, distributed a more art/*auteur* catalogue whilst appealing to a similar audience demographic; films included, *Lost in Translation* (2003), *21 Grams* (2003), *Swimming Pool* (2003) and *The Motorcycle Diaries* (2004).

Even Miramax, in its attempts to reach two different audience demographics, maintains a commitment to this demographic. Admittedly Miramax now courts a family-oriented market with films like *Finding Neverland* (2004), *Bride and Prejudice* (2004), *Hero* (2004) and *The Aviator* (2004). All of these were rated PG or PG13 in America and PG or 12A in the UK. However, it also maintains the controversial appeal with which it made its name, on the back of R-rated films such as *Reservoir Dogs* (1992). Takeshi Kitano's *Zatoichi* (2003), for instance, initially appears to simply reinforce Miramax's commitment to marketing '*auteur*' cinema. A bigger picture emerges, however, when it is coupled to their distribution of the glossy Hong Kong thriller, *Infernal Affairs* (2002). Together these very contrasting Asian films demonstrate Miramax's attempts to cash in on markets recently opened up by the mainstream appeal of hits like *Crouching Tiger Hidden Dragon* (2000), *Hero* and *House of the Flying Daggers* (2004). A large proportion of the viewers of these films, of course, are the same twenty/thirty-somethings targeted by the formulaic trend of films I isolated above.

The emergence of this recognisable, R-rated trend (and in particular, the politically engaged examples under discussion here) confirms the existence of a twenty/thirty-something demographic willing to consume it. For this reason, Jim Hillier has argued, whether films like *Being John Malkovich* are actually 'independent' is a moot point that depends on how you define the term.[35] In the past, the independent status of a film has usually been defined either by its financial independence from the major studios, or its independence of 'spirit'. Obviously the financial territory has now shifted, but in terms of 'spirit' the ground has also recently moved. As Levy, Brian Neve and Justin Wyatt have all noted, in the 1980s the political content of independent films predominantly critiqued Reaganite America.[36] [37] In the 1990s, by contrast, a mood of 'self-conscious irony, deep cynicism, and moral nihilism' became the dominant trend.[38] This new situation begged the question of whether it was still possible for such well-marketed niche films to be politically critical? Take the last two *Terminator* films for instance. Both are independent films, but although their production budgets were independent of the majors, in spirit, as I have demonstrated, they express a very mainstream stance. The presence of the majors as potential distributors undoubtedly influenced this situation. *Terminator 2* used prearranged distribution deals with the majors to secure production funding for its $100m budget.[39] *Terminator 3*, for its part, was independently produced by C2 and Intermedia. Yet although it raised its $200m budget from German film fund IMF through Intermedia Film Equities it also sold the rights to Warner and Sony,[40] and Warner's marketing campaign aimed at particularly mainstream audiences. In both cases, then, independent production funding did not purchase a license to be critical of the political status quo, as both films had huge budgets to recoup.

Yet, even though many independent films can be seen to evidence a certain market-savvy formula, this does not necessarily mean that they cannot deterritorialise the dominant voice, as my analysis of *Eternal Sunshine* will demonstrate. The only irony of this is that the major studios grow financially stronger by selling an aesthetic and political view that challenges the perspective which they also propagate in the mainstream! This result of vertical integration simply illustrates the majors' dominance of the industry and their ability, as global corporations, to co-opt the 'opposition'.

The fact remains, however, that whatever the financial motivation behind it, since 9/11 many American independent films have departed from the nihilism of the 1990s and have actively engaged with contentious political issues of the day. For instance, take Mark Wahlberg's character Tommy Corn, the disaffected fireman in *I Heart Huckabees*. Corn is openly critical of America for the impact of its oil consumption on global events, a stance which the film supports. A similar questioning of dominant American values is found in Gus Van Sant's *Elephant* (2003), which attempts to understand the motives behind the Columbine high-school massacre. Finally, *Garden State* examines a generation of twenty-something Prozac addicts attempting to feel alive again. Admittedly, at a time when films like *Fahrenheit 9/11* (2004) and *Team America* (2004) have directly addressed issues of American politics and its representation, the independent sector is not as direct in its political critique as it might be. Even so, it is worth considering how *Eternal Sunshine* smuggles in a political critique of the amnesiac state of post-9/11 America and the cinema's role in constructing it.

Contrary Mary

Eternal Sunshine is set in New York, and begins with Joel Barish (Jim Carrey) awakening in a confused state on Valentine's Day. On a sudden impulse he catches the Long Island Rail Road out to Montauk, and walks along the beach. On the way home he meets Clementine Kruczynski (Kate Winslet). They begin to date. Through a series of fragmented flashbacks the film then unravels the past that led up to this event. We discover that Joel and Clementine have been dating for the past two years. We see Joel being told by his friends Rob and Carrie that Clementine has had all memory of Joel erased by a company called Lacuna Inc. Joel then decides to have a similar operation, wiping away the past two years they spent together. Joel sleeps as Lacuna's bungling operatives Stan (Mark Ruffalo), Patrick (Elijah Wood) and Mary (Kirsten Dunst) perform the memory erasure. This process is represented in the disjointed manner of a time-image, as Joel's subconscious resists the erasure of his memories of Clementine. As the erasure does not go according to plan, Lacuna's owner–manager, Dr Howard Mierzwiak (Tom Wilkinson), arrives. He becomes momentarily entangled with Mary before his wife unexpectedly appears. It transpires that Mierzwiak and Mary previously had a fling that she then erased from her memory. Without the knowledge of its previous failure, however, she realises that she is doomed to repeat it as an unknowing dupe. Joel and Clementine, by contrast, although eventually learning of their rocky past together, decide to give their relationship another go.

As do many mainstream films to emerge after 9/11, *Eternal Sunshine* depicts characters coming to terms with a recent trauma in their personal lives. This time, however, it does not conclude that the past could never have been any different and that it can only be triumphally overcome in the future. Instead, the conclusion suggests that Joel and Clementine will retrace the two years leading up to their break up, despite the pain this entails, in order to attempt to change it. They consciously acknowledge their own complicity in creating the trauma and endeavour to stop it from happening again. Dunst's Mary, by contrast, ends the film extremely unhappy after she is told that her actions are merely unknowing repetitions of a previous mistake. It is in the contrast between these two types of remembering and forgetting, those of Joel and Clementine versus that of Mary, that the film draws its distinction between the 'right' and 'wrong' ways of coping with a recent trauma.

Nick James discusses the film's contemplation of memory in a manner that is helpful for this discussion, arguing that it reflects the 'collective amnesia about cultural history' of postmodern life.[41] He concludes,

> cinema's current refuge in memory as a site of erasable trauma – of interior cosmetic surgery – suggests a strong need for past and future denial. It's a narcissistic, isolationist point of view that wants us immediately to forget our sins and mess-ups, to purge guilt and remove pain. But it's one that also speaks of an expectation of trauma to come.[42]

Like *25th Hour*, *Eternal Sunshine* also questions the 'forget the causes' of the past trauma message of *Terminator 3* and *The Butterfly Effect*. However, as James' apolitical observations suggest, *Eternal Sunshine* does not make explicit the link between its meditation on memory and post-9/11 America. In fact, like many American films before it, it smuggles in this critique in an oblique manner. One of the ways it does this is by using the American flag to question national memory erasure. As I demonstrated in Chapter 4, *Saving Private Ryan* begins and ends with the Stars and Stripes to 'flag up' that it is a nationally representative narrative. Similarly, *Terminator 3* represents a triumphal future with the flag. In *25th Hour*, as Brogan drives towards prison and his father offers him an alternative future out west, the Stars and Stripes again appears, flying prominently on the car. In each case we are notified by the appearance of the flag that the national narrative is under discussion. In *Eternal Sunshine* the Stars and Stripes appears only once or twice, the most significant instance of which is in Joel's memory of an elephant parade that he watched with Clementine. This time, the national narrative is 'flagged up' in the context of one of two quotes that Mary cites that suggest to her the benefit of memory erasure. In this particular instance she recites Alexander Pope:

> How happy is the blameless Vestal's lot!
> The world forgetting by the world forgot.
> Eternal sunshine of the spotless mind!
> Each prayer accepted and each wish resigned . . .[43]

Figure 5.1 Dr Mierzwiak with Mary, his amnesiac automaton (Source: Focus Features/The Kobal Collection/Lee, David)

Coinciding with the appearance of the flag, Mary's commentary suggests that the 'collective amnesia about cultural identity' that James observes provides the nation with a blameless innocence. Thus memory erasure is linked with the construction of the national narrative. The film then immediately undercuts Mary's point of view as she learns that she has had a memory wipe to forget her affair with Mierzwiak. She is, quite literally, a 'blameless Vestal', but only due to her mental revirginisation through memory erasure. Mary finds this out only after seducing Mierzwiak once again, her subsequent sudden loss of faith in memory erasure ensuring that her previous ditzy platitudes are revealed as exactly that. Mary acknowledges that her quotes are from Bartlett's (a dictionary of popular quotations), and the film uses this situation to show that she is not aware of the contexts from which they are lifted, or, indeed, their ironic, and slightly sinister, implications for herself.

The same effect was created slightly earlier in the scene when Mary proposed a toast quoting Nietzsche's *Beyond Good and Evil* (1886): 'Blessed are the forgetful, for they get the better even of their blunders'. She further compares Lacuna's clients to babies, saying: 'You look at a baby and it's so pure and so free and so clean'. Immediately after this, however, Patrick visits Clementine, whose memory was also recently erased. She is in a state of great agitation as she struggles to cope with conflicting emotions in the present for which she can find no reason in the past. Entering her apartment he calls her 'Baby'. Like Mary, Clementine is confused and, without knowing why, is attempting to recreate the narrative of her romance with Joel. The reality of her confusion, however, undercuts Mary's romantic notion of the innocent, infantile state to which Lacuna reduces its clients. Clementine's distress illustrates once again that without knowledge of the past people are doomed to repeat it as unthinking automatons. In actual fact it is Mary herself who is most like a 'baby', uncomprehending and naive of the negative effect that memory erasure has had on Lacuna's clients, including herself.

Eternal Sunshine's brief reference to the Stars and Stripes adds an extra layer to its slightly unconventional narrative structure. It suggests that the amnesia propagated by American cinema after 9/11 is constructing an infantilised generation who, disconnected from their nation's own complicity in events in the recent past, are doomed to repeat the same mistakes. This is exactly the generation represented by Connor and Brewster, as they learn to repeat the Cold War stance of their terminator father figure in *Terminator 3*. In *Eternal Sunshine* the brainwashed Mary is deployed to show that this is the 'wrong' way of coping with a past trauma.

Mary's repetition of her previous mistake also illustrates the 'expectation of trauma to come' that follows memory erasure. By linking this message to the national narrative, the film uses its New York based plot to argue that the post-9/11 cinematic trend for 'forget the causes' films is extremely dangerous. It is likely to lead, as we see in Mary's actions, to the repetition of the very conditions that caused the previous trauma. In the 1990s *Memento* showed how the loss of memory could be used to manipulate the actions of a future self to commit murder. In this manner it critiqued triumphal rewritings of the past such as *Saving Private Ryan*. *Eternal Sunshine*, for its part, cautions against the consequences of national amnesia. Instead it offers Clementine and Joel's more mature decision to relive the time leading up their trauma in order to perhaps prevent it from happening again. Theirs is the 'right' way to reconstruct national identity.

In fact the film's reference to Nietzschean forgetting is interesting in that, although Mary believes the quote from *Beyond Good and Evil* to describe the memory erasures perpetrated by Lacuna Inc., it actually more accurately describes Joel and Clementine's situation. A Nietzschean forgetting like that found in the time-image is advocated in the film's ending as the two protagonists opt for the eternal return – the potential for *ungrounding* the straight line of time found in the labyrinth of time. Unlike the gung-ho stance of *Terminator 3*, *Eternal Sunshine* uses its science fiction narrative to criticise the prevailing mood of America after 9/11. As Kellner has it:

> During the hysterical fear of terrorism in the aftermath of the September 11 and anthrax attacks, there was a surge of patriotism whereby many argued that anyone who mentions political causes of Arab hostility towards the U.S. is part of the 'blame America' crowd. Indeed, even liberals resisted the 'blowback' thesis as illicitly blaming the victim. It is rather a question, first, of gaining historical understanding of the context and situation concerning those radical Islamic sectors of the Arab and Islamic world who have declared jihad against the U.S. Second, it is a question of ascribing responsibility for those in the U.S. foreign policy establishment who helped organize, fund, train, and arm the terrorists now plaguing the U.S. and other parts of the world. *If we do not understand the past, not only are we condemned to repeat it, but we also have no chance of constructing an intelligent, enlightened, and peaceful future.*[44] [my italics]

With this 'hysterical' context in mind (not to mention the financial aspirations of the studios), it is little wonder that *Eternal Sunshine* smuggles in its politically engaged critique in such a veiled manner. It argues for an examination of causes of the past as the only way to stop the mindless repetition of the same trauma. In order to assert this viewpoint cinematically *Eternal Sunshine* demonstrates the potential for deterritorialisation that is available in the time-image even as it illustrates its reterritorialisation as a movement-image. To do this the film renders Joel's dreamlike state in the manner of the time-image thereby deconstructing the reterritorialising mapping of the American psyche perpetrated in the mainstream by films like *Terminator 3*. It foregrounds the correlation between the reterritorialising mapping that the movement-image typically constructs, and the acts of national memory erasure seen in American mainstream cinema since 9/11.

Dream Mappings

Like many of Kaufman's scripts, *Eternal Sunshine* evokes the memory of another type of cinema in order to disrupt its movement-image status. It incorporates the metafictional style of European *auteurs* like Fellini, Marker and Resnais and American independents like Tom DiCillio. This is most obviously seen when the incapacitated Joel travels within his own memories much as Guido does in *8½*. Although the narrative in the present is portrayed following the conventions of the action-image, once his sensory-motor continuity is suspended Joel slips between different layers of his past like the protagonist of the time-image. In the interaction between the time- and the movement-image the film enacts its critique of the reterritorialising of the national narrative in the 'forget the causes' film trend. Admittedly this is not a new technique in American independent film. Something similar occurs in David Lynch's *Blue Velvet* (1986), when the 'memory' of European surrealism (specifically *Un chien Andalou*

(1928)) is evoked by the image of a severed ear crawling with ants. This intertextual reference comments on the film's exposure of the seedy underbelly of American life usually repressed in the sanitised Hollywood image of white picket-fenced suburbs. As I will show, a similar effect is created through the formal structure of *Eternal Sunshine*.

To facilitate the erasure of Joel's memories Lacuna Inc. instruct him to gather together all associative memorabilia associated with Clementine, both so that they can use them to 'create a map of Clementine' in his brain and so that he will have no remaining physical reminders of her left. This is exactly the same logic expressed by the ending of the theatrical release of *The Butterfly Effect*, in which Evan erases Kayleigh from his past, and then burns his journals and pictures to ensure that he is cut off from her forever. This time, however, rather than celebrating this decision on the part of its protagonist, the film then focuses on Joel's mental struggle to stop the process of memory erasure. In stark contrast to the 'you'll never change what's been and gone' lyrics heard at the end of *The Butterfly Effect*, *Eternal Sunshine* ends with a very different message. This time its Beck's, 'Everybody's Gotta Learn Sometimes':

> Change your heart
> Look around you
> Change your heart
> It will astound you
> I need your lovin'
> Like the sunshine
>
> Everybody's gotta learn sometime . . .[45]

Thus, rather than forgetting the past and moving on, changing the conditions that led to the past trauma is advocated instead.

Interestingly, however, the narrative that Lacuna constructs is a timeline that initially appears to be labyrinthine. Mierzwiak tells Joel to 'start with your most recent memories and work backwards from there' in order that they can map the 'emotional core' of his memories of Clementine. As his memories are erased, moreover, Joel's most recent memories go first and then his narrative with Clementine plays backwards until their first meeting at the party on the beach in Montauk. Rather like the memory transfer at the end of *Sliding Doors*, this is a labyrinthine movement through time from the present, backwards. However, unlike the *Sliding Doors* memory transfer the realigning of time in Joel's mind does not provide him with any substitute past to give new meaning to his identity. Thus, with memories erased, Mary, Joel and Clementine are all doomed to replay their narratives physically but without realising why. Instead of a labyrinth, then, this is simply an incomplete line.

The absence of a new identity that memory erasure entails is deliberately evoked in the choice of the firm's name. Lacuna means both an 'unfilled space or interval', and 'a missing portion in a book or manuscript'.[46] Through this choice of name *Eternal Sunshine* self-consciously highlights how the national narrative is left unfulfilled by the rhetoric of triumphal amnesia, especially in official accounts of national history like the *9/11 Commission Report*. This absence creates a situation in which many American films, especially those like *Terminator 3* which emerged after 9/11, have also selectively omitted to mention a portion of the national past. This is most clearly seen towards the end of the memory erasing process, when Joel remembers his initial meetings with Clementine in the Barnes and Noble bookstore where she works. The sudden erasure of all writing on the books illustrates the expunging of national history that Joel's memory removal allegorically reflects.

This American independent film, which is clearly influenced by the European art cinema tradition, posits a very European view of America as a nation whose population is kept ignorant of its own history, especially by its action-image dominated cinema. Joel's resistance to the process of memory erasure is figured as an attempt to stop the reterritorialising mapping of his brain, and the aesthetic of the time-image is used to render visible its resistance to the reterritorialising powers of the movement-image. As Joel realises his mistake, he attempts to hide from the map in other memories, leaping into other layers of the past that take him off the map. His evasions are deterritorialising and force the inept Lacuna operatives Stan and Mary to call Mierzwiak for help. On his arrival, father-figure Mierzwiak is able to reinstate the map. However, immediately after we witness his ability to reterritorialise Joel's memory, his authority is undermined by the revelation of his previous affair with Mary. Thus, the inevitable reterritorialisation of the time-image by the movement-image is rendered visible, but this 'triumph' is seen to be extremely damaging for the national psyche.

In this respect *Eternal Sunshine* initially appears similar to a number of its contemporaries, American films that have kept the aesthetics of the movement- and the time-image strictly separate as 'real' and 'mental' worlds including *The Cell* (2000), *Vanilla Sky* (2001), *Identity* (2003), *Gothika* (2003) and *The Jacket* (2005). Initially *Eternal Sunshine* seems similarly conservative in the distinction it seems to draw between the 'reality' of the narrative world (movement-image), and the 'virtual reality' of Joel's dreams (time-image). Yet although the organic and the crystalline regimes seem to be kept apart in a manner that confirms the Cartesian mind/body division favoured by the movement-image in fact they inform each other in a manner that formally demonstrates the deterritorialisation of the movement-image by the time-image.

At several points during the memory erasure, Joel's mental state is invaded by the goings on in his apartment. As Stan, Patrick and Mary begin to party, Joel hears Patrick talking to Clementine on the phone. From this clue he begins to solve the puzzle of who the mystery man was with whom he saw Clementine in Barnes and Noble. Similarly, on two occasions Joel attempts to awaken from his dream state in order to stop the erasure; he is unable to do so, however, as his organic form has been drugged into submission. In these moments the inhabitant of the time-image is shown attempting to bring his deterritorialising knowledge to bear on the construction of the map of national amnesia that is created by the movement-image. Literally and symbolically he is a sleeper attempting to wake from a drugged stupor in which his memories are being erased. Cinematically, he is the labyrinthine potential of the time-image to unground the straight line of time perpetrated by the movement-image. In this important respect, then, *Eternal Sunshine* is unlike these other films. It shows how the time-image and the movement-image have the potential to interact, even if the movement-image typically closes off that potential in the process of national identity construction.

Admittedly, *Eternal Sunshine* does not render movement-image and time-image (reality and dream) indiscernible as Fellini's *8½* does. However, the labyrinthine potential to unground the straight line of time found in the time-image is figured as containing the potential to deterritorialise the movement-image's reterritorialising powers. This is finally seen when Joel, facing final memory annihilation, instructs himself (through his mental incarnation of Clementine), to travel to Montauk on Valentine's Day. This is the first thing we see him do in 'reality', an action which illustrates the interaction that can occur between time- and movement-image, and the manner in which memory erasure can be deterritorialised. Here, unlike Evan in the theatrical release of *The Butterfly Effect*, Joel refuses to admit defeat and acknowledge his failure to save his girlfriend. Such a decision is not celebrated as a 'mature' acceptance of the inevitable. Instead of fixing the origin as a moment of informing loss Joel decides to try again. He posits a difference at the origin that enables his narrative with Clementine to recur eternally.

The only problem this raises is that although Joel's body initially repeats his narrative with Clementine, much as Bergson described the bodily repetition of habit, he is as yet unable to realise why. He is no better off than

Mary repeating her previous advances to Mierzwiak. This situation persists until he and Clementine recover their past together. Only then is the eternal return made available to them. As in *Memento* the body is instructed how to act, in advance, by the mind. Unlike *Memento*, however, once Joel and Clementine recover their memories, body and mind act in unison to create the eternal return. At this point the mental/time-image versus actual/action-image distinction is deterritorialised.

For this reason, at the end of the film Joel revokes his previous attempts to reduce Clementine's personality to her physical being. Previously Joel had described her spontaneous personality as an 'elaborate ruse', her changes of hair colour as 'bullshit', and had even accused her of using sex to 'get people to like her'. Defined in this way, Clementine was a purely physical entity, a body without mind. Her exterior alterations apparently made no difference to her insecure, physical (sexually defined) core being. At the end, however, Joel rejects his own previous conclusion and no longer draws a distinction between her biological identity and her outward performance of identity. The binary distinction of mind/body, like that of line/labyrinth and movement-/time-image, is thus deterritorialised. In this respect the muted performance of Carrey is also significant. Carrey's star persona was initially built on an excessive physical presence yet here he is no longer simply a comedic body as he was in the films that established his career (*Ace Ventura: Pet Detective*, *The Mask* and *Dumb and Dumber* were all released in 1994). Rather, *Eternal Sunshine* quite literally explores Joel's mind to provide a psychological depth to Carrey's character's physical actions, to show the both/and of mind and body.

In *Eternal Sunshine* the narrative of events that occur in reality cover only the course of one or two days. They begin with Joel awakening from the memory erasure, and play through his second (albeit unknowing) meeting with Clementine in Montauk on Valentine's Day. It then flashes back in time one night to Joel's arrival at his apartment after deciding to erase Clementine from his memory and plays forwards again through that night (repeatedly intercutting with Joel's mental state) as his memories of Clementine are erased. It is here, in Joel's memories, that the back story of the narrative occurring in 'reality' is filled in – ironically, just as it is erased. The time-image provides the answer to the question of 'how did we get here?' posed by the film's movement-image flashback structure. In this way *Eternal Sunshine* ungrounds the 'return to origin' circular flashback structure seen in films such as *Saving Private Ryan* by exploring the causes of the origin itself. The film illustrates the reterritorialising effect that the movement-image has on the past by fixing a false origin before which things suddenly cease to exist. Again it is worth considering the sight of the books being erased in Barnes and Noble. This erasure of national culture and history is precisely the erasure of the past that the post-9/11 movement-image enacts by focusing on the event itself rather than its causes. In the coda to its 'reality' narrative, however, *Eternal Sunshine* shows this past being returned in audiotape form to Lacuna's clients by the disaffected Mary. This provides the catalyst for Joel and Clementine's decision to try again. Hence, just as Mary returns the past to Joel and Clementine so too does *Eternal Sunshine* return the causes of the past of its movement-image narrative to the viewer. Only in this way, the film argues, can a trauma like 9/11 really be understood.

Like *Memento*, *Eternal Sunshine* also falls into Comolli and Narboni's category c as another film that does not have a political content but which becomes political in 'the criticism practised on it through its form.'[47] As these last two chapters have demonstrated, recent American independent films have formally engaged with the way national identity is constructed in mainstream American cinema. In many ways they are more deterritorialising than the European films discussed in Chapter 3, but, even so, they are not time-images. Instead they foreground, and thereby question, the manner in which the movement-image reterritorialises national identity. In the next chapter I will examine three East Asian films to see how they function in this respect.

Notes

1. Thomas Donnelly, *Rebuilding America's Defences: Strategy, Forces and Resources For a New Century* (Washington DC, 2000) http://www.newamericancentury.org/RebuildingAmericasDefenses.pdf (06/01/2005).
2. The Project for the New American Century Website. The quote is taken from their 'Statement of Principles': http://www.newamericancentury.org/statementofprinciples.htm (06/01/2005).
3. Ibid.
4 Douglas Kellner, 'Film, politics, and ideology: reflections on Hollywood film in the age of reason', *The Velvet Light Trap*, no. 27 (1991), pp. 9–24, p. 13.
5. Richard Dyer, *White* (London: Routledge, 1997), pp. 151–61.
6. Mark Jancovich, 'Modernity as subjectivity in *The Terminator*', *The Velvet Light Trap*, no. 30 (1992), pp. 3–17.
7. Ibid. p. 7.
8. Susan Jeffords, 'Can masculinity be terminated?', in Steven Cohan and Ina Rae Hark (eds), *Screening the Male* (London: Routledge, 1993), pp. 245–62.
9. Steve Neale, 'Masculinity as spectacle: reflections on men and mainstream cinema', *Screen*, 24: 6 (1983) pp. 2–16.
10. Mark Jancovich, 'Modernity as subjectivity in *The Terminator*', p. 4.

11. James Castonguay, 'Conglomeration, new media, and the cultural production of the "War on Terror"', *Cinema Journal*, 43: 4 (2004), pp. 102–8, p. 103.
12. Wheeler Winston Dixon, *Visions of the Apocalypse* (London: Wallflower, 2003), p. 81.
13. Susan Jeffords, 'Can masculinity be terminated?', p. 252.
14. Michael Paul Rogin, *Ronald Reagan, the Movie* (Berkeley: University of California Press, 1987), p. 3.
15. Ziauddin Sardar and Merryl Wyn Davies, *American Dream Global Nightmare* (London: Icon Books, 2004), p. 1.
16. Interview with director Jonathan Mostow, http://filmforce.ign.com/articles/426/426480p1.html (08/01/2005).
17. Douglas Kellner, *Grand Theft 2000* (New York: Rowman and Littlefield, 2001), p. 188.
18. Douglas Kellner, *From 9/11 to Terror War* (New York: Rowman and Littlefield, 2003), pp. 7–26.
19. Noam Chomsky, *9–11* (New York: Seven Stories Press, 2001), p. 23.
20. Patricia Mellencamp, 'TV time and catastrophe, or *Beyond the Pleasure Principle* of television', in Patricia Mellencamp (ed.), *Logics of Television* (Indiana: Indiana University Press, 1990), pp. 240–66.
21. Thomas H. Kean et al., *The 9/11 Commission Report* (New York: W.W. Norton, 2004), p. 349.
22. 'Transcript: 9/11 Panel Releases its Final Report', *Washington Post*, 22 July 2004. http://www.washingtonpost.com/wp-dyn/articles/A6014–2004 Jul22.html (07/01/2005).
23. Douglas Kellner, *From 9/11 to Terror War*, p. 171.
24. Referenced in 'Arms orders and deliveries: military expenditure, conflict areas', in Melanie Jarman, (ed.), *Campaign Against the Arms Trade News*, no. 186 (2004), p. 10–11, p. 10.
25. Renata Salecl, *On Anxiety* (London: Routledge, 2004), pp. 5–11.
26. Michael Billig, *Banal Nationalism* (London: Sage, 1995), p. 149.
27. Thomas H. Kean et al., *The 9/11 Commission Report*, p. 362.
28. The Project for the New American Century Website. The quote is taken from their 'Statement of Principles': http://www.newamericancentury.org/statementofprinciples.htm (06/01/2005).
29. Francis Fukuyama, 'The end of history?', *The National Issue*, Summer 1989, pp. 3–18, p. 4.
30. Oaisis, 'Stop Crying Your Heart Out' from *Heathen Chemistry* (Big Brother, 2002).
31. Patricia O'Neill, 'Where globalization and localization meet: Spike Lee's *25th Hour*', in *CineAction*, 64 (2004), pp. 2–7, p. 6.
32. Ibid. p. 7.
33. Emanuel Levy, *Cinema of Outsiders* (New York: New York University Press, 1999), p. 501.

34. An American R rating lies somewhere between a 15 and an 18 in the UK. For instance, R-rated *Reservoir Dogs* received an 18 certificate in the UK, whilst R-rated *Infernal Affairs* only warranted a 15 certificate. The Movie Picture Association of America (MPAA) defines an R rating as: 'RESTRICTED: Under 17 requires accompanying parent or adult guardian'. http://www.filmratings.com/ (05/05/05). The British Board of Film Classification (BBFC) classifies a film with a 15 certificate based on an examination of its depiction of a set of criteria (theme, language, nudity, sex, violence, imitable techniques, horror and drugs), and the suitability of their treatment for a 15-year-old viewer. An 18 certificate is employed 'where material or treatment appears to the Board to risk harm to individuals or, through their behaviour to societies'. The 18 certificate is usually deployed when there are sexual acts, acts of sexual violence, or illegal drug taking. For a much fuller description of these regulations, see: http://www.bbfc.co.uk/ (26/09/05).
35. Jim Hillier, 'Introduction', in Jim Hillier (ed.), *American Independent Cinema* (London: BFI, 2001), pp. ix–xvii, p. xvi.
36. Brian Neve, 'Independent cinema and modern Hollywood: pluralism in American cultural politics?' in Philip John Davies and Paul Wells (eds), *American Film and Politics from Reagan to Bush Jr.* (Manchester: Manchester University Press, 2002), pp. 123–38.
37. Justin Wyatt, 'The formation of the "major independent"', in Steve Neale and Murray Smith (eds), *Contemporary Hollywood Cinema* (London: Routledge, 1998), pp. 74–90.
38. Emanuel Levy, *Cinema of Outsiders*, p. 508.
39. Jim Hillier, 'Introduction', in Jim Hillier (ed.), *American Independent Cinema*, pp. ix–xvii, p. xv.
40. Mike Goodridge, 'Paradigm Shifts for Indies at Cannes', *Screen International*, 1404 (2003), p. 1.
41. Nick James, 'I Forgot to Remember to Forget', *Sight and Sound*, 14:5 (2004), pp. 14–18, p. 18.
42. Ibid.
43. See Alexander Pope, 'Eloise to Abelard', in John Butt (ed.), *The Poems of Alexander Pope* (London: Rutledge, 1963), pp. 252–61, p. 257 for the original text.
44. Douglas Kellner, *From 9/11 to Terror War*, p. 38.
45. Beck, 'Everybody's Gotta Learn Sometime,' *Eternal Sunshine of the Spotless Mind* (Wea, 2004).
46. Judy Pearsall (ed.), *The New Oxford Dictionary of English* (Oxford: Clarendon Press, 1998), p. 1028.
47. Jean-Luc Comolli and Jean Narboni, 'Cinema/ideology/criticism', in Bill Nichols (ed.), *Movies and Methods* (Berkeley: University of California Press, [1969] 1976), pp. 22–30, p. 26.

CHAPTER 6

The Pacific Rim

This chapter examines three films from Asian Pacific Rim countries, *Too Many Ways to be Number One* (Hong Kong, 1997), *Chaos* (Japan, 1999) and *Peppermint Candy* (South Korea, 2000). These particular films are singled out because they have, by turns, a multiple, a jumbled and a reversed narrative structure. They are examined chronologically, each time with reference to a number of other films from their respective national cinemas. Although there are numerous difficulties attached to labelling South Korea and Hong Kong 'nations' the unusual narratives of these three films are, nevertheless, again viewed as attempts to negotiate 'national' identity in the face of changing historical circumstances. Each section concludes by examining the extent to which these time-images caught in the act of becoming movement-images evidence a de- or reterritorialisation of national identity. Although it is unusual to see Asian films analysed using a Deleuzean approach, this chapter further demonstrates the applicability of his work to a number of national cinemas outside of Europe and America.

The grouping of these three national cinemas in one final chapter is not intended as a pejorative suggestion of their worth in relation to the other national cinemas discussed so far; in fact being collected in this manner avoids their homogenisation as undifferentiated works of 'Asian Cinema'. By examining each one in turn, a number of differences become apparent that are directly attributable to the specific national contexts from which each film emerged. In short, the extent to which each film de- or reterritorialises the movement-image is to a large degree a product of the national context in which it was produced.

Too Many Ways to be Number One

In recent academic writing on Hong Kong cinema it has become a commonplace to acknowledge the effect of the signing, in 1984, of the Sino-British Joint Declaration on the Future of Hong Kong, on Hong Kong cinema of the 1980s and 1990s. Along with a number of other historical events (including the Daya Bay incident of 1986, and the Tiananmen Square massacre of 1989) the declaration instigated a cinematic negotiation of Hong Kong's identity in the run up to, and following, the handover of Hong Kong to China in 1997.[1] Some examples of this type of analysis include Julian Stringer's examination of John Woo's action films *A Better Tomorrow* (1986) and *The Killer* (1989)[2], Tony Williams' discussion of Jet Li as Wong Fei Hung in the recent *Once Upon a Time in China* series (1991–7),[3] Ackbar Abbas' *Hong Kong*,[4] and various chapters in edited collections like Nick Browne's *New Chinese Cinemas* (1994), Poshek Fu and David Desser's *The Cinema of Hong Kong* (2000) and Esther Yau's *At Full Speed* (2001).[5] My analysis of *Too Many Ways* uses the same theoretical approach but emphasises the way a twice replayed narrative (like that of *Run Lola Run*) is used to negotiate the handover, the anxieties that surrounded it and the transformations to Hong Kong's identity that it initiated.

Too Many Ways is a Cantonese gangster comedy. It begins with a close-up of a watch worn by protagonist Ah Kau Wong (Ching Wan Lau).[6] Wong is having his fortune told in a cafe, although this fortune is not revealed until the narrative returns to this point for a third time at the end of the film. Leaving the cafe in the first narrative Wong returns to his flower stall (where he sells wreaths) and is met by Bo, a dubious friend with connections with the Black Star Gang in mainland China. Bo puts together a crew, including Wong, to deliver five Mercedes to China. The crew meet for dinner and a massage, but after Wong refuses to pay the bill they end up robbing the bathhouse. During the bungled get away Bo is killed and Wong and the others travel to mainland China without him. The deal with the Black Star Gang goes sour, and Wong and the rest are killed by Communist soldiers. The narrative returns to the close-up on Wong's watch and begins again. This time, however, Wong pays in the bathhouse and, through a different series of events, ends up in Taiwan with inept assassin Matt (Chun Yu Ng). Wong and Matt are hired by twin brothers Blackie and White, rival gang leaders who each want the other killed. Wong and Matt agree to kill Blackie and White, both of whom are members of the Five Lake Gang headed by Master Saint. Coincidentally, having survived in mainland China this time the rest of Bo's crew show up in Taiwan. When Blackie and White kill each other the Hong Kong crew look set to take over their territories. However, an earlier bungled robbery leads local triad kingpin Master Saint to threaten to execute several of Wong's men rather than acknowledge the crew's territorial claims. In the ensuing argument Wong is shot in the head and, although he succeeds to power, he is permanently disabled. The film returns to the watch once more, Wong's fortune is revealed and the film ends with its third narrative unexplored.

In the buddy films of John Woo, two characters were used to represent different attitudes towards Hong Kong's future. In *A Better Tomorrow*, for instance, both protagonists Ho (Lung Ti) and Mark (Yun Fat Chow) play out the dilemma that faced many Hong Kong residents in the years preceding the handover over whether to stay or leave. In *Too Many Ways* this dilemma is played out not through two different characters, but through the narrative's two attempts to find an alternative, workable future for Hong Kong migrant, Wong. Like other films of the time *Too Many Ways* evokes the desire of many Hong Kong citizens to leave their home. The centrality of this theme is apparent when, at the close of the film, Wong's future is revealed. He is told:

> within two weeks you will be asked to do something abroad. Not only once, but twice. Either Taiwan, or Mainland China. This is a test, be very careful. Either you will be rich, or you will be shit. If you can't pass the test you'll be dead meat. If you make it you'll gain money and fame.

Understandably, Wong asks for advice as to which destination he should choose. The response is:

> Taiwan or Mainland China isn't the point. The point is, your heart. You look all messed up, you don't know what you are doing now. The key to success is whether you can find yourself or not. It depends on what kind of person you want to be.

The two narratives that follow demonstrate that both outcomes (in the first Wong dies in Mainland China and in the second he gains 'money and fame' in Taiwan but is crippled as a result) are unsatisfactory; rather, Wong must learn to know himself. As allegories for the futures facing the population of Hong Kong at the time of the handover they are quite easy to construct. Leaving Hong Kong is not the preferred option, instead staying and finding a new identity is advocated.

Wong's profession is selling wreaths. Symbolically, he is shown to have accepted the death of his native Hong Kong identity in 1997 until he is sparked into life by his fortune. However, thanks to the untimely death of Bo the crew's trip to mainland China fails, the film suggesting that without the necessary contacts Hong Kong citizens are entering into a national partnership where business is unlikely to prove fruitful. This is made clear by the gang's death in mainland China as they try to take advantage of an armoured car robbery. Attempting to get your hands on Chinese state finance is seen to be a deadly business as the Communist troops do not differentiate between the Chinese and Hong Kong gangs and shoot all concerned. Thus, the future faced by Hong Kong residents once they are reunited with China is represented as one of commercial failure due to poor communication and the presence of the military state.

The second narrative then depicts a contrast to Communist China in democratic, free market Taiwan. Here Wong's ease in gaining multiple business contracts and his rise to power suggest there are a great many more opportunities available to Hong Kong migrants in Taiwan. However, the film does not allow for a simplistic 'wrong' and 'right' comparison in its contrasting treatment of these destinations. Success in this situation comes at a price, as the disabled Wong discovers.

In contrast to both *Sliding Doors* (two stories, one right, one wrong) and *Run Lola Run* (three stories, two wrong, one right) *Too Many Ways* lacks a solution in which everything goes right. This is undoubtedly owing to the emergence of the film in the year of the handover when Hong Kong's future could not be clearly seen. Unlike the European films, which celebrate a new sense of national identity as a global/local nexus, the dilemma facing Hong Kong does not have an easily identifiable solution, a 'correct' narrative of identity. In the European nations (and somewhat paradoxically in the case of an only-just reunited Germany) the regional is celebrated over previous conceptions of the national. In this Hong Kong film, by contrast, the regional identity of Hong Kong is examined in the face of fears of its imminent erasure during national reunification.

This difference is compounded by the different economic conditions facing Hong Kong and those enjoyed by the European countries. *Too Many Ways* directly acknowledges the effect of the economic recession that affected much of East Asia in the late 1990s. For instance, Wong's girlfriend in the second narrative, Number Two (Yeuk Tung Lee), states the slowness of the economy as one of the reasons for her departure to Taiwan. Unlike Berlin and London then, a 'correct' route to economic success in Hong Kong cannot be easily mapped out by Wong as it was by Helen and Lola.

Too Many Ways does go some way towards offering a solution in the interplay between the two stories, though. As was the case with both Lola and Helen, Wong has the ability to learn from mistakes in one narrative in order to enhance his life in another. In mainland China the crew blame Wong for all their troubles, for not paying the bill, for losing the money from the robbery, for burying Bo with his pager still on his person, for not being able to drive and for Bo's widow's sudden death during intercourse. However, as a result of their constant barrage, he begins to take the initiative. Although their endeavour ultimately fails, Wong becomes a powerful figure and leader of the gang in Bo's absence. The point at which he accedes to power is accentuated when the camera circles his scantily clad figure from a low angle that emphasises his underpant-clad genitalia. A distinctive fanfare is heard on the soundtrack at this point (which recurs in the second narrative), to illustrate that by fighting back he has 'found himself' in the manner his fortune predicted.

Unfortunately, on this occasion this moment of clarity comes too late. Yet, as a consequence of this, in the second narrative Wong reaches this stage much more rapidly. It is apparent that in the second retelling Wong's character is immediately more composed and authoritative and his ability to shoot and drive are much improved, suggesting his greater masculine potency. Not only does he pay for the massage, even though he has to use his watch to do so, he also leaves the massage parlour immediately afterwards, illustrating his 'knowledge' that a trip to mainland China will not help him. In this way he gains the respect of Matt, who was instrumental in berating his other incarnation whilst in mainland China. Whilst in Taiwan Wong's moment of clarity in which he 'finds himself' (again shot from below to signify his new found strength and resolve and again accompanied by the same distinctive fanfare) occurs much sooner and facilitates his rise to power. This change of character is vindicated by the tribute that Brother Li – a gang boss and peer in Wong's new Taiwanese territories – pays him in the second narrative. Wong is meeting with the bosses of the other gangs and as Li pays the restaurant bill he tells Wong: 'Do you know what a boss should learn first? When to pay!' It would seem, then, that the need to retain face by paying his own way has led to Wong's success in Taiwan. However, the narrative's final close-up of the handicapped Wong's despairing, blank stare as his crew congratulate him, intimates that this lesson in itself is not enough.

As I demonstrated in Chapter 3 in relation to *Sliding Doors* and *Run Lola Run*, multiple versions of a narrative are used to ensure that the film's chosen vision of national identity is advocated. Furthermore, the validity of this national narrative is reinforced by contrast with one or more unsuccessful versions. In this instance, like Lola and Helen, Wong learns from his previous existence in mainland China so that the narrative of his identity as a Hong Kong citizen may be more speedily advanced in Taiwan. The question the film leaves us with, then, is how will this narrative progress after Wong has learned from his time in Taiwan? In response, consider David Bordwell's passing conclusion to his analysis of *Too Many Ways*:

> Staying in Hong Kong and avoiding Bo's scheme altogether becomes a third option, one that fits into a broader theme suggesting that Hong Kong's future lies neither with the Mainland nor with Taiwan.[7]

This is precisely the note on which the film ends, although Bordwell does not elaborate on exactly what this third option may entail. Another look at the body of work that already exists on the subject casts further light on this matter.

For Stringer one of the reasons why *A Better Tomorrow* was so popular with audiences in Hong Kong was that it demonstrated how, although staying in Hong Kong might well lead to suffering once Chinese rule became effective, leaving Hong Kong was equally likely to cause emotional anxiety. In *Too Many Ways*, Wong faces the same catch-22 situation that leaving entails suffering just as staying does. Thus in the film's final return to its starting point it would seem that staying may be considered the preferable option, just as it was in *A Better Tomorrow*.

Whilst both previous narratives began with Bo accosting Wong at his wreath stall, and Wong stripping Bo of the Rolex watch, Cartier glasses, Armani shirt, Versace trousers and Calvin Klein underwear of which he is so proud, this is actually the point at which the final narrative ends. With this final image, *Too Many Ways* suggests that the search for Hong Kong's new identity continues and that to find it its citizens may need to look beyond the capitalist orientation on which so much of their economic identity has recently been based. Although *Too Many Ways* shares the same narrative structure as *Run Lola Run*, by contrast, and presumably due to its imminent reunification with China, *Too Many Ways* ends with a rejection of the identification of Hong Kong with consumer durables. The symbolic stripping of Bo's designer labels illustrates the need to once again reimagine identity. As Ackbar Abbas noted in 1997, this renegotiation has been a characteristic of Hong Kong throughout the twentieth century. After all, Hong Kong received successive waves of immigrants from China, during the 1930s when Japan invaded, during the Chinese civil war in the late 1940s and during the cultural revolution in the late 1960s. All of these impacted upon Hong Kong's regional identity. Simply by virtue of being a port, Hong Kong has been the embarkation point for numerous Chinese people leaving for other countries. In line with Abbas' work, the process of stripping and starting over with which the film ends is as much a statement on Hong Kong's ability to constantly transform as it is on the impact of the particular transformation that would occur with reunification in 1997.[8]

Under British rule the identity of Hong Kong citizens was never 'fixed' in the same way that many national identities are. Whilst discussing several Hong Kong films that deal with issues of diaspora, identity and 1997, Sheldon Lu points out that 'the question of national and cultural affiliation has been the most problematic and of the foremost importance in the minds of Hong Kong residents, for they have lived a life without a proper nationality, being neither Chinese nor British.'[9] In such a situation, Lu contends that a 'sense of rootlessness still defines the existential, emotional condition of the ordinary Hong Kong citizen.'[10] This is exactly the paradigm of identity examined in *Too Many Ways*. Unable to locate a satisfactory life in China or Taiwan, Wong is returned to Hong Kong in the third, unresolved narrative. It is as though the handover has simply reemphasised a problem which has confronted Hong Kong citizens for over a century, that of how to find identity within a 'rootless' situation. The identity of the citizens of Hong Kong is figured as a constant process of deterritorialisation, for which a fixed point of reterritorialisation (a 'correct' national narrative) has yet to be found. To give the last word on this matter to Lu, the recent history of Hong Kong is of 'a fluid, deterritorialized, transnational and mobile mechanism of national affiliation . . . This conception of flexible filiation bespeaks a process of decontextualization and recontextualization of citizenship, nationality and residence.'[11]

As a time-image caught in the act of becoming a movement-image the multiple narratives of *Too Many Ways* illustrate the labyrinthine possibilities for identity that arose for Hong Kong's citizens at the time of the handover. Noticeably, however, the film does not reterritorialise as a movement-image, reflecting the inability of Hong Kong to imagine its own future in such an uncertain situation. Its open-ended play with perpetual deterritorialisation evokes the 'existential, emotional condition of the ordinary Hong Kong citizen' that is a product of its recent history. Rather than advocating one particular future, then, the film valorises the honour and strength of character that Wong comes to express across the two narratives. Like John Woo's action heroes bravely performing their assertive masculinity in the face of suffering and inevitable defeat Wong is unable to reverse the fact of imminent reunification. It is only important that he continue to try.

In *Too Many Ways*, the physical (specifically, masculine) agency typical of the action-image always arrives a little too late, be it to save Wong's life (first narrative), or his mobility (second narrative). In this sense, the film actually has more in common with Fellini's *8½* than it does with *Sliding Doors* and *Run Lola Run*. *Too Many Ways* captures the splitting of the crystal of time, rendering visible the double time of Hong Kong's narrative of identity before it is able to reterritorialise into a dominant, or 'correct', national narrative after reunification. Like Guido before him, our first glimpse of Wong (after the repeated establishing shot of the watch) is a close-up of his hand as his fortune is told. This hand has yet to seize its new identity and, although it is unlike Guido's grasping hand, it is still an open hand, trying to read its own future. Its sensory-motor continuity also remains unfulfilled as it searches for a manner in which to act. The question of whether Wong will be able to successfully regain his sensory-motor continuity (to overcome his death and then wheelchair-bound states) in a manner that will resolve Hong Kong's narrative of identity into a movement-image, remains purposefully unresolved at the film's conclusion.

Chaos

In contrast to *Too Many Ways*, the narrative structure of Hideo Nakata's *Chaos* is designed – somewhat like that of *Memento* – to reveal informing events only after the viewer has experienced their consequences. In this manner it creates confusion (as the viewer is often unaware of why events are occurring), a certain degree of suspense (as to whether events are 'real' or not) and the prevailing black mood that we might expect of a *noir* thriller. However, despite this apparent similarity with its American counterpart, *Chaos* actually has more in common with *Vertigo* than it does with *Memento*. *Chaos* uses the same plot device as *Vertigo* – the murder of the glamorous wife of a successful businessman and her impersonation by a working-class doppelganger – in order to examine the changing role of women in contemporary Japanese society. Moreover, its meditation on gender roles and female performance is foregrounded by the confusion over identities thrown up by the jumbled narrative. In effect, the film formally reflects the theme of its narrative, its exploration of how changing gender roles in Japan have recently created instability in the dominant narrative of national identity. As a *noir* thriller, *Chaos* reterritorialises into a movement-image in a very conventional sense, with the *femme fatale* (like Judy/Madeleine in *Vertigo*) leaping to her death. The final image of her smiling face, however, creates a recollection-image unlike that which closes *Vertigo*. It not only exposes but also challenges the movement-image's powers of reterritorialisation. To a certain extent, then, *Chaos* (like *8½* and *Too Many Ways*) also captures the suspended moment during which the national narrative searches for reterritorialisation.

A detailed synopsis is necessary to describe the temporal structure of this film. It begins with the title, 'Chaos', superimposed on a close-up shot of rain pelting onto a road surface. This is actually the defining moment in the film, but as in a time-image, at this point we cannot tell if it is a flashback or the present that we are witnessing. We then cut to the present moment of the narrative as a couple eat lunch in a chic restaurant called 'L'. They are Mr Takayuki Komiyama (Ken Mitsuishi) CEO of a large company called Shinko Enterprises and a woman who appears to be his wife, Saori Komiyama (Miki Nakatani). Saori is kidnapped and a ransom demanded. Komiyama calls the police. We see him arrive at the proposed handover, but no kidnapper appears. We flashback to the events immediately following

Saori's disappearance from 'L'. Saori arrives at the house of handyman Goro Kuroda (Masato Hagiwara) disguised as a teenaged girl. We learn that the kidnapping is a fake. The story unfolds as Saori takes Kuroda to apartment 303 of the Seiwa Heights complex. Kuroda ensures the kidnapping looks real by making Saori dress up glamorously once again, frightening her and tying her up. A brief ellipsis occurs and Kuroda is shown returning to apartment 303 only to find Saori dead. He takes a phone call in which a disguised voice blackmails him into disposing of her body.

The next day, whilst driving his son back to his estranged wife, Kuroda spots a doppelganger of Saori. After much sleuthing he tracks her down, and in a subjective flashback, realises that he has met her previously in his capacity as handyman. Saori's impersonator is female model, Tsushima Satomi (Miki Nakatani). Satomi and Komiyama meet in a hotel room, and it becomes clear that they were both in cahoots over the killing of the real Saori (whose was the body in apartment 303) and the fake kidnapping of Satomi/Saori. The film flashes back once again, this time to the opening shot of rain on a road surface. Saori arrives at apartment 303 brandishing a large knife. An ellipsis shifts us to a moment after her sudden death before a subjective flashback from Satomi's point of view shows the struggle in which she and Komiyama killed Saori. We return to the present, Kuroda confronts Satomi, transforms her into Saori once more and uses her to bait an elaborate trap for Komiyama. Kuroda returns Saori's body to apartment 303 where the police find Komiyama. However, a happy ending is denied as Satomi and Koruda are unable to trust each other and Satomi commits suicide by jumping into the sea.

As I demonstrated in Chapter 2, the indiscernible female double of *Vertigo* does not illustrate a crystal of time but, rather, a recollection-image. The Judy/Madeleine circuit becomes actual in the present, with the copy (Judy/Madeleine) replacing the original (Madeleine) in an act of reterritorialisation. This action recreates the past that was (a singular, actual definition of the past) as opposed to opening up the deterritorialising possibilities of the virtual past that is. In terms of national identity this process exposes the manner in which a past marked by colonial difference is replaced in the present with an image of class difference. Thus *Vertigo* shows the constant need to realign the national narrative in order to suggest an unbroken lineage to the past that was. In a somewhat similar manner *Chaos* deals with the issue of changing gender roles in contemporary Japan. This time, however, although both the makeover of Satomi into Satomi/Saori and her final death scene create recollection-images, as a consequence of its rather different context *Chaos* goes much further than *Vertigo* in deterritorialising the movement-image.

In the early 1990s the Japanese economy that had been so buoyant during previous decades suddenly faced an economic depression. Working practices that had previously sustained the bubble economy had to change, and this had an effect on the performance of gender roles in Japanese society. For instance, the white-collar salaryman was no longer guaranteed a job for life; many became unemployed and found their masculinity degraded as wives and children referred to them as *sodaigomi* (oversized garbage).[12] Even so, according to Yumiko Iida, the slightly greater equality surrounding employment that emerged out of this new context did not have a terribly huge impact on female opportunities. What did change were female attitudes towards their previously accepted normative gender roles. As Iida has it:

> The commodification of what used to be considered 'sacred' in Japan – the family and women's sexuality – has in many ways contributed to the liberation of women, who in the 1990s enjoy more options in life . . . Their status was in some measure set back in the 1990s due to the general economic decline and the tightening of the job market. On the level of consciousness and lifestyle, however, there have been significant changes among the younger generations of women who began to challenge long uncontested gender roles and family relations. For one thing, many women simply begin to reject marriage and childbearing, no longer considering the role of wife and mother as an attractive option. For another, as sexuality became increasingly commercialised, the conventional belief in the family and women's bodies as the last remaining bastions of morality, supposedly 'sacred' private realms free from commercial enterprise, have undergone substantial changes.[13]

It is this shift in thinking concerning the performance of femininity, the commercialisation of women's bodies and women's role in public society generally that *Chaos* negotiates through its two identical women. *Chaos* is extremely self-conscious in its examination of the performance of identity. With the exception of the police, very few people are what they seem to be, and the film's disrupted narrative delights in exposing each character's facade retrospectively. For instance, despite initial events we soon learn that Komiyama is certainly not a man concerned for his kidnapped wife. Kidnapper Kuroda indeed, is really only a handyman, although he is more than capable of playing the roles of both kidnapper and policeman if necessary. In fact the only role he seems incapable of playing effectively is that of father. Most central to the film though, is Satomi, whose identity is constantly in flux. It is impossible to fix one identity as essentially hers because the very first time we see her she is performing the role of another, pretending to be dutiful wife Saori in restaurant 'L'. In fact her masquerading abilities are constantly foregrounded by the film, as we variously see her acting out the parts of teenager, *femme fatale*, child, wife, lover, model, and we even hear her voice disguised as a blackmailing male on the phone.

In conjunction with the narrative's disrupted schema this constant fluxing of Satomi's identity is used to illustrate the stuttering of the national narrative that is created when women perform their expected gender roles differently. With each leap forward or backwards in narrative time the film presents us with another face of Satomi. Her constantly shifting identity makes it extremely difficult to follow the narrative as who she is to different people constantly changes. For instance, we first know her as Saori, doting wife of Komiyama, cutting up his steak for him as his hand is incapacitated; we are then immediately introduced to her through Kuroda's eyes, as Saori, self-kidnapper with dubious motives disguised as a teenaged girl. Next we meet her as Satomi the model, and so on. Each shift in the narrative (each flashback, ellipsis or simply shift of location) provides us with a different Satomi. Somewhat akin to the time-travelling Guido in *8½*, Satomi's identity is constantly transforming as it slips between different faces, different aspects of the crystal of time. This formal effect again evokes Butler's thinking on performative identity and its labyrinthine ability to unground the repetition of the same on which identity is based. In terms of national identity Satomi physically demonstrates the state of flux within the national narrative that changing gender roles have created in Japan. Like the young women that Iida describes, she refuses to remain stable in the doting wife role in which we first meet her. As a professional model, working for the rather pointedly titled 'Act Promotion' agency, Satomi perfectly illustrates Iida's observations on the newfound ability of women in contemporary Japan to use their body for commercial gain, as opposed to familial duty.

Just as in *Vertigo*, so too in *Chaos* the performance of femininity is bound up with male desire for a certain image of womanhood, specifically the role of wife. Very like Judy when she is made-over into Madeleine by Scottie, Satomi fights a losing battle against Kuroda's attempts to reterritorialise her various identities into the image of Saori. This struggle is first seen when Satomi appears at Kuroda's door in her teenage-girl disguise. Kuroda insists on creating a realistic image of a kidnap, which involves them both adopting the appearances and emotions that come with their respective kidnapper/kidnapped roles. Thus he takes away and destroys her disguise and insists that she wear Saori's dress, jewellery and make up before he binds her. Initially Satomi is able to escape this position of Saori's double, but only by replacing her own body with that of Saori. Yet after Kuroda finds Satomi again the process is repeated with Kuroda interfering to the point of applying Satomi's lipstick for her. Indeed, at the end of the film, after using Satomi/Saori to trap Komiyama, Kuroda seduces her, repeatedly rubbing his thumb over her made up lips and commenting on how much the colour becomes her. At this point, Satomi has effectively taken the place of Saori, of potential wife for Kuroda. She has been reterritorialised into the recollection-image that Kuroda desires, just as Judy/Madeleine was by Scottie. Thus, despite his apparently valiant quest for justice for the dead Saori, Kuroda is actually little different from Komiyama in his desire for everything that Saori represents. Kuroda, himself estranged from his wife and seemingly unable to empathise emotionally with his son, still longs for the ideal figure of the wife into which he reterritorialises Satomi/Saori.

It is interesting, then, that the film does not end with Satomi replaying Saori's death in quite the same manner as deployed in *Vertigo*. Satomi and Kuroda's sexual foreplay is interrupted by Kuroda's discovery of a knife on Satomi's person. This was given to Satomi by Komiyama just prior to his arrest. A knife-wielding woman, Satomi is, in yet another respect, the double of Saori. Saori is only seen alive once in the film – as she arrives at apartment 303 in the driving rain bringing with her a large kitchen knife and the 'chaos' of the title. Kuroda's horrified reaction to the knife illustrates that even if Satomi/Satori becomes the image of the dutiful wife she always contains the submerged, castrating potential to derail the national narrative by breaking from this role and appropriating the phallus. It was Saori's initial attack on Komiyama that injured his hand, a symbolic castration that left him dependent on Satomi (seen initially in her appropriation of the knife as she cuts up of his steak in restaurant 'L'). The knife here functions as a symbol of the ungrounding force that lurks beneath the surface and threatens to derail the comfortable life of the salaryman and, by extension, the sensory-motor continuity through which the national narrative is rendered in the movement-image. In *8½*, Guido's grasping hand represents a sensory-motor discontinuity that illustrates the Italian search for national identity. In *Saving Private Ryan*, Miller's shaking hand represented national identity rendered unstable by war. In *Memento*, Shelby's tattooed hand ('remember Sammy Jankis') illustrated the construction of a false history to national identity. In *Too Many Ways*, Wong's open palm renders the unknown future in which Hong Kong's fortune will be read. Now, in *Chaos*, Komiyama's injured hand represents the faltering of the national narrative that occurs when a knife-wielding woman symbolically rejects the role of wife and mother.

However, unlike the parallel act in *Vertigo*, Satomi's doubling of Saori is ultimately not the cause of her death. Determined not to repeat Saori's fate Satomi throws the knife away and runs into the forest. As she attempts to escape Kuroda it begins to rain. In her final leap from the cliff the soaking wet Satomi turns and smiles at Kuroda. A brief freeze on her features

Figure 6.1 Satomi grasps her opportunity in 1990s Japan (Source: Kino International/The Kobal Collection)

creates a matching image with the earlier image of her in her bathroom that Kuroda had previously dredged up in his subjective flashback. When they first met Satomi was struggling with a leak in her apartment. After handyman Kuroda turned off the water she stood, dripping wet, beaming at him. In his memory, Kuroda's face established recognition (an act which was obviously impossible at the time when they actually met) but which retroactively reveals this point in the narrative to be their first meeting. As Satomi leaps from the cliff the exact same shot/reverse shot and freeze frame pattern is repeated as was used in Kuroda's flashback. This ensures that Kuroda and the audience are left with a different recollection image than that of Satomi/Saori the dutiful wife that Kuroda previously created. In her smiling leap, *femme fatale* Satomi matches herself to her past incarnation as a working woman, someone unable to deal with simple domestic occurrences like a leaky bathroom, and who makes a living instead by performing a number of different roles as a model. Admittedly Satomi/Saori's identity is still fixed by this creation of a recollection image. After all, in death her crystalline status is ultimately reterritorialised. However, unlike Judy/Madeleine, whose death matches that of the real Madeleine, Satomi/Saori escapes the symbolic strangulation at the hands of her husband that was Saori's fate. Instead she returns to the role of single, working woman. In a sense, then, the freeze frame could be interpreted literally as the suspended moment of the national narrative, as it struggles to reterritorialise in a manner that accommodates the changing face of female identity in contemporary Japan.

The film illustrates the fear of 'chaos' that occurs when feminine traits that were once thought essential are revealed to be culturally determined performances. Unlike *Vertigo*, however, which can only conclude by exposing the death of the woman that the reterritorialisation of the national narrative entails, *Chaos* attempts to challenge this conclusion. Thus, once again, it is to a large degree the different historical context which determines the extent to which the film is able to deterritorialise the movement-image. Just as *Vertigo* does, the film uses the indiscernibility between original and copy (between real and fake wife; real and fake kidnapping) to illustrate a fluxing state of national identity. However, neither film concludes with simply the unresolved crystal of time seen in *8½*. Instead, to differing degrees, *Vertigo* exposes and *Chaos* challenges the reterritorialisation of the national narrative.

The association of Satomi with water throughout the film adds another dimension to this interpretation. Through this imagery *Chaos* engages with several other Japanese films to emerge since the late 1990s, not least of which are the two Hideo Nakata films that bracket *Chaos*: *Ring* (1998) and *Dark Water* (2002). A brief examination of the similarities between these and certain other Japanese films of the period under discussion will enable *Chaos*' examination of national identity to appear much more starkly. Both *Ring* and *Dark Water* are adaptations of literary works by Kôji Suzuki whilst *Chaos* is loosely based on a story by Shogo Utano. Even so, *Chaos*, ultimately the product of scriptwriter Hisashi Saito, shares their preoccupation with femininity and water (specifically rain, domestic bathrooms and the sea), dysfunctional families, absent fathers, working women, the 'problem' of motherhood and the impact of contemporary life on Japanese children.

Like her counterparts in *Ring* and *Dark Water*, Satomi is associated throughout with water. This would appear to be an attempt to demonstrate the chaos that accompanies the dissolution of the nuclear family. Where the monstrous Sadako (Rie Inou) in *Ring* is somehow an unnatural product of the sea, the 'chaotic' Satomi dies by leaping into the sea. Where Yoshimi Matsubara (Hitomi Kuroki) in *Dark Water* is unable to resolve the supernatural leakages that threaten her domestic interior so Satomi is unable to stop her leaking bathroom from filling with water. As though combining these characteristics, and again illustrating her lack of essential identity, Satomi is at once figured as a woman who is incapable of providing a safe domestic environment *and* as a threatening force aligned with nature, which threatens to invade the civilised environs of the home.

Ultimately, both Matsubara in *Dark Water*, and the protagonist of *Ring*, Reiko Asakawa (Nanako Matsushima), are reterritorialised when they enter confined, man-made womb-like spaces (a water tank and a well respectively) to soothe a tormented ghost child. The physical constraining of these working mothers could be said to illustrate a rather conservative message of the continued need for nurturing mothers in contemporary Japanese society, especially now that the nuclear family is, as all three films demonstrate, dissolving. In *Chaos*, however, the wife and mother role is rejected by Satomi. When viewed in relation to her association with water, her sodden leap into the sea could be seen as an attempt to preserve her uncertain identity. Her multiple selves become dispersed within a nature that is represented by all three films as potentially invasive of civilisation, and therefore 'chaotic'. Although it creates a recollection-image, in her final leap Satomi's identity becomes unknowable once again. Satomi literally vanishes into the sea, her body, unlike the uncomfortably recurrent presence of Saori's corpse, is nowhere to be seen. It is as though *Chaos*, with its disrupted narrative, acknowledges its inability to capture the essence of this slippery crystalline referent, the 'chaos' that threatens to unground the hegemonic order of the national narrative.

Indeed, this analysis can be taken a step further by briefly considering the resonances between Takashi Miike's *Audition* (1999) and Satomi's transformation from her teenaged-girl disguise into the image of glamorous wife at the hands of Kuroda. *Audition* is an exposé of the masculine construction of the female into the role of dutiful wife.[14] The humour in the film is created by Aoyama's (Ryo Ishibashi) projection of his ideal type onto Asami (Eihi Shiina), a young woman who, due to abuse suffered as a young girl, has developed psychopathic tendencies. When Aoyama fails to demonstrate that his love for her is exclusive, as he promised, she begins to transform him into a dog-like creature, entirely dependent on her for life. In *Audition* the psychopathic Asami is – if we follow Barbara Creed's seminal work on the topic–a monstrous female.[15] She has been warped by repression, and her return is therefore disruptive of the very patriarchal economy that she was manufactured to sustain. As Alvin Lu puts it, when discussing recent Japanese horror films in general, these films took 'Japan's pre-eminent bubble economy icon – the teenage girl – to her ultimate baroque incarnation as diseased vengeful spirit'.[16] In both *Ring* and *Audition* the vengeful female teen can also be seen as the monstrous return of the repressed, illustrating that with the burst of the bubble economy the normative gender roles on which it was based have now been undermined.[17] From the 'chaos' that such a situation creates emerges the supposedly monstrous female. Similarly, in *Chaos*, Satomi's decides to reject her transformation from her teenage-girl disguise (pony tails, sunhat, skirt and t-shirt) to glamorous wife at the hands of Kuroda. In place of this identity she initially leaves Saori's dead body and then her smiling suicide. Aware of the numerous identities that are now available to her, Satomi settles on that of working woman, illustrating her rejection of the process of reterritorialisation seen in *Vertigo*.

Admittedly, *Chaos* treads a very fine line between its celebration of currently deterritorialising female identity, and the need to reterritorialise dominant gender roles. The most damning return of the repressed is Saori's corpse, whose sudden reappearance in the bathroom of apartment 303 convicts Komiyama and serves, perhaps, as a warning against the dangers of marital infidelity. After all, it was his affair that created the situation in the first place. When read in this way the film seems to condemn Satomi for her part in this process, reterritorialising her into a cliched *femme fatale* who is punished by death. However, as with many films in which a monstrous femininity appears, the ambiguity of *Chaos* lies mainly in the way it is interpreted. On the one hand, films like *Chaos, Ring* and *Audition* can be read as a backlash against the recent transformation of femininity in Japan, and especially the rejection of the role of wife and mother. On the other, they can be seen as subversive celebrations of the new-found power of this reemergent section of society. If we return momentarily to Iida's work, it would seem that it is actually the second such interpretation that most accurately describes *Chaos*. Drawing on Sharon Kinsella's work on *rorikon manga* (a style of comic book named after the Japanese for Lolita-complex that became very popular in the 1990s), Iida notes that

> this popular genre of 'sexy little girls' merged in some sense with the long-established discourse of the 'cute-girls' of the 1980s, which many young Japanese women had endorsed, but in the general cultural context of the 1990s, it became more exclusively the fantasy object of young males. Referring to this shift in cultural landscape, Sharon Kinsella argued that the popularity of *rorikon manga* 'reflects simultaneously an awareness of the increasing power and centrality of young women in society, and also a reactive desire to see these young women disarmed, infantized and subordinated.' In other words, these sexualised cute-girl figures serve as idealised substitutes for what does not exist, and also as sites of fantasy for those wishing to avoid facing the difficulties and imperfections of the real world and real women.[18]

Audition, Ring and *Chaos* all examine this ambiguity over the increased 'centrality' of young women, and the desire of many to see them if not infantised then certainly disarmed and subordinated. As the male protagonists of both *Audition* and *Chaos* attempt to transform their female counterparts into dutiful wives, they unleash instead murderous *femme fatales*. Yet both films explicitly resist the reterritorialisation of their female protagonists' monstrous or chaotic powers. Whilst they both end with the deaths of their respective monstrous *femmes* (and could therefore be read as disarming and subordinating them) neither one simply condemns her for the disruptions she has caused. Rather, both *Audition* and *Chaos* foreground the part played by patriarchal society in the construction of the ideal role of wife that these protagonists ultimately mis- or rather, reinterpret for themselves.

Rather as in *Vertigo*, then, it is perhaps not so much the return of the repressed that creates the sense of 'horror' in these films. Instead, as I showed in Chapter 2 using Powell's work on the horror film, it is the indiscernibility between past and present that shocks, the glimpse of the virtual past that 'is' that is obtained during a moment of national transformation. As these films show, the bubble economy's reterritorialisation of the little girl into the role of wife in the recent past still haunts the present. It creates an indiscernibility of past and present identities (all these films investigate the identities of their female characters, often by examining their pasts) whose shocking presence is allegorically figured as a ghostly, murderous or otherwise monstrous performance of female identity. The recent past and the present oscillate in this way to illustrate the moment of historical transformation that the new economic situation has created in which female identity is 'adrift', having lost its previous historical fixity in the role of wife and mother.

Chaos continually attempts to find the origin of the historical moment in which the female role-player 'usurped' the traditional position of wife. Unable to grasp this slippery, crystalline referent the film shows instead (particularly through its twice repeated shot of the rain falling on tarmac) how this 'chaos' exists in the very inception of civilisation. As Satomi's return to the sea illustrates, it continues to subsist in nature as civilisation's other. The chaotic structure of the film's narrative, then, reflects the chaotic state of the national narrative. In a far more formally pointed fashion than *Vertigo*, *Chaos* demonstrates the inconclusiveness of the movement-image, its temporary nature as an order that reterritorialises chaos, but whose reign is only ever precarious at best. Like the peculiar relationship that exists between the deterritorialising time-image and the reterritorialising movement-image, the deterritorialising effect of chaos will always return, no matter how it is reterritorialised, or 'repressed'. For this reason, despite their obvious formal similarities *Chaos* is extremely different from *Memento*, whose narrative goes a long way towards exposing the reterritorialisation of national identity that is effected by the movement-image, but which is unable to fully break out of the classical model of narrative time. *Chaos*, for its part, attempts to show how the reterritorialisation of national identity in the recollection-image can be either constructed by patriarchal determinants (the image of the 'dead' wife) or by a female play with the transformative (here rendered as 'chaotic') performance of identity. Once again, then, a close examination of the national context in which a film emerged illustrates that, although this Japanese film is in many ways (especially thematically and formally) similar to its American predecessor *Vertigo* in other ways (particularly in respect of the conclusions it draws on changing gender roles) it is rather different.

Peppermint Candy

Peppermint Candy does not offer the possibility of an open-ended, or undecided future to the national narrative in quite the same way that *Too Many Ways* and *Chaos* do. Rather than taking place in the present *Peppermint Candy*'s narrative surveys the past twenty years, its meditation on the past forcing a questioning of the present, and the direction South Korea's national narrative may take in the future. This is achieved in large part through the self-conscious examination of the progress of history that the film offers in its reversed narrative time scheme. *Peppermint Candy* is a tragedy. Due to its reversed narrative structure the viewer knows from the very first scene that its protagonist is doomed to die. Using this unusual narrative structure it demonstrates precisely the process of reterritorialisation that has shaped South Korea's national narrative over the last twenty years. It examines the reasons why it was unable to deterritorialise at crucial moments, primarily because of the constraints placed on the population by a series of repressive military dictatorships. This film is a formal meditation on the movement-image that exposes its reterritorialising, linear workings in order to demonstrate how the national narrative is constructed cinematically. Its formal experimentation, then, mirrors its emphasis on institutional, physical constraints. Its narrative illustrates how the performance of individual identity is often no match for the institutions that contain this potentially deterritorialising activity, whilst its structure formally demonstrates this exact same phenomena.

As with the previous films it is worth acknowledging the cinematic context in which *Peppermint Candy* emerged. In certain respects it stands at the crossroads of recent South Korean cinema. Aesthetically it is very similar to several much discussed films of the 1980s and 1990s that are often grouped together as works of New Korean Cinema. Until very recently much of the academic writing in English on South Korean cinema tended to focus rather exclusively on films like *Mandala* (1981), *Black Republic* (1990), *Sopyonge* (1993) and *A Single Spark* (1995).[19] These films were often singled out as worthy of note because they were 'different' from much mainstream South Korean genre cinema. At the risk of somewhat oversimplifying the Western appreciation of South Korean cinema, previously it was the films most familiar to European categories of 'quality' cinema (art, *auteur*, period and social-realist films) that tended to garner the most critical interest. Since the late 1990s, however, things have begun to change somewhat, with the international success of a number of Korean films (especially those following a blockbuster model) rejuvenating critical interest in the diversity of genres that exist in South Korean cinema. However, in one of the most important books to appear on the topic, *The Remasculinization of Korean Cinema* (2004), Kyung Hyun Kim continues the previous trend by focusing precisely on the New Korean Cinema of the 1980s and 1990s, those films which stand in contrast to the genre cinema of the time.

Kim examines the use of masculinity in New Korean Cinema of the 1980s and 1990s, particularly its use as a filter through which much South Korean national identity was explored. Kim argues that

> the New Korean Cinema of the last two decades has incessantly pursued themes, characterizations and narratives that center on a particular notion of subjectivity: the image of an individual modern *man* desperate to free himself from institutional repression, familial responsibilities, and personal anxieties.[20]

New Korean Cinema expressed the psyche of a nation whose 'national traditional culture', especially its Confucian heritage, was disappearing due to the influence of global capitalism.[21] Thus, Kim notes, any number of films of the period followed traumatised, alienated or otherwise emasculated male characters symbolic of the population's lack of agency under successive military regimes.

Kim concludes this study with the emergence of the blockbusters *Shiri* (1999) and *Joint Security Area* (2000), products of a new era of filmmaking in South Korea that saw the end of the New Korean Cinema. As symptomatic of this shift, Kim notes that in *Shiri*, South Korean masculine agency is reestablished through the depiction of active South Korean agent Jong-won Yu (Suk-kyu Han), and specifically through 'the destruction and erasure of the North Korean Other that is embodied in the female'[22] agent Bang-hee Lee (Yoon-jin Kim). Within this scheme Kim posits *Peppermint Candy* as the culmination of the films of the New Korean Cinema movement that preceded it, arguing that, due to its examination of the preceding twenty years, *Peppermint Candy* 'drew the curtain on the period'.[23] This is true to a large degree. After all, Kim's argument – that Korean films since the late 1990s, have not focused on incapacitated males as cinema of the previous twenty years did – seems extremely valid. Kim's analysis of *Shiri* demonstrates this succinctly. Yet *Peppermint Candy* is actually a product of the new situation that has emerged in South Korea since the late 1990s, which has seen a huge explosion of film production. Is it entirely fair, then, to position it as the final act in the development of the New Korean Cinema of the 1980s and 1990s? In spite of its similarities to the predecessors that Kim identifies it actually resonates strongly with popular films of the late 1990s and 2000s. To ascertain exactly where this film stands it is worth examining its industrially liminal position in more detail.

In 1997, South Korea was hit by the Asian economic crisis (often referred to in parts of East Asia as the International Monetary Fund crisis). It was one of several so-called East Asian Tiger economies (along with Hong Kong, Singapore and Taiwan) that had previously been upheld as exemplars of market capitalism's apparent ability to both generate wealth and self-regulate. However, especially in South Korea, the crash illuminated an until then thinly veiled secret. In fact it was free market incentives, combined with a strong, centralised military power base, that helped regulate many of these economies. Moreover, this type of economic success was often achieved at the expense of sectors of the population, and with the tacit support of supposedly pro-democracy countries like the USA. For this reason South Korea has seen so many violent clashes between labour movements, student protestors, the police and the army, in the postwar era.

Like many of its Asian neighbours in the Pacific Rim, South Korea's currency sharply devalued because of the crash, and certain working practices were reconsidered.[24] Owing to the new economic situation that subsequently emerged, South Korean cinema is now resurgent. The *chaebols* (business conglomerates who had previously dominated the film industry) either streamlined production or withdrew from film production altogether leaving a vacuum that was soon filled by venture capital. This new money took advantage of a growing domestic market for South Korean cinema, as the devalued Won ensured that domestic films were, comparatively, far cheaper to distribute than Hollywood imports. These factors, along with the continued presence of the protectionist screen quota system – whereby cinemas in South Korea must show Korean films at least 40 per cent of the time[25] – and a shift in emphasis towards popular genre films with higher production values (many following the Hollywood blockbuster model), have ensured South Korean cinema's rejuvenated status in Asia since the late 1990s.

However, *Peppermint Candy*'s status in relation to this emergent situation is not unambiguous. Its finance came from UniKorea, a 'relatively young'[26] venture capital firm founded in 1999, making it a product of the new economic situation. Can it therefore be viewed as the final word on New Korean Cinema? Well, UniKorea is actually slightly unusual in that it is supportive of films that attempt to exist outside of mainstream genres. UniKorea's heritage is most clearly seen in the presence of its cofounder, actor Sung-keon Moon, who starred in such works of New Korean Cinema as *Black Republic* and *A Single Spark*. Moreover, as Kim's work on masculinity convincingly demonstrates, *Peppermint Candy* engages with the history of South Korea in the latter decades of the twentieth century in a similar way to films such as *Black Republic*. Indeed, its formal experimentation is similar to that of director Sang-su Hong (a director also discussed by Kim) whose work also avoids glossy attempts to approach mainstream audiences. For instance, his *The Virgin Stripped Bare by Her Bachelors* (2000) has a parallel universe narrative akin to *Run Lola Run*, whilst his *The Day a Pig Fell Into the Well* (1996) was well received in the West and is sometimes discussed, for instance by Han Ju Kwak,[27] as the inheritor of the tradition exemplified by *Black Republic* and *A Single Spark*.

Yet, in spite of all these factors that justify Kim's positioning of *Peppermint Candy* as an alternative to recent mainstream South Korean films, it also has certain similarities with many of its contemporaries that do aim at mainstream audiences. For instance, it explores national identity through a foregrounded allegorical exploration of national history. In this respect it actually has a lot in common with blockbusters like *2009: Lost Memories* (2002), a science-fiction film that examines South Korea's current national identity by speculating on the effect of a Japanese 'victory' in the Second World War. Indeed this examination of national identity through an exploration of national history and/or the legacy of partition, is prevalent in any number of South Korean films of the late 1990s and 2000s. Consider, for instance, thrillers like *Memories of Murder* (2003), blockbusters like *Shiri* and *Joint Security Area* and violent underworld films like *Oldboy* (2003). Admittedly it could be argued that a Western viewer could perceive that historical engagement is a trend in these films because it is precisely this type of film that gains distribution in Western markets, and therefore it is inaccurate to extrapolate this into a general trend in South Korean cinema. However, this is also true of films that are not so widely distributed in the West. This engagement with questions of history and national identity is evident, for instance, in the spate of romantic time travel melodramas that have emerged since the late 1990s.[28] It is especially clear in *Ditto* (2000), a film that, a little like *Frequency*, splits its narrative between 1979 and 2000 to uncover the continuities between the two periods in spite of the politically turbulent interim.

Thus, thematically at least, *Peppermint Candy* is not altogether different from these more popular films (*Shiri* and *Joint Security Area* are two of the biggest box office hits of South Korean cinema history)[29] as South Korean cinema continues to place the relative merits and limitations of Western categories of film genres and types in perspective, by mixing a discourse on politics usually associated with 'serious' cinema with popular genres. As Chris Berry notes, whilst adopting recognisable Western aesthetics such as the blockbuster model to appeal to global audiences, recent Korean films since the late 1990s have retained an interest in local, political issues.[30]

Moreover, the search for the 'modern *man*' that Kim defines still exists in recent popular Korean cinema. Kim also acknowledges its immediate reappearance, after *Shiri*, in *Joint Security Area*.[31] Alternatively, for instance, consider Dae-ho Yim (Kang-ho Song), protagonist of the popular wrestling comedy *The Foul King* (2000). He is a young man precisely like those Kim described in the New Korean Cinema of the 1980s and 1990s, as 'desperate to free himself from institutional repression, familial responsibilities, and personal anxieties'. It is not a straightforward matter, then, to say that *Peppermint Candy* draws the curtain on, or marks the end of, an era in South Korean cinema. Most obviously, the existence of UniKorea illustrates that the new industrial conditions have created a space for niche products such as *Peppermint Candy* to exist in, alongside the resurgent blockbuster and a host of other popular genres. The fact that its director, Chang-dong Lee stood as Korean Minister of Culture and Tourism from 2003 to 2004, suggests that this type of film still has a part to play in the international development of South Korean cinema.

Kim's stance on *Peppermint Candy* is perhaps a consequence of a certain bias, which recurs throughout the book, that 'meaningful' cinema is both socially reflective and cinematically reflexive, whilst genre cinema is dehistoricised by its market orientation.[32] For the purposes of this work it should be clear that my choice of *Peppermint Candy* for its formal distinctiveness is not a judgement on its supposedly superior worth as an art film. Rather, like *Eternal Sunshine*, I view it as a film that aims at a certain niche market. Admittedly, in this context it neither covets nor achieves quite the same crossover into the mainstream as the American independent film. On the other hand, it does use its unusual narrative form both to flag up its difference from the mainstream and to create a different type of viewing experience, a different appreciation of the construction of narrative and identity. Thus, like the other films discussed in this book, it offers another opportunity to examine the emergence of hybrid movement- and time-image films at times of historical transformation.

At this point a detailed plot synopsis is necessary. *Peppermint Candy* begins with the final episode in its linear narrative. It then jumps back in time to a preceding episode, plays it through to its completion, leaps back in time again and so on. In this respect it is different from *Memento*, which, as I showed in Chapter 4, utilises a classical flashback structure to order its jumbled narrative. Instead *Peppermint Candy* uses its unusual structure to chart the changing identity of protagonist Yong-ho Kim (Kyung-gu Sol) in reverse. Yong-ho is initially introduced to us as a belligerent, obnoxious and evidently disturbed middle-aged man. He arrives at a 'twenty-years on' riverside reunion picnic, of the Bongwoo Club (a factory worker's group formed in 1979), in spring 1999. After disrupting events for a brief while, Yong-ho commits suicide by standing in front of an approaching train. As he dies there is a freeze frame on his face. He screams, 'I am going back'. The next section then begins and we see Yong-ho, three days prior to his suicide, purchase a gun, attempt to shoot his ex-business partner and visit his ex-wife and daughter one last time. Yong-ho lives in a seedy shack, his business having failed, and he is obviously meant as a victim of the economic crisis of the late 1990s.

Yong-ho is visited by an unknown man, who reveals himself to be the husband of Sun-im Yun (So-ri Moon), Yong-ho's first love. Together they travel to visit Sun-im in hospital, where she lies in a critical state. On their way there, Sun-im's husband buys Yong-ho a new suit. The next flashback finds Yong-ho a successful businessman, enjoying the economic boom in the summer of 1994. However, his personal life is in crisis. He is spying on his wife as she has an affair, and pursuing an affair of his own. Whilst out with his mistress he bumps into a man whom he recognises and Yong-ho tells him that he quit the police two years previously. The next flashback is to spring 1987. Yong-ho arrests a suspect, one Myung-sik Park, who turns out to be the man from the restaurant in the previous sequence. Yong-ho and his colleagues torture him brutally until he gives up a student activist, Won-sik Kim, residing in Kunsan. On a stakeout in Kunsan, Yong-ho has a one-night stand with a young woman, but he is unable to meet her for breakfast as his colleagues insist they return to Seoul.

Next we see Yong-ho in autumn 1984, fresh out of military service, and newly recruited to the police. He unwillingly tortures his first ever victim, who defecates on his hands. Sun-im visits him, but Yong-ho deliberately upsets her by seducing the waitress in the local cafe. She is Hong-ja (Yeo-jin Kim), the woman who later becomes his wife. The penultimate episode takes place in May 1980. Yong-ho is in military service and Sun-im has travelled all the way from Seoul to visit him. Yong-ho's division is called into Kwangju to quell a civilian antigovernment uprising. Yong-ho is shot in the leg, and accidentally kills an innocent civilian woman (whom he initially mistakes for Sun-im).

Finally, we return to the original Bongwoo Club picnic, a gathering of idealistic young friends. Yong-ho, a shy and sensitive young man, talks to Sun-im. He describes a feeling of déjà vu, and she gives him a peppermint candy. Breaking off from the group, Yong-ho goes to the railway where, in twenty years time, he will commit suicide. A final freeze frame is employed on his face, as though he were experiencing a foretaste of his disastrous end.

Each episode is interspersed by a brief interlude of footage shot from the rear of a moving train. This is played backwards and accompanied by soft music. The interlude is used to show that the narrative is moving back in time, as we variously see cars and people moving backwards, and even at one point a bird flying in reverse. Significantly, the very first image of the film is shot from a train emerging from a tunnel into the light.

Most obviously, the main effect of this reverse structure is to render the initially unlikeable Yong-ho a tragic character. We are left with the image of an innocent, sensitive man, whom we know was then brutalised by the social order of South Korea over the previous two decades. The film's allegorical status is fairly evident throughout with Yong-ho representing a generation whose innocence was smashed by police and military brutality during the 1980s and 1990s. The changing identity of the protagonist is seen to directly mirror the changing identity of South Korea by focusing on the traumas he personally suffered at defining moments of national history. Although the historical events around which Yong-ho's episodic narrative is structured would be fairly well known to South Korean audiences it is briefly worth teasing out their significance for non-Korean nationals.

The film begins after the economic crash of the late 1990s. Yong-ho's suicide is a rather literal rendering of the national situation that then existed, as there were several instances of small businessmen killing themselves (and often their families as well) on finding themselves ruined after 1997. The episode that precedes this, set in 1994, illustrates South Korea's then booming economy through Yong-ho's successful small business venture. Yong-ho's transformation into an entrepreneur after he has left the police represents the country's gradual movement away from the authoritarian state that began with the first democratic presidential elections of 1987 and significantly altered after 1992, the year Yong-ho states that he left the police force. The episode set in 1994, then, illustrates the changing state of South Korea under its first civilian president, Young-sam

Kim, during a period when military and police control was gradually reduced.

Yong-ho's actions in Kunsan in April 1987 take place during the military/police crackdown on the pro-democracy movement that preceded the first election in June of the same year. At this election, due to an opposition split, Major General Doo-hwan Chun's hand-picked successor, Tae-woo Roh was elected president. Yong-ho's desire to meet the young woman who – for him at least – is a double of Sun-im, and his lack of enthusiasm for capturing Won-sik, both illustrates his growing desire to end his participation in the repressive regime and reflects the growing disillusionment expressed by the protestors.

Prior to this, in 1984, we see Yong-ho torture his first suspect, a man who was a worker from the same district as him. Thus, once again, through Yong-ho the population of South Korea is shown being divided by the military/police state. The torture sequence is primarily rendered through the facial contortions of Yong-ho, with the victim mostly obscured by the bottom of the frame. Thus, the 'unseen' brutality of the regime is shown to affect both those who were subjected to it and also those who participated in it. This is made obvious both when the suspect defecates on Yong-ho and, again, when Yong-ho, traumatised by the whole affair, is unable to connect with Sun-im as a consequence of his own feelings of lost innocence. As Sun-im compliments him on his 'sweet' hands (the only part of him that seem unchanged to her), Yong-ho, knowing his hands to be capable of killing and torture, uses them to seduce waitress Hong-ja, to deliberately disillusion Sun-im.

The pivotal moment of the film, the events in Kwangju in 1980, are infamous in South Korea. It was the biggest civilian massacre in modern-day South Korea. Official figures state that around 200 people died, with unofficial estimates suggesting around 2,000. This was the culmination of a series of events. In 1979 Major General Chung-hee Park (who had held power since a military coup in 1961) was assassinated. During the months that followed, Major General Doo-hwan Chun consolidated power. In 1980 he declared martial law, and abolished the National Assembly. Protestors took to the streets and in 1980 the Kwangju massacre occurred. In *Peppermint Candy* this event is played out through the nervous, wounded Yong-ho's accidental shooting of an innocent young woman, which again suggests that many of those who perpetrated the massacre were – like Yong-ho, on military service – as much victims of military oppression, or at least of institutionalised militarism, as were those who died.

Moreover, the incidents in Kwangju are used to reflect on the larger division that exists within Korea. During this sequence it is unclear where the bullet that strikes Yong-ho's leg comes from. Certainly none of the civilian protestors that we briefly see are carrying weapons and it may be that he is accidentally shot by one of his equally scared colleagues in arms. The injury he suffers (which, as I shall further explore in a moment, recurs at significant moments during the narrative) is seen to be a result of the country's divided nature. Not only of the division within South Korea at that time between the military and the civilian population but also the division between North and South Korea since the end of the civil war in 1953 that necessitated the maintenance of a standing army and the mandatory period of military service undertaken by Yong-ho. Rather than blaming the military *per se*, *Peppermint Candy* points to the institutionalisation of the population, especially into the military, as the reason for the massacre. This is most obviously seen in the image of soldiers' boots trampling on the peppermint candy (symbols of innocence and love) that Sun-im sent Yong-ho, and again in Yong-ho's identification of the young woman he accidentally shoots with Sun-im. In *Peppermint Candy* the recent history of the nation is rendered as a traumatic period during which individuals on both sides of the law were equally brutalised. To create this impression the violence perpetrated on the protestors by the South Korean army's special forces, especially the Special Warfare Command paratroopers, or 'black berets', is excluded from the frame. Instead, the film focuses on the participation of the regular army in the retaking of the city, on the bungled actions of equally scared people on either sides of the conflict.

Finally, the film leaves us in autumn 1979, around the time of the assassination of Major General Chung-hee Park. Highlighting the innocence and youth of Yong-ho, Sun-im and their friends illustrate that there was potential at that time for the country to have developed in a markedly different manner than it did. In the interim period between the assassination of Park and Chun's accession to power was the period now known as the 'Seoul Spring'. of which Donald Stone MacDonald notes:

> The mood of the 'Seoul Spring' interlude was one of anticipation of a return to civilian government . . . The democratic mood also fostered happenings that were anathema to south [sic] Korean conservatives, such as worker's strikes and demonstrations objecting to compulsory military service and police surveillance on campuses.[33]

The film uses Yong-ho's participation in the picnic of 1979, an image reminiscent of the Seoul Spring, to evoke a time when national identity could have developed in a very different direction. Therefore, by beginning the film with the reunion, *Peppermint Candy* notes the continued possibility of change in South Korea. After all, the Bongwoo Club still exists, in spite of Yong-ho's alienation from it and its more middle-aged satisfaction with material success and comfort. Their reunion or 'recurrence' at this point in history suggests that another moment for change exists in South Korea in 2000, just as it did in 1979.

However, this allegorical reading is obviously determined by the film, which chooses its moments of historical significance with great care. It is perhaps more important, then, to examine the added dimension that its formal structure provides. In particular, I will now examine the film's negotiation of the movement- and the time-image in its attempt to represent the opportunities that national identity had to change at each of these historical moments.

Writing on the effect of watching the reversed narrative film *Betrayal* (1983), Slavoj Žižek argues that although the final outcome of the story is always known to the viewer a greater sense of the possibility of change is suggested than when watching a conventional linear narrative. For Žižek 'it is precisely the reversal of the temporal order that makes us experience in an almost palpable way the utter contingency of the narrative sequence, i.e. the fact that, at every turning point things might have taken another direction'.[34] This is precisely the effect achieved by the narrative structure of *Peppermint Candy*, which shows each significant moment in the narrative of South Korean national identity as another moment of lost innocence for Yong-ho. Each episode shows a moment of potential change in both an individual's and a nation's narrative, and then shows its reterritorialisation. The reverse structure continually pauses to play out events that occurred at a fork in the labyrinth of time, only to demonstrate how all possible deterritorialisations were curtailed by the police state at these potential moments of national transformation.

Each moment of potential change is marked by a moment of temporary sensory-motor incapacity for Yong-ho. Despite the wound he sustained during the Kwangju uprising, for most of the film Yong-ho walks, runs, cycles and tortures without any difficulty. His limp recurs, then, for psychological reasons. Each such incident is closely connected to the possible deterritorialisation of identity (both for Yong-ho, and by extension, for South Korea) that is symbolically offered by Sun-im. Thus, at each such moment in the narrative the film suggests the possibility that a time-image could appear. Yong-ho's sensory-motor stutter reminds us that the possibility existed for the past (Yong-ho's youthful innocence) to reappear in the gap between perception and action, and thereby to break up the seemingly inevitable national narrative. By playing its movement-image narrative backwards, the film does indeed show the possibility of contingency that Žižek notes, but this contingency is the result of a fork appearing in the narrative of national identity. Although Kyung Hyun Kim discusses Yong-ho's limp in relation to other South Korean films that use such symbolism to express failing masculinity,[35] there is another way of viewing this physical disability when a Deleuzean methodology is employed.

The limp first appears as Yong-ho leaves Sun-im's hospital bedside towards the beginning of the film. As he walks downstairs his leg buckles, allowing Sun-im's husband to catch up with him and hand him the camera that Sun-im previously offered him as a gift. The camera represents his youthful desire to capture beauty, a doorway through time that, the belated return of this gift suggests, may still be open to Yong-ho. His youthful ideals are not lost to him, then, but become so once he decides to sell the camera immediately and use the money to buy a gun with which to shoot himself. By this time a product of the military state, Yong-ho chooses the 'wrong' direction through time. His limp suggests a moment of sensory-motor discontinuity, a point at which, his body slowed, the past attempts to appear in the interval between perception (and here it is no coincidence that the gift is a camera) and action, much as it did in *Vertigo*. However, Yong-ho 'limps along' to his inexorable death just as the country limps along in the route it has taken for the previous two decades.

The limp next recurs in 1987, on the eve of the first democratic election and just after Yong-ho's meeting with the young woman in Kunsan. As his colleagues attempt to catch Won-sik, Yong-ho is knocked over and his limp returns. Here the psychological association is much clearer as it is the act of policing a protestor that damages his sensory-motor continuity just as it was in Kwangju. Indeed, as Yong-ho is no help to his colleagues, it is as though his sensory-motor stillness is almost an unconscious attempt at aiding the escape of Won-sik.

Despite this, however, Yong-ho is again unable to take a different direction from his colleagues, to take advantage of this temporary aberration in his sensory-motor continuity. Although he wants to meet the anonymous girl for breakfast, he is quickly reterritorialised by the need for the policemen to return to Seoul with their suspect. As the girl is associated with Sun-im it is as though the events of Kwangju are being replayed, with Yong-ho's institutionalisation into the military (and now the police) and his subsequent deployment against the population once again destroying his ability to connect with his lover. This is again seen in the episode that takes place in 1980, when Sun-im visits the military base but is unable to gain access to see Yong-ho. Instead he is sent on manoeuvres, gets shot in the leg and kills the innocent girl. It also recurs when Sun-im visits Yong-ho in 1984, after the torture of his first victim. After breaking her heart, Yong-ho sees Sun-im to her train, and as he hands her back the camera he turns to leave – only to suddenly start limping again.

When Yong-ho is injured in Kwangju and has to rest in the railyard he initially perceives the innocent woman to be Sun-im. As he awaits the return of his comrades we see, from Yong-ho's point of view, a woman who is clearly Sun-im hiding in the shadows. When the girl reappears she is, of course, a totally different person. Into the interval created by his sensory-motor stillness, Sun-im, the past, reappears in the 'made-over' image of a woman from Yong-ho's past. However, in attempting to aid her in her escape from the returning soldiers, Yong-ho accidentally kills not only the innocent young woman but also that way back to his past.

It is understandable that Kim should consider Kwangju as a primal scene, identified by the film as the cause of the nation's present state.[36] Yet this is perhaps to miss the point of the film's final scene at the picnic in 1979. Here *Peppermint Candy* identifies not the cause of an historical trauma, but the moment of hope that preceded it. Therein lies its potential cure. Through the perpetually recurring Sun-im and the liberatory possibility that she offers Yong-ho to recapture his identity before its reterritorialisation in the military regime, the film questions the singular nature of the national narrative. It suggests that each historical episode should not be seen as just another chapter in an inevitably linear saga of repression but as a moment in which change was possible, only the repressive state apparatus was too powerful, and traumatised individuals like Yong-ho too powerless, to effect change. Thus in *Peppermint Candy*, national history appears as a series of layers in the Bergsonian cone of time.[37]

Like Guido in *8½*, *Peppermint Candy* searches through different layers of the national past for an image with which to match the present. In this respect, the film's discovery of potential recollection-images is interesting, particularly the ghost-like double of Sun-im that Yong-ho accidentally shoots, and the anonymous woman that he meets in Kunsan. Initially discussing Kunsan as the hometown of his first love, Yong-ho cynically seduces the anonymous woman with his well-practised line as dreamy romantic. However, after sex, when she asks him to call her Sun-im, and to tell her anything he likes, Yong-ho begins to break down and weep. His desire to meet her for breakfast the next morning, although unfulfilled due to the capture of Won-sik, again represents his desire to reconnect to the past through a recollection-image of Sun-im. Although he is unable to meet her, the film goes out of the way to show this incidental character waiting for him, as though to represent the continued possibility of such an encounter with the pre-Kwangju past. Here, unlike its counterpart in *Chaos*, the recollection-image of the made-over woman verges on becoming a crystal of time that captures the past and present in its virtual/actual oscillation. Unfortunately, Yong-ho is unable to use this moment in time productively to actualise a different future for himself. Instead, his return to Seoul reaffirms the linearity of the national narrative.

Indeed, when Sun-im visits policeman Yong-ho in 1984, their conversation about his hands illustrates once again the potential for change that still exists but which he is unable to grasp after Kwangju. In *8½, Saving Private Ryan, Memento, Too Many Ways* and *Chaos* a grasping, shaking, tattooed, fortune telling, or injured hand is used to illustrate a moment of indecision in the exercise of sensory-motor power, a moment of potential historical change. By contrast, Yong-ho's hands, praised as 'sweet' by Sun-im (but to his mind covered in the shit of his first torture victim), are used to seduce his future wife Hong-ja, rather than Sun-im. Once again, when offered a chance to change his life he was unable to due to his reterritorialisation within the police state. The return of Sun-im and the potential that she offers as crystalline representative of his part is spurned by Yong-ho.

The recollection-image on which the film does ultimately settle is that of Yong-ho's face, in freeze frame, as seen by the railway tracks in both 1979 and 1999. These images bracket the narrative and show how the virtual potential of the young Yong-ho was actualised into the brutal figure that he became as soldier and policeman. As they frame the flashback that is the film's narrative they confirm its linearity. Was the flashback structured in the conventional manner – beginning with Yong-ho's suicide, then returning to the picnic in 1979 before replaying events leading up to this initial image – then the film would be much more easily identified as a movement-image in the style of *Saving Private Ryan*. However, as the narrative plays backwards we are finally left with the image of the young idealistic Yong-ho. In this way *Peppermint Candy* attempts to show how the virtual potential offered by the crystal of time always coexists with its actual manifestation. Thus, although it begins with Yong-ho's suicide, it also points out that if he had managed to act differently at any of the turning points in his life this did not necessarily have to be the ending of his story. Here the appearance of a recollection-image is defamiliarised, and rather than creating an actual image that overlays the virtual past, it is deterritorialised. This time the actual present is stripped away to reveal the virtual past that it disguises in a manner that makes us reconsider how we feel about this present-day image of the nation.

Undeniably, *Peppermint Candy* demonstrates formally the power of the movement-image to reterritorialise the national narrative, just as it illustrates it through the story of Yong-ho. Yet it also evokes the deterritorialising power of the time-image and its potential to stutter this linear pathway through time. As a reverse narrative, the film foregrounds the potential for undermining the movement-image whilst simultaneously evoking the awesome power of the movement-image to reterritorialise this deterritorialising power. In fact, this Asian film puts Butler's early theoretical stance on performative identity into perspective. Through the actions of the institutionally brutalised Yong-ho we see the idea that the labyrinth of time can provide the possibility of a new identity as betraying a very European/North American perspective on the individual's power to effect their own destiny. As the repressive institutions that Yong-ho encounters in South Korea show, the individual is unlikely (even in large numbers) to be able to change national identity at a single moment in time. Rather, change is a culmination of a series of events (after all, South Korea is no longer a military dictatorship), but these events occur in these unique historical moments not as part of an inevitable, linear, evolutionary series.

As one final point in this respect it is worth briefly considering Yong-ho's appearance in the film with the similarly revealing character metamorphosis seen in *Memento*. When Yong-ho first appears his apparel suggests that he is a respectable and perhaps successful businessman. However, this image is almost immediately debunked as the following sequence shows Sun-im's husband buying him a suit in which to visit her in hospital. In *Memento*, Shelby's reverse transformation from white-collar to blue-collar worker with the murder of Jimmy Grants in the abandoned oil refinery deconstructed the shift from Fordist to post-Fordist wealth and the foreign policy on which it was based. For its part *Peppermint Candy* illustrates how the wealth of the Tiger economy that the besuited Yong-ho initially seems to represent, was actually based on the military repression that was administered (here, literally by Yong-ho) to the population. This parallel between the two films is extremely interesting when you consider that it was a typical piece of US gunboat diplomacy in Asia that effectively legitimised Chun's accession to power and the perpetrators of the Kwangju massacre. Two aircraft carriers were sent to Pusan in May 1980, not to support the civilian demonstrators but to ensure that no other foreign power (especially no foreign Communist power) intervened in the military crackdown. It is the same US foreign policy that is critiqued in both films.

Yet *Peppermint Candy* focuses on South Korea's history as something that occurred as a result of the Korean people's strengths and weaknesses rather than as a product of the actions of other countries. In this respect it is similar to its contemporary *Memories of Murder*. Here the police's recourse to America for vital forensic evidence to determine a serial killer's identity does not provide a satisfactory conclusion as to exactly who he was. At the point in the film when this inconclusive news from America arrives, the chief suspect is released from the clutches of a police officer who, with the best intentions, has resorted to brutal violence in the face of uncertainty over the killer's identity. The suspect disappears into a railway tunnel, symbolising that the killer's identity is lost forever to the past. The film's meditation on police brutality peaks here with the awkward question of whether tacit but ultimately inconclusive American support can 'excuse' the violence perpetrated by the South Korean state in the 1980s.

The correlation between this film and the use of the railway tunnel in *Peppermint Candy* is interesting. Both films use this image to suggest the past. In *Memories of Murder* this portal is a blank, a past in which guilt remains unknowable in line with its stance that the blame for these past events is a 'collective' one.[38] In *Peppermint Candy*, by contrast, the opening shot of the film takes us from the darkness of the tunnel into the light as we move backwards through time. Yet, in a manner similar to *Memories of Murder* we travel back in time to uncover a collective 'guilt' – that of the South Korean people subject to a repressive military state. The train, then, so often a symbol of progress and modernity, is here used to repeatedly question the cost of economic progress in South Korea.

The difference between *Peppermint Candy* and a film like *Memories of Murder* or *2009: Lost Memories*, is that it formally foregrounds its examination of both the historical and cinematic construction of national identity. In this respect it corresponds to Comolli and Narboni's category b, of films that operate against the 'prevailing ideology' in both their content and their form.[39] It is for this reason that it, like the other Asian films considered in this final chapter, is extremely interesting to view through a Deleuzean filter, even whilst the concerns of them all remain specific to their particular nations of origin.

Notes

1. Daya Bay is in the Guangdong Province, in the southern, Cantonese, area of China to the northeast of Hong Kong. When the Chinese began to build a nuclear power plant there the people of Hong Kong raised a million-signature petition opposing its construction. Construction went ahead anyway. Li Cheuk-To, 'The return of the father: Hong Kong new wave and Its Chinese context in the 1980s', in Nick Browne et al. (eds), *New Chinese Cinemas* (Cambridge: Cambridge University Press, 1994), pp. 160–79, pp. 174–5.
2. Julian Stringer, '"Your tender smiles give me strength": paradigms of masculinity in John Woo's *A Better Tomorrow* and *The Killer*', *Screen*, 38:1 (1997), pp. 25–41.
3. Tony Williams, 'Under "western eyes": the personal odyssey of Huang Fei-Hong in *Once Upon a Time in China*', *Cinema Journal*, 40:1 (2000), pp. 3–24.
4. Ackbar Abbas, *Hong Kong* (Minneapolis: Universtiy of Minnesota Press, 1997).

5. Nick Browne et al. (eds), *New Chinese Cinemas: Forms, Identities, Politics* (Cambridge: Cambridge University Press, 1994), Esther C. M. Yau (ed.), *At Full Speed: Hong Kong Cinema in a Borderless World* (Minneapolis: University of Minnesota Press, 2001) and Poshek Fu and David Desser (eds), *The Cinema of Hong Kong* (Cambridge: Cambridge University Press, 2000).
6. A brief note regarding names. To avoid confusion I have rendered all Asian names as first name followed by surname. Names of fictional characters have been rendered in the clearest way possible and usually as per the film. This means that at times I have used the first name, in order to avoid confusion elsewhere (for instance, between Saori Komiyama and Takaynki Komiyama in *Chaos*, or between Yong-ho Kim and Won-sik Kim, characters in *Peppermint Candy*, not to mention Kyung Hyun Kim the author, and Jeong-kwon Kim the director etc). The majority of names have been taken from either the film itself, or the *Internet Movie Database*.
7. David Bordwell, 'Film futures', *Substance: A Review of Theory and Literary Criticism*, Issue 97, 31:1 (2002), pp. 88–104, p. 93.
8. Ackbar Abbas, *Hong Kong*, pp. 1–15.
9. Sheldon H. Lu, 'Filming diaspora and identity: Hong Kong and 1997', in Poshek Fu and David Desser (eds), *The Cinema of Hong Kong* (Cambridge: Cambridge University Press, 2000), pp. 273–88, p. 275.
10. Ibid. p. 278.
11. Ibid. p. 276.
12. Yumiko Iida, *Rethinking Identity in Modern Japan* (New York: Routledge, 2002), p. 230.
13. Ibid. p. 229.
14. Tom Mes, *Agitator: The Cinema of Takashi Miike* (Guildford: FAB, 2003), pp. 181–91.
15. Barbara Creed, *The Monstrous Feminine* (London: Routledge, 2003).
16. Alvin Lu, 'Horror Japanese Style', *Film Comment*, 38: 1 (2002), p. 38.
17. For a more sustained analysis of this topic, see Jay McRoy, 'Introduction', in Jay McRoy (ed.), *Japanese Horror Cinema* (Edinburgh: Edinburgh University Press, 2005), pp. 3–4, and Tateishi, Ramie, 'The Japanese horror film series: *Ring* and *Eko Eko Azarak*', in Steven Jay Schneider (ed.), *Fear Without Frontiers* (Guildford: FAB Press, 2003), pp. 295–304.
18. Yumiko Iida, *Rethinking Identity in Modern Japan*, p. 227.
19. See for instance: Isolde Standish, 'Korean cinema and the new realism', in Wimal Dissanayake (ed.), *Colonialism and Nationalism in Asian Cinema* (Bloomington: Indiana University Press, 1994), pp. 65–89; Rob Wilson, 'Melodramas of Korean national identity: from *Mandala* to *Black Republic*', in Wimal Dissanayake (ed.), *Colonialism and Nationalism in Asian Cinema*, pp. 90–104; Tony Rayns, *Seoul Stirring* (London: Institute for Contemporary Art/Toshiba, 1994); Hyangjin Lee, *Contemporary Korean Cinema* (Manchester: Manchester University Press, 2000); Kyung Hyun Kim, 'Post-trauma and historical remembrance in recent South Korean cinema: reading

Park Kwang-su's *A Single Spark* (1995) and Chang Sŏn-u's *A Petal* (1996)', *Cinema Journal*, 41:4 (2002), pp. 95–115; Han Ju Kwak, 'Discourse on modernization in 1990s Korean cinema', in Jenny Kwok Wah Lau (ed.), *Multiple Modernities: Cinemas and Popular Media in Transcultural East Asia* (Philadelphia: Temple University Press, 2003), pp. 90–113; Eungjun Min, Jinsook Joo and Han Ju Kwak, *Korean Film* (Westport, CT: Praeger, 2003).

20. Kyung Hyun Kim, *The Remasculinization of Korean Cinema* (Durham: Duke University Press, 2004), p. x.
21. Ibid. p. x.
22. Ibid. p. 266.
23. Ibid. p. 22.
24. Ibid. p. 271.
25. Peter Harry Rist, 'Korean Cinema Now', *CineAction* 64 (2004), pp. 37–45, p. 43.
26. Anthony C.Y. Leong, *Korean Cinema: The New Hong Kong* (Victoria: Trafford Publishing, 2002), p. 14.
27. Han Ju Kwak, 'Discourse on modernization in 1990s Korean cinema', in Jenny Kwok Wah Lau (ed.), *Multiple Modernities*, pp. 90–113.
28. Anthony C.Y. Leong, *Korean Cinema*, pp. 117–54.
29. See Eungjun Min, Jinsook Joo and Han Ju Kwak, *Korean Film: History, Resistance and Democratic Imagination* (Westport, CT: Praeger, 2003), p. 171, and Chris Berry, '"What's big about the big film?": "de-Westernizing" the blockbuster in Korea and China', in Julian Stringer (ed.), *Movie Blockbusters* (London: Routledge, 2003), pp. 217–29, p. 224.
30. Chris Berry, '"What's big about the big film?"' p. 226.
31. Kyung Hyun Kim, *The Remasculinization of Korean Cinema*, p. 11.
32. Ibid. p. 274.
33. Donald Stone Macdonald, *The Koreans* (Oxford: Westview Press, 1996), p. 58.
34. Slavoj Žižek, *Looking Awry* (Cambridge, MA: The MIT Press, 1991), p. 70.
35. Kyung Hyun Kim, *The Remasculinization of Korean Cinema*, pp. 23–4.
36. Ibid. pp. 22–3.
37. Since the time of writing, Aaron Han Joon Magnar-Park has expressed a somewhat similar conclusion concerning the coexistence of the past with the present in *Peppermint Candy* albeit from a different theoretical direction. Aaron Han Joon Magnar-Park, '*Peppermint Candy*: The Will Not to Forget', in Chi-Yon Shin and Julian Stringer (eds), *New Korean Cinema*. (Edinburgh: Edinburgh University Press, 2005), pp. 159–69.
38. Tony Rayns, 'Suspicious minds', *Sight and Sound*, 14:9 (2004), pp. 18–20, p. 19.
39. Jean-Luc Comolli and Jean Narboni, 'Cinema/ideology/criticism', in Bill Nichols (ed.), *Movies and Methods* (Berkeley: University of California Press, [1969] 1976), pp. 22–30, p. 26.

Conclusion: *Blind Chance* and Possible Futures

The films discussed in this book are contemporary manifestations of a tradition that can be traced back to directors such as Hitchcock, Fellini, Godard, Rivette, Tarkovsky, Resnais et al., those same directors that Deleuze drew on in constructing his taxonomy of images. The appearance of a labyrinthine model of time in many of these films is particularly indebted to Alain Resnais' *oeuvre*, which includes such films as *L'année dernière a Marienbad* (1961), *Je t'aime je t'aime* (1968), *Providence* (1977) and *Smoking/No Smoking* (1993). Moreover, *Run Lola Run* and *Peppermint Candy* both self-consciously acknowledge their debt to Krzystof Kieslowski's *Blind Chance* (1981) as does *Sliding Doors* to his *Double Life of Veronique* (1991).

However, this study was never an attempt to construct an evolutionary time-line as though progressing from these predecessors to their contemporary 'offspring'. Rather, it was to show, through a specific focus on particular nations, the historical shifts and resulting transformations of national identity that these films negotiate. This book attempts to account for the widespread proliferation of this type of film across different national cinemas (to the point at which they can perhaps be considered an international genre in their own right) and to examine exactly how they have each deployed different aspects of the movement- and the time-image to negotiate recent transformations of national identity.

At first glance these films do seem to evidence, as Deleuze's work suggests, a general epistemic shift that occurred in the postwar era. However, on closer inspection it becomes clear that the manifestations of this genre that have emerged since the late 1990s and particularly those discussed in this book actually foreground, to a greater or lesser degree, the reterritorialisation of the time-image by the movement-image in the service of the construction or reconstruction of national identity. In many cases the shift in thinking that was formally demonstrated by the time-image has very quickly come to serve a more classical, linear view of history, existing often as a temporary other that is soon reterritorialised by the movement-image. In others it is used to expose, critique or deterritorialise this very process.

That this phenomenon also exists in various American and Asian films demonstrates the need for a more context specific analysis of these films than Deleuze undertook. Put simply, it is no longer enough to simply posit the time-image as the European other of the American movement-image. Rather, a global picture must be considered in which these films engage with issues of national identity for both local and international markets.

As a final example that illustrates the need for this localised analysis I will briefly discuss *Blind Chance*. Kieslowski's famous film replays the story of protagonist Witek Dlugosz (Boguslaw Linda) three times. It begins with a close-up on his mouth as he screams, 'No' (later referenced by both *Run Lola Run* and *Peppermint Candy*) at the moment his plane explodes in midair. We then flash back to his birth, and briefly recap his childhood and adolescence to the point where he is running to catch the Łódź Warsaw train. This becomes the starting point of each story, the fork in the labyrinth of time from which it deviates with each retelling. The first time he catches the train, joins the Communist party, is betrayed by them and finds himself trapped in Poland at the end. On the second occasion he misses the train, gets into a fight with the station guard, and, disillusioned with the party, joins the Catholic Youth Organisation instead. Unfortunately he is eventually ostracised by the Catholics and is again unable to leave Poland. In the third retelling he avoids all form of social commitment (political or religious) and instead finds happiness in professional and marital success. However, as Witek leaves on a plane for Paris, the story ends with the explosion with which it began. In short, in no story is there any escape from Communist Poland.

The contrast between this conclusion and that of *Run Lola Run* is striking. As I showed in Chapter 3, the order of the three retellings of Lola's run through Berlin creates a linear narrative structure in which an upbeat 'correct' ending (that emphasises the value of entrepreneurial activity in the new German global city) is contrasted with the two previous 'incorrect' versions of the same story. In *Blind Chance*, by contrast, a final 'correct' solution is entirely missing, expressing the inability of Kieslowski's film to find a viable national narrative. Thus, in a different set of historical circumstances to those of recently reunified Germany, the same formal structure yields a very different outcome.

Tadeusz Sobolewski argues of *Blind Chance* that the film illustrates the 'arbitrariness of every choice of world view'.[1] In a manner that also explains *Peppermint Candy*'s take on history it illustrates how the same person could turn out radically differently given a tiny variation in their path through life, showing that 'On the other side of the barricades are people just like us!'[2] *Blind Chance*, then, whilst formally demonstrating the search for national identity, is unable to offer a new political direction, either in the predetermined way that *Sliding Doors* or *Run Lola Run* do, or even in the undefined manner of *Too Many Ways*. Rather, it shows how all attempts to deterritorialise national identity are dead ends in Communist Poland. For this reason it is possible to see more similarities between *Blind Chance* and *Peppermint Candy* than between *Blind Chance* and *Run Lola Run* or between *Blind Chance* and *Too Many Ways*, despite the fact that the latter couplings contain the most obvious formal similarities. This is because of the more questioning negotiation of the role the state plays in constructing national identity that is evident in the first coupling.

As this conclusion illustrates, the approach that I have taken stands in contrast to the stance taken by a number of other writers: that films like *Blind Chance* and *Run Lola Run* express a manner of conceiving of the world most clearly seen in new media forms, especially the internet, computer games and MTV. This argument is typified by Ruth Perlmutter's article of 2002, 'Multiple Strands and Possible Worlds' and is simply a contemporary spin on Deleuze's notion that postwar European cinema expresses a new way of conceiving time.[3] As Paul Coates has noted it is not enough to consider *Run Lola Run*, as Slavoj Žižek does, as a more 'developed' version of *Blind Chance*,[4] or to see *Run Lola Run* as 'more adequate to the basic matrix of alternative spins of the narrative' whilst condemning *Blind Chance* as 'clumsy and artificial'.[5] Although this stance fits the hypothesis that these films express the same thinking as computer-game narratives or the labyrinthine passageways of the internet it fails to take into consideration the objections I have raised above. To reiterate, these films should not simply be considered solely in formal terms. Rather, the differences that exist between them can more usefully be uncovered when they are viewed in their national contexts. Žižek's argument in particular betrays a linear, evolutionary mind set that does not pay sufficient attention to the existence of these films within their own layers of national history.

In the interaction between such approaches I have tried to further the fusing of a Deleuzean-inspired analysis of narrative, form and time, with an historical understanding of the way these films negotiate national identity. In this way, theory is brought to bear on the historical context of these films, accommodating a consideration of their social and industrial construction and function. The emergence of several films from East Asia around the time of the economic crisis of 1997 would seem to confirm the validity of this approach over the more general context evoked by Deleuze and maintained by many who examine multiple narrative films.

Admittedly there is a great deal of scope for more work on this area. As more and more examples of such films emerge the situations negotiated by the particular examples of the late 1990s and early 2000s contained in this book continue to change. For instance, consider the difference between the French films *Épouse-moi* (2000) and the more recent *Irreversible* (2002) and *5×2* (2004). *Épouse-moi* has a triple narrative scheme similar to *Run Lola Run*, and like both Tykwer's film and *Sliding Doors*, it attempts to sell a rosy vision of life in a newly gentrified, extremely wealthy Paris. It is to *La Haine* (1995) what *Sliding Doors* is to *Nil By Mouth* (1997). *Irreversible* and *5×2*, however, are markedly different. They are both reverse-order narratives, like *Peppermint Candy* although without quite the same obviously allegorical examination of history. These films meditate on the teleological drive of narrative, and its conflation with the normative (or even compulsory) position afforded to heterosexuality by the classical narrative. *Irreversible* is a rape–revenge drama in which the genre's usual narrative motives are questioned, rather as they are in *Memento*, by the backwards revelation of motivation and cause to events already witnessed. The fact that the rape is mistakenly avenged is the film's rather horrible conclusion. For its part, *5×2* questions the romance genre in a similar way, by beginning with a divorce and anal rape (*Irreversible*'s most disturbing sequence is also an anal rape) and then playing backwards to the first meeting of the couple. It is as though these films are noting the implausibility (or perhaps, impossibility) of a conventional, happy ending in contemporary French art cinema. Both films also meditate on the construction of contemporary French national identity, specifically in relation to class difference. As Leighton Grist suggests, their probing narrative structures mirror the recent national self-examination that arose over the Jean-Marie Le Pen presidential poll outcry in 2002.[6] However, constraints of space and time leave a full discussion of these films beyond the scope of this work.

There are any number of films that can be examined in this way. A comprehensive list would include at least the following: *Blind Chance*, *Betrayal*, *Groundhog Day*, *Smoking/No Smoking*, *Before the Rain*, *Too Many Ways*, *Lost Highway* (1997), *Sliding Doors*, *Run Lola Run*, *Me Myself I* (1999), *Calla* (1999), *Being John Malkovich*, *Chaos*, *The Virgin Stripped Bare by Her Bachelors*, *Épouse-moi*, *Possible Worlds* (2000), *Memento*, *Peppermint Candy*, *Family Man*, *The Cell*, *Vanilla Sky*, *Mulholland Drive* (2001), *Bungee Jumping of their Own* (2001), *Irreversible*, *Ditto*, *2009: Lost Memories*, *The I Inside* (2003), *21 Grams*, *Elephant*, *Gothika*, *Identity*, *5×2*, *Eternal Sunshine of the Spotless Mind*, *Trauma* (2004), *Melinda and Melinda* (2004), *The Jacket* and a host of others which I have no doubt neglected to mention. As I have shown, using Deleuze's taxonomy of images enables us to approach these films through their formal similarities, providing a consideration of the interplay between movement- and time-image that occurs in these films. At the same time it facilitates a greater understanding of exactly how they are negotiating recent transformations of national identity.

That is not to say, of course, that this work provides the only approach that it is possible to take to these films. Nor indeed, is it the only way to deploy Deleuze's theories. Emma Wilson, for instance, in her book on Kieslowski's French cinema, *Memory and Survival* (2000) uses Deleuze's work on the time-image to show how Kieslowski's later works 'disrupt the easy mapping of his cinema into separate time bands and national boundaries'.[7] Further exploration may well suggest that not all films with a manipulated narrative structure are as involved with questions of national identity as those that I have examined clearly are. This is the case even if Wilson's work is tacitly framed by the question of the nation and precisely how it is renegotiated by Kieslowski's later films.

Similarly, my focus on narrative structure leads me to draw conclusions that a different approach – especially one that examines images for their iconic or figural significance – may dispute. After all, the narrative/spectacle debate is unlikely to be resolved by any one book! Even so, the point I have made in this work remains valid. Using Deleuze's philosophy to examine recent films that self-consciously manipulate narrative time adds another dimension to our understanding of the way national identity is constructed in cinema.

Notes

1. Tadeusz Sobolewski, 'Ultimate concerns', in Paul Coates (ed.), *Lucid Dreams: The Films of Krzystof Kieslowski* (London: Flick Books, 1999), pp. 19–31, p. 22.
2. Ibid.
3. Ruth Perlmutter, 'Multiple strands and possible worlds', *The Canadian Journal of Film Studies*, 11:2 (2002), pp. 44–61.
4. Paul Coates makes this point in an as yet unpublished conference paper, Paul Coates, 'Just gaming: Kieslowski's *Blind Chance*, Tykwer's *Run Lola Run* and a note on *Heaven*', delivered at the Society for Cinema and Media Studies Conference, 31 March –3 April 2005. This is scheduled to appear in Stephen Woodward (ed.), *After Kieslowski: The Legacy of Krysztof Kieslowski* (Detroit: Wayne State University Press, forthcoming).
5. Slavoj Žižek, *The Fright of Real Tears: Krzystof Kieslowski between Theory and Post-Theory* (London: BFI, 2001), p. 82.
6. The link between *Irreversible*'s narrative structure and political events in

France was discussed in a conference panel on *Irreversible* at the University of Amsterdam. Of particular relevance was Leighton Grist's paper '*Irreversible*: essentialism, ideology, politics', in, Leighton Grist, Shaun Kimber, Laura Hubner and Paul Carter, '*Irreversible*', at *Cinema in Europe: Networks in Progress*, University of Amsterdam, 22 – 26 June 2005.

7. Emma Wilson, *Memory and Survival: The French Cinema of Krzystof Kieslowski* (Oxford: Legenda, 2000), p. 3.

Select Bibliography

Books

Abbas, Ackbar (1997), *Hong Kong: Culture and the Politics of Disappearance*, Minneapolis: University of Minnesota Press.

Anderson, Benedict (1983), *Imagined Communities: Reflections on the Origin and Spread of Nationalism*, London: Verso.

Ansell Pearson, Keith (1999), *Germinal Life: The Difference and Repetition of Deleuze*, London: Routledge.

Ashby, Justine and Andrew Higson (eds) (2000), *British Cinema Past and Present*, London: Routledge.

Bennis, Phyllis and Michel Moushabeck (eds) (1992), *Beyond the Storm: A Gulf Crisis Reader*, Edinburgh: Canongate.

Bergson, Henri [1896] (1991), *Matter and Memory*, New York: Zone Books.

Bergson, Henri [1911] (1998), *Creative Evolution*, New York: Dover Publications Inc.

Bergson, Henri [1921] (1999), *Duration and Simultaneity*, Manchester Clinamen Press.

Bhabha, Homi K. (ed.) (1990), *Nation and Narration*, London: Routledge.

Bhabha, Homi K. (1994), *The Location of Culture*, London: Routledge.

Billig, Michael (1995), *Banal Nationalism*, London: Sage.

Bogue, Ronald (1989), *Deleuze and Guattari*, London: Routledge.

Böhm, Steffen, Campbell Jones, Chris Land and Mat Paterson (eds) (2006), *Against Automobility*, Oxford: Blackwell.

Bondanella, Peter (ed.) (1978), *Federico Fellini: Essays in Criticism*, Oxford: Oxford University Press.

Bondanella, Peter (1983), *Italian Cinema: From Neorealism to the Present*, New York: Frederick Ungar Publishing Co.

Bondanella, Peter (1992), *The Cinema of Federico Fellini*, New Jersey: Princeton University Press.

Bordwell, David and Nöel Carroll (eds) (1996), *Post Theory*, Wisconsin: University of Wisconsin Press.

Borges, Jorge Luis (1964), *Labyrinths*, London: Penguin.

Brill, Lesley (1988), *The Hitchcock Romance*, New Jersey: Princeton University Press.

Browne, Nick, Paul G. Pickowicz, Vivian Sobchack and Esther Yau (eds) (1994),

New Chinese Cinemas: Forms, Identities, Politics, Cambridge: Cambridge University Press.

Brunsdon, Charlotte (1997), *Screen Tastes*, London: Routledge.

Bruzzi, Stella (1997), *Undressing Cinema*, London: Routledge.

Buchanan, Ian (ed.) (1999), *A Deleuzean Century?* Durham: Duke University Press.

Buchanan, Ian and Claire Colebrook (eds) (2000), *Deleuze and Feminist Theory*, Edinburgh: Edinburgh University Press.

Burgoyne, Robert (1997), *Film Nation: Hollywood Looks at U.S. History*, Minneapolis: University of Minnesota Press.

Butler, Alison (2002), *Women's Cinema*, London: Wallflower.

Butler, Judith (1990), *Gender Trouble: Feminism and the Subversion of Identity*, London: Routledge.

Cameron, Keith (ed.) (1999), *National Identity*, Exeter: Intellect.

Carroll, Nöel (1998), *Interpreting the Moving Image*, Cambridge: Cambridge University Press.

Certeau, Michel de (1984), *The Practice of Everyday Life*, Los Angeles: University of California Press.

Chomsky, Noam (2001), *9–11*, New York: Seven Stories Press.

Corrigan, Timothy (1991), *A Cinema Without Walls*, London: Routledge.

Creed, Barbara (2003), *The Monstrous Feminine*, London: Routledge.

Cubitt, Sean (2004), *The Cinema Effect*, Cambridge, MA: The MIT Press.

Davies, Philip John and Paul Wells (eds) (2002), *American Film and Politics from Reagan to Bush Jr*, Manchester: Manchester University Press.

Deleuze, Gilles [1964] (1972), *Proust and Signs*, New York: George Baziller.

Deleuze, Gilles [1962] (1983), *Nietzsche and Philosophy*, London: The Athlone Press.

Deleuze, Gilles [1963] (1984), *Kant's Critical Philosophy: The Doctrine of the Faculties*, London: The Athlone Press.

Deleuze, Gilles [1983] (1986), *Cinema 1: The Movement-Image*, London: The Athlone Press.

Deleuze, Gilles [1986] (1988), *Foucault*, London: The Athlone Press.

Deleuze, Gilles [1967] (1989), *Masochism: A Study in Coldness and Cruelty*, New York: Zone Books.

Deleuze, Gilles [1985] (1989), *Cinema 2: The Time-Image*, London: The Athlone Press.

Deleuze, Gilles [1969] (1990), *The Logic of Sense*, London: The Athlone Press.

Deleuze, Gilles (1990), *Negotiations*, New York: Columbia University Press.

Deleuze, Gilles [1966] (1991), *Bergsonism*, New York: Zone Books.

Deleuze, Gilles [1988] (1993), *The Fold: Leibniz and the Baroque*, London: The Athlone Press.

Deleuze, Gilles [1968] (1997), *Difference and Repetition*, London: The Athlone Press.

Deleuze, Gilles and Félix Guattari [1972] (1983), *Anti-Oedipus*, Minneapolis: University of Minnesota Press.

Deleuze, Gilles and Félix Guattari [1975] (1986), *Kafka: Towards a Minor Literature*, Minneapolis: University of Minnesota Press.

Deleuze, Gilles and Félix Guattari [1980] (1987), *A Thousand Plateaus: Capitalism and Schizophrenia*, London: The Athlone Press.

Deleuze, Gilles and Félix Guattari [1991] (1994), *What is Philosophy*, London: Verso.

Deleuze, Gilles and Claire Parnet [1977] (1987), *Dialogues*, London: The Athlone Press.

Deutsch, David (1997), *The Fabric of Reality*, London: Allen Lane.

Dijkink, Gertjan (1996), *National Identity and Geopolitical Visions*, London: Routledge.

Dissanayake, Wimal (ed.) (1994), *Colonialism and Nationalism in Asian Cinema*, Bloomington: Indiana University Press.

Dixon, Wheeler Winston (2003), *Visions of the Apocalypse*, London: Wallflower.

Doherty, Thomas (1999), *Projections of War: Hollywood, American Culture and World War II*, New York: Columbia University Press.

Dyer, Richard (1997), *White*, London: Routledge.

Dyer, Richard and Ginette Vincendeau (eds) (1992), *Popular European Cinema*, London: Routledge.

Eleftheriotis, Dimitris (2001), *Popular Cinema of Europe: Studies of Texts, Contexts and Frameworks*, New York: Continuum.

Engelhardt, Tom (1995), *The End of Victory Culture*, New York: Basic Books.

Flaxman, Gregory (ed.) (2000), *The Brain is the Screen: Deleuze and the Philosophy of Cinema*, Minneapolis: University of Minnesota Press.

Foucault, Michel [1966] (1970), *The Order of Things*, New York: Pantheon Books.

Foucault, Michel (1976), *The History of Sexuality Volume I*, London: Penguin.

Foucault, Michel [1975] (1977), *Discipline and Punish*, London: Penguin.

Foucault, Michel (1984), *The History of Sexuality Volume II*, London: Penguin.

Foucault, Michel (1984), *The History of Sexuality Volume III*, London: Penguin.

French, Sean (1996), *The Terminator*, London: British Film Institute.

Fu, Poshek and David Desser (eds) (2000), *The Cinema of Hong Kong*, Cambridge: Cambridge University Press.

Gardiner, Michael (2004), *The Cultural Roots of British Devolution*, Edinburgh: Edinburgh University Press.

Glover, Carol J. (1992), *Men, Women and Chain Saws*, London: British Film Institute.

Goodchild, Philip (1996), *Gilles Deleuze and the Question of Philosophy*, Madison: Fairleigh Dickinson University Press.

Grainge, Paul (ed.) (2003), *Memory and Popular Film*, Manchester: Manchester University Press.

Harvey, David (1990), *The Condition of Postmodernity*, Oxford: Blackwell.

Higson, Andrew (1995), *Waving the Flag: Constructing a National Cinema in Britain*, Oxford: Clarendon Press.

Hillier, Jim (ed.) (2001), *American Independent Cinema*, London: British Film Institute.

Holmlund, Chris and Justin Wyatt (eds) (2003), *Contemporary American Independent Film*, London: Routledge.

Iida, Yumiko (2002), *Rethinking Identity in Modern Japan*, New York: Routledge.

Insdorf, Annette (1999), *Double Lives, Second Chances: The Cinema of Krzystof Kieslowski*, New York: Miramax Books.

Jäckel, Anne (2003), *European Film Industries*, London: British Film Institute.

Kean, Thomas H., Lee H. Hamilton, Richard Ben-Veniste, Bob Kerrey, Fred F. Fielding, John F. Lehman, Jamie S. Gorelick, Timothy J. Roemer, Slade Gorton and James R. Thompson (2004), *The 9/11 Commission Report*, New York: W.W. Norton.

Kellner, Douglas (1992), *The Persian Gulf TV War*, Boulder: Westview Press.

Kellner, Douglas (2001), *Grand Theft 2000*, New York: Rowman and Littlefield.

Kellner, Douglas (2003), *From 9/11 to Terror War; The Dangers of the Bush Legacy*, New York: Rowman & Littlefield.

Kennedy, Barbara (2000), *Deleuze and Cinema: The Aesthetics of Sensation*, Edinburgh: Edinburgh University Press.

Kim, Kyung Hyun (2004), *The Remasculinization of Korean Cinema*, Durham: Duke University Press.

King, Anthony D. (1990), *Global Cities: Post-Imperialism and the Internationalization of London*, London: Routledge.

King, Geoff (2005), *American Independent Cinema*, London: I.B. Taurus.

Landy, Marcia (2000), *Italian Film*, Cambridge: Cambridge University Press.

Landy, Marcia (ed.) (2001), *The Historical Film*, London: The Athlone Press.

Landy, Marcia (1996), *Cinematic Uses of the Past*, Minneapolis: University of Minnesota Press.

Lee, Hyangjin (2000), *Contemporary Korean Cinema*, Manchester: Manchester University Press.

Leong, Anthony C. Y. (2002), *Korean Cinema: The New Hong Kong*, Victoria: Trafford Publishing.

Levy, Emanuel (1999), *Cinema of Outsiders*, New York: New York University Press.

Lewis, Jon (ed.) (1998), *The New American Cinema*, Durham: Duke University Press.

Lewis, Jon (ed.) (2001), *The End of Cinema as we Know It: American Film in the Nineties*, London: Pluto Press.

Liehm, Mira (1984), *Passion and Defiance*, Berkeley: University of California Press.

Lyotard, François [1979] (1984), *The Postmodern Condition*, Manchester: Manchester University Press.

Macdonald, Donald Stone (1996), *The Koreans: Contemporary Politics and Society*, Oxford: Westview Press.

MacKenzie, Scott and Mette Hjort (eds) (2000), *Cinema and Nation*, London: Routledge.

Marks, Laura U. (2000), *The Skin of the Film: Intercultural Cinema, Embodiment and the Senses*, Durham: Duke University Press.
Marshall, Bill (2001), *Quebec National Cinema*, Montreal: McGill-Queen's University Press.
Marshall, Ian and Danah Zohar (1997), *Who's Afraid of Schrödinger's Cat?*, London: Bloomsbury.
Massumi, Brian (1992), *A User's Guide to Capitalism and Schizophrenia*, Cambridge: The MIT Press.
McRoy, Jay (ed.) (2005), *Japanese Horror Cinema*, Edinburgh: Edinburgh University Press.
Mendik, Xavier and Steven Jay Schneider (2002), *Underground U.S.A.*, London: Wallflower.
Mercer, Kobena (1994), *Welcome to the Jungle*, London: Routledge.
Merrick, Greg (2000), *Celluloid Mavericks: The History of American Independent Film*, New York: Thunder Mouth Press.
Mes, Tom (2003), *Agitator: The Cinema of Takashi Miike*, Guildford: FAB.
Min, Eungjun, Jinsook Joo and Han Ju Kwak (2003), *Korean Film*, Westport, CT: Praeger.
Mottram, James (2002), *The Making of Memento*, London: Faber & Faber.
Mullarkey, John (1999), *Bergson and Philosophy*, Notre Dame: University of Notre Dame Press.
Mullarkey, John (ed.) (1999), *The New Bergson*, Manchester: Manchester University Press.
Murphy, Robert (ed.) (2000), *British Cinema in the 90s*, London: British Film Institute.
Nairn, Tom (2000), *After Britain*, London: Granta Books.
Neale, Steve (2000), *Genre and Hollywood*, London: Routledge.
Neale, Steve (ed.) (2002), *Genre and Contemporary Hollywood*, London: British Film Institute.
Neale, Steve and Murray Smith (eds) (1998), *Contemporary Hollywood Cinema*, London: Routledge.
Nietzsche, Friedrich [1888] (1968), *Twilight of the Idols/The Anti-Christ*, London: Penguin.
Nietzsche, Friedrich [1885] (1969), *Thus Spoke Zarathustra*, London: Penguin.
Nietzsche, Friedrich [1886] (1973), *Beyond Good and Evil*, London: Penguin.
Nietzsche, Friedrich, [1888] (1979), *Ecce Homo*, London: Penguin.
Nowell Smith, Geoffrey (ed.) (1998), *Hollywood and Europe*, London: British Film Institute.
Olkowski, Dorothea (1999), *Gilles Deleuze and the Ruin of Representation*, Berkeley: University of California Press.
Penley, Constance (1989), *The Future of an Illusion*, London: Routledge.
Pidduck, Julianne (2004), *Contemporary Costume Film*, London: British Film Institute.

Pisters, Patricia (ed.) (2001), *Micropolitics of Media Culture*, Amsterdam: Amsterdam University Press.
Pisters, Patricia (2003), *The Matrix of Visual Culture: Working With Deleuze in Film Theory*, California: Stanford University Press.
Powell, Anna (2004), *Deleuze and Horror Film*, Edinburgh: Edinburgh University Press.
Prigognine, Ilya and Isabelle Stengers (1984), *Order out of Chaos*, London: Heinemann.
Rayns, Tony (1994), *Seoul Stirring*, London: Institute for Contemporary Art/Toshiba.
Rodowick, David (1991), *The Difficulty of Difference*, New York: London.
Rodowick, David (1997), *Gilles Deleuze's Time Machine*, Durham and London: Duke University Press.
Rodowick, David (2001), *Reading the Figural, Or, Philosophy after the New Media*, Durham and London: Duke University Press.
Rogin, Michael Paul (1987), *Ronald Reagan, The Movie*, Berkeley: University of California Press.
Russo, Vito (1985), *The Celluloid Closet*, New York: Harper & Row.
Ryan, Michael and Douglas Kellner (1988), *Camera Politica*, Bloomington: Indiana University Press.
Salecl, Renata (2004), *On Anxiety*, London: Routledge.
Sardar, Ziauddin and Merryl Wyn Davies (2004), *American Dream Global Nightmare*, London: Icon Books.
Sassen, Saskia (1991), *The Global City: New York, London, Tokyo*, Princeton: Princeton University Press.
Sassen, Saskia (1994), *Cities in a World Economy*, London: Pine Forge Press.
Schrift, Alan (1995), *Nietzsche's French Legacy*, London: Routledge.
Shaviro, Steven (1993), *The Cinematic Body*, Minneapolis: University of Minnesota Press.
Shin, Chi-Yun and Julian Stringer (eds) (2005), *New Korean Cinema*, Edinburgh: Edinburgh University Press.
Silverman, Kaja (1992), *Male Subjectivity at the Margins*, London: Routledge.
Smith, Anthony D. (1991), *National Identity*, London: Penguin.
Sokal, Alan and Jean Bricmont (1988), *Intellectual Impostures*, London: Profile.
Sorlin, Pierre (1980), *The Film in History*, Oxford: Basil Blackwell.
Sorlin, Pierre (1996), *Italian National Cinema 1896–1996*, London: Routledge.
Sterrit, David (1993), *The Films of Alfred Hitchcock*, Cambridge: Cambridge University Press.
Stewart, Ian (1989), *Does God Play Dice?*, London: Penguin.
Thrift, Nigel and Peter Williams (eds) (1987), *Class and Space*, London: Macmillan.
Truffaut, François (1983), *Hitchcock*, New York: Simon & Schuster.
Turim, Maureen (1989), *Flashbacks in Film*, London: Routledge.

Wilson, Emma (2000), *Memory and Survival: The French Cinema of Krzystof Kieslowski*, Oxford: Legenda.
Wilson, Rob and Wimal Dissanayake (eds) (1996), *Global/Local*, Durham: Duke University Press.
Wood, Robin (1989), *Hitchcock's Films Revisited*, London: Faber & Faber.
Yau, Esther C. M. (ed.) (2001), *At Full Speed: Hong Kong Cinema in a Borderless World*, Minneapolis: University of Minnesota Press.
Žižek, Slavoj (1991), *Looking Awry*, Cambridge, MA: The MIT Press.
Žižek, Slavoj (2001), *The Fright of Real Tears: Krzystof Kieslowski between Theory and Post-Theory*, London: British Film Institute.

Articles/Book Chapters

Auster, Albert (2002), '*Saving Private Ryan* and American triumphalism', *Journal of Popular Film and Television*, 30: 2, pp. 98–104.
Berry, Chris (2003), '"What's big about the big film?": "de-westernizing" the blockbuster in Korea and China', in Julian Stringer (ed.), *Movie Blockbusters*, London: Routledge, pp. 217–29.
Bordwell, David (2002), 'Film futures', *Substance: A Review of Theory and Literary Criticism*, Issue 97, 31:1, pp. 88–104.
Bordwell, David (1979), 'Art cinema as mode of film practice', *Film Criticism*, 4:1, pp. 56–64.
Brunsdon, Charlotte (2001), 'London films: from private gardens to utopian moments', *Cineaste*, 26: 4, pp. 43–6.
Butler, Judith (1991), 'Imitation and gender insubordination', in Diana Fuss (ed.), *Inside/Out: Lesbian Theories, Gay Theories*, New York: Routledge, pp. 13–31.
Castonguay, James (2004), 'Conglomeration, new media, and the cultural production of the "War on Terror"', *Cinema Journal*, 43:4, pp. 102–8.
Comolli, Jean-Luc and Jean Narboni [1969] (1976), 'Cinema/ideology/criticism', in Bill Nichols (ed.), *Movies and Methods*, Berkeley: University of California Press, pp. 22–30.
Corber, Robert J. (1999), '"You wanna check my thumbprints?": *Vertigo*, the trope of invisibility and cold war nationalism', in Richard Allen (ed.), *Alfred Hitchcock: Centenary Essays*, London: British Film Institute, pp. 301–14.
Dark, Chris (2000), 'Mr Memory', *Sight and Sound*, 10:11, pp. 24–6.
Davies, Jude (1995), 'Gender, ethnicity and cultural crisis in *Falling Down* and *Groundhog Day*', *Screen*, 36:3, pp. 214–32.
Foucault, Michel (1979), 'The lives of infamous men', in Meaghan Morris and Paul Patton (eds), *Michel Foucault*, Sydney: Feral Publications.
Fukuyama, Francis (1989), 'The end of history?', *The National Issue*, Summer Issue, pp. 3–18.
Garwood, Ian (2002), 'The autorenfilm in contemporary German cinema', in Tim Bergfelder, Erica Carter and Deniz Gö (eds), *The German Cinema Book*, London: British Film Institute, pp. 202–10.

Geraghty, Christine (2002), 'Crossing over: performing as a lady and a dame', *Screen*, 43:1, pp. 41–56.

Goodridge, Mike (2003), 'Paradigm shifts for indies at Cannes', *Screen International*, 1404 (2003), p. 1.

Haase, Christine (2003), 'You can run, but you can't hide: transcultural filmmaking in *Run Lola Run*', in Randall Halle and Margaret McCarthy (eds), *Light Motives: German Popular Film in Perspective*, Detroit: Wayne State University Press, pp. 395–415.

Hammond, Michael (2002), 'Some smothering dreams', in Steve Neale (ed.), *Genre and Contemporary Hollywood*, London: British Film Institute, pp. 62–76.

Hodgkins, John (2002), 'In the wake of Desert Storm', *Journal of Popular Film and Television*, 30:2, pp. 74–84.

Hutton, Patrick H. (1988), 'Foucault, Freud, and the technologies of the self', in Luther H. Martin, Huck Gutman and Patrick H. Hutton (eds), *Technologies of the Self: A Seminar with Michel Foucault*, Amherst: University of Massachusetts Press, pp. 121–44.

James, Nick (2004), 'I forgot to remember to forget', *Sight and Sound*, 14:5 (2004), pp. 14–8.

Jancovich, Mark (1992), 'Modernity as subjectivity in *The Terminator*', *The Velvet Light Trap*, Issue 30, pp. 3–17.

Jeffords, Susan (1993), 'Can masculinity be terminated?', in Steven Cohan and Ina Rae Hark (eds), *Screening the Male*, London: Routledge, pp. 245–62.

Jeffords, Susan (1993), 'The big switch: Hollywood masculinity in the nineties', in Jim Collins, Hilary Radner and Ava Preacher Collins (eds), *Film Theory Goes to the Movies*, London: Routledge, 1993, pp. 196–208.

Kellner, Douglas (1991), 'Film, politics, and ideology: reflections on Hollywood film in the age of reason', *The Velvet Light Trap*, no. 27, pp. 9–24.

Kim, Kyung Hyun (2002), 'Post-trauma and historical remembrance in recent South Korean cinema: reading park Kwang-su's *A Single Spark* (1995) and Chang Sŏn-u's *A Petal* (1996)', *Cinema Journal*, 41:4, pp. 95–115;

Krutnik, Frank (1997), 'Something more than night', in David B. Clarke (ed.), *The Cinematic City*, London: Routledge, pp. 83–109.

Kwak, Han Ju (2003), 'Discourse on modernization in 1990s Korean cinema', in Jenny Kwok Wah Lau (ed.), *Multiple Modernities: Cinemas and Popular Media in Transcultural East Asia*, Philadelphia: Temple University Press, pp. 90–113.

Li, Cheuk-To (1994), 'The return of the father: Hong Kong new wave and its Chinese context in the 1980s', in Nick Browne, Paul G. Pickowicz, Vivian Sobchack and Esther Yau (eds), *New Chinese Cinemas*, Cambridge: Cambridge University Press, pp. 160–79.

Lu, Alvin (2002), 'Horror Japanese style', *Film Comment*, 38: 1, p. 38.

Magnan-Park, Aaron Hanjoon (2005), '*Peppermint Candy*: The Will Not to Forget', in Chi-Yun Shin and Jalian Stringer (eds), *New Korean Cinema*, Edinburgh: Edinburgh University Press.

Martin-Jones, David (2002), 'Laura U. Marks, *The Skin of the Film*', *Screen*, 43:4, pp. 442–6.

Martin-Jones, David (2004), '*Orphans*, a work of minor cinema from post-devolutionary Scotland', *Journal of British Cinema and Television*, 1:2, pp. 226–41.

Martin-Jones, David (2006), 'No literal connection: images of mass commodification, US militarism, and the oil industry, in *The Big Lebowski*', in Steffen Böhm, Campbell Jones, Chris Land and Mat Paterson (eds), *Against Automobility*, Oxford: Blackwell.

Mellencamp, Patricia (1990), 'TV time and catastrophe, or *Beyond the Pleasure Principle* of television', in Patricia Mellencamp (ed.), *Logics of Television*, Indiana: Indiana University Press, pp. 240–66.

Mesch, Claudia (2000), 'Racing Berlin: the games of *Run Lola Run*', in *M/C: A Journal of Media and Culture*, 3:3 http://journal.media-culture.org.au/0006/berlin.php (06/07/05).

Murphy, Timothy S. (1998), 'Quantum ontology: a virtual mechanics of becoming', in Eleanor Kaufman and Kevin Jon Heller, *Deleuze & Guattari: New Mappings in Politics, Philosophy and Culture*, Minneapolis: University of Minnesota Press, pp. 211–29.

Neale, Steve (1981), 'Art cinema as institution', *Screen*, 22:1, pp. 11–39.

Neale, Steve (1983), 'Masculinity as spectacle: reflections on men and mainstream cinema', *Screen*, 24:6, pp. 2–16.

O'Neill, Patricia (2004), 'Where globalization and localization meet: Spike Lee's *25th Hour*', in *CineAction*, 64, pp. 2–7.

Perlmutter, Ruth (2002), 'Multiple strands and possible worlds', *The Canadian Journal of Film Studies*, 11:2, pp. 44–61.

Ramie, Tateishi (2003), 'The Japanese horror film series: *Ring* and *Eko Eko Azarak*', in Steven Jay Schneider (ed.), *Fear Without Frontiers: Horror Cinema Across the Globe*, Guildford: FAB Press, pp. 295–304.

Ranciere, Jacques (1977), 'Interview: the image of brotherhood', *Edinburgh 77 Magazine*, vol. 2, pp. 26–31.

Rayns, Tony (2004), 'Suspicious minds', *Sight and Sound*, 14:9, pp. 18–20.

Rist, Peter Harry (2004), 'Korean cinema now', *CineAction*, 64, pp. 37–45.

Smith, Dina M. (2002), 'Global Cinderella: *Sabrina* (1954), Hollywood, and postwar internationalism', *Cinema Journal*, 41:4, pp. 27–51.

Sobolewski, Tadeusz (1999), 'Ultimate concerns', in Paul Coates (ed.), *Lucid Dreams: The Films of Krzystof Kieslowski*, London: Flick Books, pp. 19–31.

Stam, Robert and Louise Spence (1983), 'Colonialism, racism and representation – an introduction', *Screen*, 24:2, pp. 2–20.

Stoddart, Helen (1995), 'Auteurism and film authorship', in Joanne Hollows and Mark Jancovich (eds), *Approaches to Popular Film*, Manchester: Manchester University Press, pp. 37–58.

Storey, John (2003), 'The articulation of memory and desire: from Vietnam to the

Persian Gulf', in Paul Grainge (ed.), *Memory and Popular Film*, Manchester: Manchester University Press, pp. 99–119.

Stringer, Julian (1997), '"Your tender smiles give me strength": paradigms of masculinity in John Woo's *A Better Tomorrow* and *The Killer*', *Screen*, 38:1, pp. 25–41.

Tomasulo, Frank P. (2001), 'The empire of the gun', in Jon Lewis (ed.), *The End of Cinema as We Know It*, London: Pluto Press, pp. 115–30.

Trifonova, Temenuga (2002), 'Time and point of view in contemporary cinema', *CineAction*, no. 58, pp. 11–31.

Truffaut, François [1954] (1976), 'A certain tendency of the French cinema', in Bill Nichols (ed.), *Movies and Methods*, Berkeley: University of California Press, pp. 224–36.

Tubrett, Dion (2001), 'So where are you?', *CineAction*, no. 56, pp. 2–10.

Wallace, Michele Faith (2003), 'The good lynching and *The Birth of a Nation*', *Cinema Journal*, 43:1, pp. 85–104.

Whalen, Tom (2000), 'Run Lola Run', *Film Quarterly*, 53:3, pp. 33–40.

Whitehouse, Charles (2004), 'Capital Co-ordinates', *Sight and Sound*, 14:6, p. 6.

Williams, Tony (2000), 'Under "western eyes": the personal odyssey of Huang Fei-Hong in *Once Upon a Time in China*', *Cinema Journal*, 40:1, pp. 3–24.

Wyatt, Justin (1998), 'The formation of the "major independent"', in Steve Neale and Murray Smith (eds), *Contemporary Hollywood Cinema*, London: Routledge, pp. 74–90.

Yacowar, Maurice (1999), '*Run Lola Run*: *Renn* for your Life', *Queen's Quarterly*, 109:4, pp. 557–67.

Select Filmography

Année dernière à Marienbad, L' (France/Italy, Alain Resnais, 1961)
Audition (Japan/South Korea, Takashi Miike, 1999)
Being John Malkovich (USA, Spike Jonze, 1999)
Better Tomorrow, A (HK, John Woo, 1986)
Big Lebowski, The (USA/UK, Joel Coen, 1998)
Birth of a Nation (USA, D. W. Griffith, 1915)
Blind Chance (Poland, Krzystof Kieslowski, 1982)
Butterfly Effect The (USA, Eric Bress & J. Mackye Gruber, 2004)
Chaos (Japan, Hideo Nakata, 1999)
Dark Water (Japan, Hideo Nakata, 2002)
Ditto (South Korea, Jeong-kwon Kim, 2000)
Dolce Vita, La (Italy/France, Federico Fellini, 1960)
8½ (Italy, Federico Fellini, 1963)
Eternal Sunshine of the Spotless Mind (USA, Michel Gondry, 2004)
Family Man (USA, Brett Ratner, 2000)
Frequency (USA, Gregory Hoblit, 2000)
Groundhog Day (USA, Harold Ramis, 1993)
Handsworth Songs (UK, John Akomfrah, 1986)
Irreversible (France, Gaspar Noé, 2004)
It's a Wonderful Life (USA, Frank Capra, 1946)
Jacket, The (USA/UK/Germany, John Maybury, 2005)
Jetée, La (France, Chris Marker, 1962)
Joint Security Area (South Korea, Chan-wook Park, 2000)
Lone Star (USA, John Sayles, 1995)
Makin' Up (Germany, Katja von Garnier, 1993)
Memento (USA, Christopher Nolan, 2000)
Memories of Murder (South Korea, Joon-ho Bong, 2003)
Notting Hill (UK/USA, Roger Michell, 1999)
Peppermint Candy (South Korea/Japan, Chang-dong Lee, 2000)
Pretty Woman (USA, Gary Marshall, 1990)
Ring (Japan, Hideo Nakata, 1998)
Rules of Engagement (USA/Canada/UK/Germany, William Friedkin, 2000)

Run Lola Run (Germany, Tomas Tykwer, 1998)
Sabrina (USA, Billy Wilder, 1954)
Saving Private Ryan (USA, Steven Spielberg, 1998)
Shiri (South Korea, Je-gyu Kang, 1999)
Sliding Doors (UK/USA, Peter Howitt, 1997)
Star Wars (USA, George Lucas, 1977)
Terminator, The (USA, James Cameron, 1984)
Terminator 2 (France/USA, James Cameron, 1991)
Terminator 3 (USA/Germany/UK, Jonathan Mostow, 2003)
Three Kings (USA/Australia, David O Russell, 1999)
Time Machine, The (USA, George Pal, 1960)
Too Many Ways to be Number One (Hong Kong, Ka-Fai Wai, 1997)
25th Hour (USA, Spike Lee, 2000)
Top Gun (USA, Tony Scott, 1986)
Vertigo (USA, Alfred Hitchcock, 1958)
You've Got Mail (USA, Nora Ephron, 1998)

Index